Why
the
Wild
Things Are

WHY THE WILD Things Are

Animals in the Lives of Children

GAIL F. MELSON

HARVARD UNIVERSITY PRESS

CAMBRIDGE, MASSACHUSETTS, AND LONDON, ENGLAND

First Harvard University Press paperback edition, 2005

Library of Congress Cataloging-in-Publication Data

Melson, Gail F.
Why the wild things are : animals in the lives of children /
Gail F. Melson.
p. cm.
Includes index.
ISBN 0-674-00481-7 (cloth)
ISBN 0-674-01752-8 (pbk.)
1. Pet owners—Psychology.   2. Pets—Psychological aspects.
3. Pets—Social aspects.   4. Children and animals.
5. Human-animal relationships.   I. Title.

SF411.47 .M45 2001
636.008′7′019—dc21
00-046201

For Robert, always

ACKNOWLEDGMENTS

Purdue University and my home department, Child Development and Family Studies, provided me a precious sabbatical, and the Henry A. Murray Center for the Study of Lives at Radcliffe College supplied a nurturing setting in which the idea for this project gestated.

I am grateful to Alan Beck, A. G. Rud, and Frank Ascione for their careful reading of portions of this book and their helpful comments. In particular, Alan Beck alerted me to many valuable but overlooked sources, gave me many insights to consider, and freely bestowed countless hours of reflection. I learned from many conversations with parents, educators, therapists, scholars, humane society professionals, and, of course, children. I especially want to thank the following individuals who shared with me their insights about children's lives with animals: Cindy Adams; Doug Allen; Phil Arkow; Suzanne Barnard; Jo Bernofsky; Robert Bierer; Barbara Boat; Mary Pat Boatfield; Michelle Brock; Susan Brooks; John Caruso; Susan Cohen; the Cornell family—Rex, Debra, Latisha, Phillip, Chanel, and Emily; Debbie Coultis; Sharon Coyle; Joan Dalton; Jill DeGrave; Karen Diamond; Amy and Kate LeFurgy; Sandra Diskin; Dan Dunten; Jim and Laura Elicker; Maureen Frederickson; Jane Harvey; Ina Jacobs; Aaron Katcher; Nancy Katz; Marianne Klingel; Rice Lilley; Nancy Lind; Lynn Loar; Randall Lockwood; Dee Dee Long; Nancy Lynn; Meridyth MacLaren;

Jill May; Joan McGroarty; Vicky Mehl; Myrna Milani; Sally Mohler; Amanda and Bethany Moseley; Hedy Nuriel; Marcia Paterson; Sam, Myra, and Lisa Ross; Laurie Rovin; Caroline Schaffer; Jane Shaw; Tom Skeldon; Peggy Smith; Robin Squier; Linda Stillabower; Volker, Erica, and Philip Thomas; Barbara Valereious; and Linn Veen.

I have been priviledged to collaborate with outstanding graduate and undergraduate students on studies of children's relationships with animals. Among those who contributed as students to work discussed in these pages are Patricia da Costa, Fiona Innes, Susan Peet, Laura Richards, Rona Schwarz, Cheri Sparks, Madhavi Vyas, and Hsiu-Wen Yu. Ting Liu cheerfully made countless runs to scattered libraries gathering and returning materials. I thank Jennifer Courtney for timely editorial assistance.

My editor, Elizabeth Knoll, and literary agent, Kristen Wainwright, both knew just when to prod, when to make space, when to encourage, and when, ever tactfully, to redirect.

Sara Melson's incisive and encouraging editing and Josh Melson's thoughtful reflections on animals in therapeutic settings were of enormous help. My husband, Robert, was my constant sounding board, cheering section, quintessential ideal reader, *sine qua non*: I deeply thank him. Last, I salute Audrey Marilyn, that gorgeous, verbal, blond bombshell of a tabby cat who faithfully perched on the keyboard, slept on my notes, and paced on top of my desk as she "supervised" the writing of this book. She made sure I stopped to appreciate fully the human-companion animal bond every time I turned to this work.

CONTENTS

Why
the
Wild
Things Are

Introduction

The boy must be about ten, a Huck Finn wannabe in this university town smack in the heartland of the country. His scuffed sneakers are untied, the shoelaces trailing on the floor. The baseball cap visor is determinedly pointing backward, and his oversize T-shirt hangs down over ripped jeans. He sits at the far end of the veterinary clinic waiting room, crowded with whimpering, barking, and howling patients, next to a man who must be his father—the John Deere hat is at the same angle. The boy is folded over something I can't quite see, slowly stroking it with smooth, rhythmic circles. His voice is soft, a low murmur of endearments in a babyish singsong. I crane my neck to glimpse a small shivering mass of black and white fur plastered to the boy's T-shirt. The father, too, is patting the dog and whispering to it.

I am struck by the softness, the tenderness of their ministrations. Back in our child development laboratory, my colleague has been filming new mothers each week as they cuddle and coo to their babies. He is constructing a documentary record of how the mother-child attachment bond emerges during the first few years of life. What I am seeing now in the vet clinic seems to be striking evidence of an attachment bond between boy and dog, a bond that resonates with emotion as deeply as the videotaped mother-baby sessions. The lilting singsong as the mothers croon to their babies, the reassuring hugs and pats as mothers cradle them, are mirrored by the boy and his dog. The terrified, clinging animal is clearly eliciting pint-sized nurture from the boy much as a baby signals, with gesture and gaze.

That moment in the veterinary hospital piqued my curiosity. Here was an important relationship for this child and for many other children. Here, a child's deepest feelings were engaged. Here, too, was a bond in which children, however small and helpless they might feel in the world of towering adult authority, could reassure someone more vulnerable than they. Here were mutual devotion, comfort, and care.

In the ensuing days and weeks, my thoughts often returned to that scene. Something that had not registered at the time now swam into sharper focus. I had been watching a ten-year-old *boy*, one, moreover, who looked like a poster child for all-American masculinity. Both he and his John Wayne–lookalike father had been in tender public embrace of a small, needy creature. Where else were boys or men to be seen displaying such gentle caregiving? The answer seemed obvious—nowhere.

At the university, the department where I taught housed a preschool and day-care center where children from the community cheerfully served as "guinea pigs" for the early childhood education undergraduates practicing their story-hour and snack-time skills. There were also real guinea pigs in each classroom, and these creatures were instrumental in distracting a tearful, homesick child or quietly holding the attention of an overactive one. I had watched the children's fascination when guinea pig babies suddenly appeared one morning. I remembered somber faces at a guinea pig funeral in the play yard some months later.

In all the interviews that my students, colleagues, and I had conducted over the years about parent-child relationships, about significant events in the family, about the child's bonds with others, we had never thought to ask about nonhuman family members. Yet in how many homes had family portraits displayed a self-satisfied-looking dog or cat front and center? How many visits had begun with noisy, wet animal greetings as children proudly introduced their pets and showed off their special tricks (often no more than rolling over for a tummy scratch)?

Soon I realized it was not just real animals that figured so ubiquitously in children's lives. Animal characters fill children's stories and screens, both television and computer. Big Bird, Barney, Ninja Turtles, Carebears, and stuffed animals of every sort populate the toy shelf and decorate the playroom. Their images saturate the huge market of children's gear, from training mugs, to backpacks, lunchboxes, and funmeals. Animals real, fanciful, and long gone from the earth become a child's "significant other" for a time. Here is a dinosaur-besotted kid with paleolithic expertise worthy of a Ph.D. There is a Curious George– fixated child, surrounded by mischievous-monkey paraphernalia. Everywhere, it seems, are Sendak wild beasts and Seuss lorax. Animals crowd the symbolic life of children, but thin out from their imaginations as they mature into teenagers. This affinity of children for animal characters, from Mickey Mouse to Babar the elephant, seemed as self-evident and unremarkable as children's love of ice cream.

The relationship between children and animals was one I had ignored in my teaching, writing, and research even as I explored the significant human ties—parents, relatives, teachers, peers—that shape children's lives. I began to ask myself incredulously, how *could* I have missed it? My own two children, then teenagers, had grown up with their beloved dog, Liba, and a succession of high-maintenance cats as the much-fussed-over center of our family. After school, when my son joined the knot of neighborhood children who gathered in the vacant lot for pickup games of ball, assorted mutts and purebreds tagged along and vainly took up positions in the outfield. Their names and personalities drifted into our conversations at home. The pets of the neighborhood and of their schoolmates were part of my children's social world, tightly bound together in the tangle of best friends, so-so buddies, chums, cliques, and enemies that make up the society of children.

What about my own childhood? How many childhood reminiscences evoked Trixie, the small, neurotic blond mutt who appeared in our driveway one day in miraculous answer to the tearful pleas of my younger sister for a dog? I recalled the eponymous Fluffy, the kitten I acquired as half of a matched set when my cousin received her kitten on that unforgettable joint birthday. There they all were, our child selves and these long-gone animals, together in the old albums that passed into my hands when my parents died.

Animals were so *there* as part of the woof and web of childhood, including my own, that I had never noticed them. Neither had most other scholars, I discovered, while searching in vain through child development textbooks for an index entry under "pets" or "animals: relationships with." A trek through the abstracts of research studies yielded little more pay dirt.

A handful of psychologists, veterinarians, animal behavior specialists, and therapists was turning to what they called "the human-animal bond" and its effects on adjustment and well-being, but their focus was mainly on the second half of life, not the first few decades. The results of that work, however, were startling. An animal behaviorist, Alan Beck, and a child psychiatrist, Aaron Katcher, had teamed up to demonstrate that "the touch-talk dialogue we establish with pets" reduces stress, lowers blood pressure, and promotes relaxation. Even passive observation of animals had stress-reducing benefits. Simply watching, for no more than ten minutes, tropical fish swimming in an aquarium proved to be as effective as hypnosis in reducing the anxiety and discomfort of adult patients about to undergo dental surgery. Other studies documented decreased cardiovascular reactivity among adult women in the presence of their pets and improved survival following a heart attack for pet owners, compared to non-pet-owning adults.[1] Contact with companion animals was emerging as a significant source of support and well-being for adults.

These findings raised questions about children's development. Might these benefits apply to children as well? Could animals be even more important for children's lives than for those of adults? Are animals significant for children only when kids are stressed? What other roles might they play? These questions prompted others, opening a new terrain of exploration, the animal world of children.

My goal in the following pages is to chart this new terrain in the study of children. I propose a "biocentric" view of development, one that recognizes the pervasiveness of real and symbolic animals in children's lives.[2] I argue that the study of children has been largely "humanocentric," assuming that only human relationships—with parents, siblings, relatives, friends, teachers, other children—are consequential for development.[3] This humanocentric perspective on development is at best a seriously incomplete portrait of the ecology of children. At worst, it misses potentially significant influences on children's development. By contrast, the biocentric view assumes that animal presence in all its forms merits neither facile sentimentalizing nor quick dismissal, but serious investigation. Because scholars are just now venturing into this new terrain, many fundamental questions remain unanswered. Even basic descriptive information about children's daily lives with their pets or contacts with other animals is incomplete. The terrain of a biocentric account of childhood is largely unmapped, with only a few landmarks sketched in. This book, I hope, will raise questions, stimulate research, and thus begin to fill in the map. As befits a new area of inquiry, I see my task as hypothesis generating rather than hypothesis testing.

Chapter 1 documents how theory and research on children's development have ignored animals and suggests ways in which attention to children's animal connections recasts many issues in social and cognitive development, among them the formation of attachments to others, the development of ideas about the social and nonsocial world, and moral reasoning. Chapter 2 traces the evolution of petkeeping, domestication of animals, and changes in the family that together have made children intimate partners with the animals who reside with them. Chapter 3 focuses on the emotional bond between child and pet. I suggest that this bond shares many of the same features as children's significant ties with humans—reassurance, support, and the "contact comfort" of touch, for example. I also explore those qualities of children's relationships with their pets that are distinctive—an emphasis on sensory, nonverbal communication, the experience of nurturing a dependent being different from oneself, a nonevaluative, in-the-present availability. Chapter 4 goes into the classroom, home, yard, park, and zoo to ask what children might be absorbing from observing and interacting with living animals. From this perspective, animals are rich lodes of information for children about fundamental cognitive puzzles—how living beings and inanimate objects differ, how one can try to know other minds, how one is connected to other species. These issues carry moral and ethical urgency as well. Chapter 5 considers therapies for troubled children that incorporate contact with animals and nature. I assess the potential of—and the unanswered questions about—using animals to treat a wide range of problems, from extreme shyness to hyperactivity, to learning disabilities. Chapter 6 considers animals as symbols, both as offered up by adults for children and as products of children's imagination. I suggest that young children use monsters, dragons, teddy bears, and creatures great and small to explore, clarify, and reflect different facets of the child's sense of self. Chapter 7 examines the troubled side of the child-animal relationship—children's mistreatment of animals, possible links between animal abuse and family violence, and animal neglect and abandonment. These issues illustrate that, notwithstanding popular imagery of mutual devotion between child and creature, there is no single master narrative that can capture the complexity of children's relationships to other species, whether pets, wild animals, or domestic farm animals. Children often reflect society's ambivalent and contradictory messages about human and humane treatment of other species. Finally, Chapter 8 sketches a research, teaching, and program agenda based on a biocentric perspective for studying children's development and enriching their lives. It focuses on deepening and shaping rather than discouraging children's intuitive affinity for other forms of life.

1

Animals and the Study
of Children

Scholars of child development have traditionally had little to say about animals' presence in children's lives and what that might mean for their development. Many of the more influential accounts simply ignore the issue. Consider cognitive development. Jean Piaget, the great Swiss observer of children, wrote voluminously about how children come to understand the world around them. Early childhood, before age seven, lay in the grip of what Piaget called *animism,* the belief that inanimate objects are as alive as animate things. Therefore, in his view, distinctive experiences with animals were impossible until children's thought processes matured and became more rational and logical.

Relationship-focused scholars of child development might have been expected to provide more insight into the child-animal connection, yet influential theorists in this area have likewise ignored it. A good example is John Bowlby, the British psychiatrist who developed attachment theory. More than fifty years ago, his observations of the grief, withdrawal, depression, and even death of hospitalized infants who had been separated from their mothers sensitized psychologists to the importance of early bonds. When young children can rely on a responsive caregiver for reassurance when upset or stressed, they derive a sense of security and well-being that is essential to the ability to thrive.

Bowlby saw mothers as the primal attachment figures and relegated others in children's lives—fathers, grandparents, older siblings, caregivers—to secondary status. Recently, however, psychologists have disputed this hierarchy of attachments, showing that children simultaneously develop multiple attachments. Fathers, older brothers and sisters, grandparents, and paid caregivers often function as sources of security and can be as effective as, and sometimes preferable to, mothers in reassuring young children.

Nowhere do attachment theorists mention the possibility of bonds with nonhumans. This is surprising, given the ubiquitousness of pets and ample evidence of strong attachment to them, based on reports from both parents and children in North America and western Europe. In light of the emotional investment many children make in their resident animals and their ready availability, might pets function as a source of security and reassurance in the face of stress? Under what conditions would they do so? Is attachment to an animal distinct quantitatively or qualitatively from attachments to other humans? Attachment theorists have never posed such questions, much less undertaken research into them.[1]

If any perspective might have included child-animal relationships, it surely would have been ecological theory, first elaborated by Urie Bronfenbrenner of Cornell University in 1979 in his influential book, *The Ecology of Human Development*. There he made a plea for scholars of child development to turn to serious study of children's real-life environments. No more laboratory studies of children, no more psychological testing disconnected from the everyday contexts of children's lives. Researchers would leave the lab, shed their white coats, and go to homes, playgrounds, schoolyards, back alleys, and malls. There they would understand children as they really lived, not "the strange behavior of children in strange situations," as Bronfenbrenner described the artificiality of laboratory studies.[2]

From an ecological perspective, he argued, children grow up in a variety of nested, interrelated contexts—home, school, neighborhood play group, religious institution, extended family, among others. Each setting can be deconstructed into a set of significant ties and a blueprint of normative expectations. The family, in particular, is viewed as a complex web of reciprocal influences, a system of circular feedback loops, in which all family members affect the child, who is simultaneously affecting them. Other environmental influences filter down to children indirectly. For example, parents may bring tensions from their workplace and snap at their children. School funding cuts cancel the school orchestra, depriving a child of music instruction. Cultural values and broad social trends, what Bronfenbrenner calls the *macrosystem,* color all those contexts more directly impinging on the child.

In their nuanced, multilayered depiction of children's environments, Bronfenbrenner and other ecologically oriented psychologists sketched out contexts inhabited by other humans but never those inhabited by animals. In a 1960 book, *The Non-Human Environment,* Harold Searles had argued that physical settings of nonhuman objects and animals influenced personality and should be the focus of study. But the very inclusion of animals with "nonhuman objects" seemed to relegate them to the status of furniture or toys. In any event, the ambitious agenda Searles outlined for a new science—the study of the nonhuman environment as a developmental context, including animals—never caught fire.

Even as assessment of children's environments became ever more detailed, no one thought to ask about the presence of animals and what children were doing with them. Psychologists Mihaly Csikzentmihalyi and Reed Larson have amassed reams of data on the where, what, and when of adolescents' daily lives, by giving teenagers beepers and then beeping them at intervals throughout the day. In their 1984 *Being Adolescent: Conflict and Growth in the Teenage Years,* for example, we find out what percentage of time teens watch TV, listen to music, study, and even take a nap. (They spend about as much time napping—a little over 3 percent of the day—as reading nonschool materials.) We learn that they spend about a quarter of the day alone, and on average 19 percent of their waking time with family. This family time is broken down for parents, siblings, and other relatives, in all possible combinations. Yet there is no category for those nonhuman family members, pets, that are undoubtedly there for most of the teenagers when their beepers go off.

When social psychologists began asking adults and, later, children about their *personal networks*, the queries were restricted to the people to whom they were linked. Among their many functions, personal networks proved to be an important conduit of social support, conveying feelings of being cared for, loved, and valued, providing an often literal shoulder to cry on, and dispensing advice, information, and material aid. In turn, social support emerged as a key coping resource, predicting psychological well-being, particularly when children or adults were under stress. Personal network assessments, with instructions like "Tell me the names of all the people who are important to you in one way or another," guaranteed that ties to nonhuman animals would be missed.[3]

Social connections also have been of paramount importance to psychologists who explore how a child's sense of self grows from infancy into adulthood, so that each individual comes to experience a unique subjective sense of "I" and at the same time is seen by others (and can be reflected on by oneself) as a unique personality, "me." For pioneering social psychologists like George Herbert Mead (1863–1931) and Charles H. Cooley (1864–1929), a child's sense of self and indeed all of human thought emerge through interaction with others. Cooley coined the term "looking-glass self" to capture how the self is built from the qualities seen reflected in the eyes of others. Those others, by definition, could only be other humans.

Object relations and self psychologists, such as Heinz Hartmann, Margaret Mahler, and Heinz Kohut, also focused on the child's development of a sense of self out of relationships with others ("objects"). Kohut's work, for example, suggests at least seven kinds of interpersonal experiences, called "selfobject experiences," needed to establish and maintain a cohesive and balanced sense of self: mirroring (feeling recognized and affirmed), merging (feeling one with the other), idealizing (being accepted by an admired other), alter-ego (feeling essentially like the other), adversary (being able to assert oneself against an available and responsive other), efficacy (feeling able to elicit a response from the other), and vitalizing (feeling the other is attuned to one's shifting moods and emotions). Although Kohut and other self psychologists assumed that only humans could provide such selfobject experiences, we shall see that for many children, their pets serve mirroring, merging, vitalizing, and other functions.[4]

A prominent theme in many accounts of children's development is the importance of peer relationships—the ties that children form with age-mates. Not only do other children provide "selfobject" experiences; they also create "horizontal" or egalitarian ties, in contrast to the "vertical" authority structure of parent over child. In this view, children's play and games are the crucible of the first democracy, as taking turns, sharing, and collaborating work themselves out in peer conflict and compromise. Play with other children serves other functions as well. Its unstructured, unhurried quality is the font of all later creativity, according to Csikzentmihalyi and many other developmentalists. In the "as if" of pretend play, young children put together props (this seashell is a teacup), roles (the waiter serves the tea to the customer), and plot or story line (going out for teatime) to construct a hypothetical reality. Such symbol manipulation stimulates reasoning; children observed to engage in lots of pretend play in their preschool or child-care center score higher several years later on tests that require them to manipulate abstract symbols.[5]

Children play with their pets. Does it make sense to think of some pets as interactive partners, similar in some ways to other children? Play with pets might well have the "horizontal" and symbolic properties shown to be developmentally beneficial. Perhaps play with a pet combines the egalitarian elements of age-mates with the hierarchical structure of parent-child relations, making it similar in this respect to the older-younger sibling relationship. The child directs and structures the play, using the pet sometimes as a prop, at other times as a more immature play partner. Speculation about the nature and significance of children's play with pets remains just that, since nowhere can animals be found in the voluminous literature on children's play and peer relationships.

Freud and some other psychoanalytically oriented scholars at least took note of children's fascination with animals. Freud himself was struck by how frequently animals appeared in the dreams of children. For him, animal figures represented projections of powerful adults, usually parents, who were too threatening to the child to pop up undisguised in the dream world. From a psychoanalytic point of view, children and animals shared a natural kinship, since biological urges not subject to human reason held sway over both of them.[6] Even more than Freud, Jung stressed that animal symbols often expressed facets of the self, an insight that self psychologists missed. One Jungian psychologist stated: "The Self is often symbolized as an animal, representing our instinctive nature and its connectedness with one's surroundings. (That is why there are so many helpful animals in myths and fairy tales.)"[7]

Such was the frequency of animal imagery in children's dreams and associations that psychoanalytically oriented psychologists developed projective tests using animal images for children and even for the purported "inner child" of adult patients. The psychoanalytic gloss of animals as instinct was overly narrow, however. It cut off investigation into a wider range of developmental needs, serving ego and superego, not just id, that animal themes and characters in dreams, play, fantasies, and stories might address. Curiously, psychoanalytic emphasis on animal symbolism did not lead to any attempts to decipher the multiple meanings of real pets and other living animals for children.

In short, children's ties to animals seem to have slipped below the radar screens of almost all scholars of child development. At the same time, a few pioneering therapists were reporting startling results about the power of animals to affect emotionally troubled children. Boris Levinson, in his 1969 classic, *Pet-Oriented Psychotherapy,* and a few years later, in *Pets and Human Development,* described how the presence of a friendly dog in a therapy session helped create a safe environment within which highly withdrawn children began to respond to someone outside themselves. The nascent field of therapeutic horseback riding was showing how children with disabilities improved balance and coordination and gained feelings of self-confidence and mastery behind the reins of a horse. Testimonials were proliferating attesting to the dramatic benefits of assistance dogs for children with hearing, sight, or mobility impairments.

A few researchers, impressed with these accounts and with findings on the power of animals to be stress reducers for adults, set out to demonstrate that animals could calm children. In a series of studies, Erika Friedmann, James Lynch, Aaron Katcher, and Alan Beck showed that, as with adults, children's blood pressure decreased in the company of a friendly dog.[8] Such intriguing results inspired a small band of scholars to explore the child-pet relationship more broadly. Their work began to appear in academic journals, conference proceedings, and therapists' case reports.

Meanwhile, new perspectives on children's development were creating more fertile ground for considering the significance of animals. Cognitive psychology was challenging Piaget's account of animism by uncovering a child's "naïve biology," a core domain of knowledge about living things. Its first glimmers are discernible in infancy, and by the preschool years, far earlier than Piaget had thought, this knowledge base, particularly about animals, already is well established.[9] From ages four to ten, children continue to refine their reasoning about the biological processes underlying "alive" versus "dead" and "inanimate" (never alive), "animal" versus "human" and nonanimal thing. This early and progressively more accurate cognitive mapping of animals raises further questions: Besides cognitive maturation, what influences children's "naïve biology"? How does children's involvement with real animals—observing, touching, caring for, talking to them—contribute to biological knowledge? How do children use their "naïve biology" to make sense not only of animals, but of their own aliveness? And conversely, how do children apply understanding of themselves and other humans as living entities to the puzzle of distinguishing and understanding other species?

In recent years, evolutionary biology has been prompting psychologists to ask about the evolutionary basis for human behavior. The coevolution of modern humans, not just alongside but interdependently with animal and plant species, makes it probable that built into the human psyche are interest in, use of, and feelings about animals. From this perspective, interspecies relations may be just as fundamental a building-block of human development as intraspecies ties. Petkeeping, apparently universal among human groups and so old it coevolved with modern humans, is intriguing. While the reproductive advantages that pets enjoy from the arrangement seem clear—protection from predators, diseases, and the elements—the payoffs for humans are less obvious. Might pets provide children with experiences that would benefit them developmentally? As we shall see, children show strong interest not just in their pets but in domesticated farm animals, wild animals, and animal representations as well. What might be the evolutionary basis for such behavior?

New computer-aided technologies are joining with robotics to make us rethink fundamental assumptions about human-nonhuman interactions. Plush animals with sophisticated computers embedded in them, called *personal embodied agents* or *relational artifacts,* are capable of remarkable responsiveness. ActiMates Barney, the Furby, Tama, AIBO, and Tamagotchi are likely to be joined by ever more sophisticated "agents" that further blur the lines between animate beings and inanimate things. Virtual pets are proliferating, and children are developing relationships with these "creatures." Research has yet to catch up with this exploding market. However, early findings make clear that children form emotional attachments to their virtual pets. One five-year-old said about her Furby: "Well, I love it. It's more alive . . . because it sleeps with me. It likes to sleep with me."[10] If we learn more about children's interactions with real pets and other real animals, as well as children's use of animal symbols, we should be better able to understand this emerging domain of robotic pets. We then may have the tools to influence the development of this technology in directions that benefit children.

About a decade ago, with colleagues and students I began to study children's ties to their pets and the meaning of those relationships for their development. Over the ensuing years we interviewed children and their parents, queried teachers, and observed children and their pets at home, in parks, and at playgrounds. We scanned national surveys of parents and children for overlooked information about pets and their significance for families. The search took us back to earlier psychological studies for hints of animals' impact on the lives of children. We also began to examine evidence of how children were responding to the wide range of "up close" animal contacts in their daily lives—bees circling a picnic lunch, squirrels, chipmunks, rabbits, and birds in the backyard, spiders spinning by the back door. We considered children's ideas about animals. For example, how do children develop an understanding of "animal" as a category, of mammals versus reptiles, and of species of mammals? How are children framing the moral claims of animals (or lack thereof)? Does the development of moral reasoning about others encompass nonhumans?

Decoding the symbolic roles that animal characters play required a fresh look at children's picture books, stories, and school readers, many of which are tales told by and about animal characters. Folklorists have long viewed animal tales as vehicles to convey a culture's ideas about relationships, both among humans and between humans and animals. Anthropologists—notably the French scholar Claude Lévi-Strauss—have documented animal symbolism permeating traditional cultures of North and South America, Australia, Africa, and Asia. In a landmark study of totemism, Lévi-Strauss claimed that for traditional cultures around the world, "animals are good to think."[11] By this he meant that animal species and behaviors functioned as a symbol system that mapped onto human actions and emotions and made them intelligible. This insight, if applied to children's development, suggests that animals may function as a meaning system through which children make sense of both themselves and their surrounding environments.

Therapists have been exploring the healing potential of animals for children with emotional and physical problems. Treatment programs like Green Chimneys Children's Services, in New York State, and the Devereux Foundation, in Pennsylvania, are models for infusing animals throughout the therapeutic process. A close examination of animals as healing "partners," however, reveals a complex, as yet poorly understood dynamic. Animals in the therapeutic milieu, like children's "naïve biology," family bonds with pets, or animal storybook characters, raise further questions about animals as significant developmental influences.

In open-ended, in-depth interviews, many pet-owning children spoke with deep feeling about what animals mean in their lives. We also talked to parents and teachers, to child therapists, social workers, animal shelter workers, veterinarians, pet store owners, children's zoo directors—all those whose work and lives make them keen observers of what animals mean to children.

These sources—interviews, research studies, therapists' reports, stories for and by children provide the basis for this book and its simple argument that expanding our understanding of children to encompass their contacts with nonhuman living forms, especially animals, can illuminate important questions about development. Although we do not have the answers to most of these questions, asking them is a crucial first step toward a broader and more accurate picture of children. How do children understand different ways of being alive? How do their encounters with distinct forms of life affect their comprehension of what life is, what being human is, and what comprises their own selves? How do encounters with animals affect developing capacities for empathy and sympathy? Does moral reasoning reach across species lines? Does that reach affect judgments about morality toward humans? Are the ties that children form with pets reducible to proxies for human relationships, like sibling, friend, or parent? Do ties with animals complement, substitute for, or amplify human bonds? Might animals provide children unique experiences not readily available from fellow humans?

The ties that children forge with their pets are often among the most significant bonds of childhood, as deeply affecting as those with parents, siblings, and friends. Like parents or grandparents, children's pets can give them feelings of being loved, reassure them in times of stress, counteract loneliness, and provide emotional support. Like siblings, animals can be at-home play companions, or afterschool company in an empty house. Like friends, pets can be confidants, keepers of secrets, and members in good standing of what psychologist William Corsaro calls "children's peer culture."[12]

In other respects, of course, children's experiences with animals differ from those with humans. Animals enact the dramas of birth and death in a visible, accessible way at a time when these human events are hidden from children. Unlike humans, familiar, friendly pets are social partners who tend to induce physiological relaxation, making new situations less stressful and more approachable. Animals are especially effective bridges to other children and to adults. Since cross-species communication is nonverbal, at least in one direction, children face particular challenges in decoding body motion, gesture, and sound. An animal pushes a child to recognize the distinct subjectivity of a being who moves and communicates in ways very different from those of the child.

Because pets live in at least 75 percent of all American households with children and are the only family members who never grow up, they function as a potential training ground for learning about nurturing others. Unlike caregiving to babies, young children, or dependent adults, pet care is gender-neutral, not associated with what males versus females should do. As Alan Beck and Aaron Katcher put it, "A pet may be the only being that a man, trained in the macho code, can touch with affection."[13]

As the only household members usually smaller and less powerful than the child, pets can also provide a context for playing out themes of power and domination. The "one-down" position of a pet as the only family member whom a child owns, coupled with the animal's constant presence and apparent responsiveness, makes it an ideal "transitional object," a being who can represent a child's wishes without fear of contradiction.[14] If, as Karl Menninger argued, all relationships are ambivalent, then children's ties to their pets will reflect the same rich stew of emotions served up in children's relationships with parents, siblings, or friends. Pets challenge children to temper the role of master with kindness, to blend domination with solicitude. Few relationships of childhood require this same balancing act; perhaps the role of older sibling comes closest.

Kindness—or cruelty—toward animals has long been seen as a lit-
mus test of a child's character. Contemporary research, however, has
failed to turn up evidence that kindness or cruelty to animals *causes* children to act in parallel fashion toward other people. Rather, psychologists
like Frank Ascione, of Utah State University, an authority on children's
cruelty toward animals, view repeated, extreme, and intentional cruelty—seen in only a small percentage of those who ever mistreat an animal—as an early warning of psychological disturbance. The far more
common casual mistreatment, indifference, or occasional neglect does
not seem to be diagnostic. Equally unclear, and in urgent need of research, is the connection, if any, between children's concern for animal
well-being—their active doing of good for animals, as distinct from refraining from harming them—and their prosocial behavior toward
humans.[15]

The links between treatment of animals and other people emerge,
on closer examination, as far from simple and linear. In many countries,
institutionalized cruelty toward animals—bullfights, cockfights—coexists with relatively low rates of violence toward humans. Similarly, culturally mandated kindness toward animals can be paired with vicious destruction of fellow humans, as the stringent Nazi animal protection laws
attest.[16]

In stories, television, movies, video games, and ads, not to mention
children's dreams and fantasies, animals are a ready cast of characters
through which children explore facets of themselves—the wild beast,
the cunning fox, the faithful dog, the huge and toothsome dinosaur. Because adults create them, these symbolic images are also a window into a
culture's ideas about children and animals and how they are related.
The subtext of animal images is replete with "boundary issues" about
human-animal distinctiveness, with ethical implications for animal welfare, animal rights, and ecological consciousness.[17]

For at least the last hundred years, American cultural images weave
together child and animal into the same cloth. Like animals, children
represent the wild and unsocialized in the midst of the "civilized" family.
Like pets, who are unbridled by social conventions, babies' messy

instinctual life of ingestion and elimination is on public display. From the vantage point of the verbal adult, babies and pets share the same vocabulary of nonverbal communication, the language of gesture, grunt, and howl. Like the puppy to be housebroken and trained, the human baby must rein in unchecked impulses to learn the rules of human society and earn a place at (or, in the dog's case, under) the family dinner table.

Historically, relationships between adults and children and between adults and pets have changed in similar ways.[18] Both have lost their utilitarian functions to become sentimental objects of affection. Both (often juxtaposed) have become shorthand markers of warmth, domesticity, and approachability. Inserted into ads and movies, they say "cute," "small," "needy," and "safe." In 1999, when Mercedes-Benz wanted a visual image to convey the loyalty and devotion the car company inspired in its customers, it enlarged a photograph of a young boy cradling his puppy, slapped a single-word caption—loyalty—under it and took out full-page ads in major publications like the *New York Times*.

Is the link between children and animals solely a cultural creation? Are adults imposing their fantasies of the childlike pet and the animal-like child? Because we associate children with pets and other small animals, are we imagining a special kinship and then making it real by filling children's lives with pets, stuffed animals, animal picture books, and trips to the zoo? Is the apparent fascination of many children with all things animal simply proof of their cultural conditioning?

I argue that many cultures, including our own, are elaborating a natural attraction children have to animals. The biophilia hypothesis, first advanced by the biologist E. O. Wilson, suggests that a predisposition to attune to animals and other living things is part of the human evolutionary heritage, a product of our coevolution as omnivores with the animals and plants on which our survival depends.[19] Biophilia depicts children as born assuming a connection with other living things. The emotions and personalities of animals, real and symbolic, are immediate to children in the same way that the emotions and personalities of people are. Because of this, animals enter the drama of a child's life in direct and powerful ways. Children readily access animals as material in the development of a sense of self. Every human child begins life situated in what adults call "the animal world." As Freud put it in his 1913 essay, *Totem and Taboo,* denying human bonds with animals "is still as foreign to the child as it is to the savage or to primitive man."[20]

Many cultures recognize the affinity of children for animals and build on it images that link children to animals. At the same time, children in Western cultures gradually absorb a worldview of humans as radically distinct from and superior to other species, the human as "top dog" on the evolutionary chain of being. What one scholar calls "the categorically human self" emerges—a strict division between human attributes and often negatively valued animal characteristics.[21]

This belief is nowhere better articulated than by Sarah Trimmer, whose school text, *Fabulous Histories: Designed for the Instruction of Children Respecting Their Treatment of Animals,* was in every classroom in England throughout the nineteenth century:

> The world we live in seems to have been principally designed for the use and comfort of mankind, who, by the Divine appointment, have dominion over the inferior creatures . . . Some creatures have nothing to give us but their own bodies; these have been expressly destined by the Supreme Governor as food for mankind . . . These we have an undoubted right to kill, but should make their short lives as comfortable as possible. Other creatures seem to be of no particular use to mankind, but . . . serve to furnish our minds with contemplations on the wisdom, power and goodness of God, and to exhilarate our spirits by their cheerfulness.[22]

Cultural messages are considerably more complex than an initial fusion of child with animal, followed by a simple assertion of human superiority at the pinnacle of the evolutionary ladder. Children grapple with a complicated, often contradictory, mix of social codes governing animals and their treatment. There are creatures incorporated as family members, stamped out as pests, saved from extinction, and ground into Big Macs. The result is that children often mirror societal unease with culturally sanctioned uses of animals. If we wish to redefine those uses and recast them in more ecologically responsible terms, children's relationships with animals may be the place to begin.

2

Reaching across the Divide

It is an Ice Age evening over 100,000 years ago.[1] A wolf inches closer to the fires of *Homo sapiens sapiens* and the intoxicating smell of roasted flesh. A child discards a bone, and the wolf creeps nearer. Gradually the wolf comes to expect the leavings of the hunt. Or maybe some children stumble upon mewling wolf pups abandoned in their den. The feistiest of the bunch wiggles toward a child's fingers and latches on. The child's mother puts the pup to her breast to nurse. The hand-raised wolf soon "adopts" its human family, hanging around the group. The first "pet" takes up residence.

Humans and wolves probably first formed a loose alliance of mutual benefit: wolves got a ready supply of food, and humans profited from wolves' hunting and scavenging skills. (Some scholars credit wolves, lured by the protection and food supply of human packs, with taking the initiative.) Anthropologists consider the taming of the wolf to be the beginning of a fundamental transformation in the relations of the human species with other animals. Within 5,000 years the tamed wolf would evolve into the dog, the first species existing primarily as a human companion.[2] However, both before the wolf's entry into human society and for many thousands of years afterward, animals remained powerful and emotionally charged equals of humans. Small bands would hunt down game, sometimes tracking prey for days, and mark their kill with ceremony and rituals of respect for a worthy adversary.[3] For the most part, however, these foragers gathered grains, berries, and nuts; hence the term "hunter-gatherer" peoples.

Children would have had close encounters with many animals whose "flight distance," the point at which prey will begin to run from a predator, would have been much shorter than that of contemporary wild species. Human hunters, armed only with short spears, small arrows, or stones, would have had to approach quite close to animal prey, who, in turn, would have learned to tolerate the proximity of human presence. Mothers and children scouring for berries through the brush would have occasionally stumbled upon a large predator, perhaps a resting lion, watchful in the tall grasses. The mothers and children would have spoken to the lion cautiously but with firm insistence on their rights to gather berries there. They would have recognized this particular lion as an individual, not "a lion," an interchangeable exemplar of its kind. In turn, the lion would have read the body language, movements, and voice tone of these familiar human animals.[4] As Juliet Clutton-Brock notes, "It is difficult to picture the close association that must have existed between these early hunter-gatherer societies and all the other animals within the environment."[5]

Small rodents, birds, and mammals shared the berry patches, woods, and grasslands with human young. What small child could resist sticking a twig down a burrow to unearth a field mouse, or picking up an injured bird for closer inspection? Children must have played at hunting—stalking, cornering, and moving in for the kill—in this teeming space of diminutive creatures. But there would have been moments when the hunting game lost its urgency, and the whiff of a new relationship would present itself. A child might stop to pick up a momentarily stunned mouse, cup it in her hands or wrap it in large leaves, and carry it back to the encampment. There the child would hide it for a few days, sneaking away to hold and gaze at it. The child might feed the mouse, which would soon learn to go to the food source in the outstretched hand. Or a child might happen on animal young, abandoned after their mother had been killed. Whatever the circumstance, taming of animal young is probably as old as humanity itself, a by-product of the sharing, nurturing, and protecting instincts honed in our highly social species.[6]

The long period of human immaturity, far more extended than in other mammals, may have drawn children more directly to animals. Human young, like juveniles of other species, exhibit more curiosity, playfulness, interspecies approach, and flexibility, as well as less fearfulness, than adults. (This is why animal young of many species are readily tamed, only to revert to their "wild" nature when mature.) The decade-plus span of human immaturity bequeaths to children a luxurious stretch of time for investigating the life forms around them.

The nature of early human evolution remains murky, extrapolated from anthropologists' observations of modern forager peoples and archaeologists' analyses of early human finds.[7] Nonetheless, it is plausible that children were part of the first "domestic alliance" between humans and other animal species and may even have taken an active role.

From Wolf to Lassie

With domestication—the captive breeding of species so as to induce permanent changes in bone structure and behavior—humans would gradually become keepers of other species, extending control over their lifespans and deaths. The domestication of species other than dogs apparently began only around 10,000 years ago—a mere blip of evolutionary time—when animal husbandry and agriculture slowly began to replace hunting. Sheep and goats were domesticated around 9,000 years ago, followed by cattle, pigs, and horses, asses, camels, water buffalo, and domestic fowl around 5,000 years ago. Wild cats began hanging around the granaries of early agricultural settlements in the Near East at least 9,000 years ago, launching an arrangement of mutual advantage with humans, who welcomed the free rodent-clearing service. About 4,000 years ago, Egyptians began to confine cats to temples and deliberately breed them.[8]

Humans and animals evolved a set of complex relationships. Humans hunted and raised animals as products for human consumption.

Humans also were caretakers of other animals who served as helpers, companions, amusement, and loved ones.[9] The two relationships were not contradictory, but simply two complementary aspects of domestication. Only a limited number of species could be successfully domesticated. The ideal candidate possessed a hierarchical social organization, a short flight distance, a slow response to danger, and weak territorial instincts. Within suitable species, the process of domestication further selected for immature, tractable characteristics, such as minimal fearfulness. As a result, the most common household pets, dogs and cats, as well as other domesticated animals, exhibit *neoteny*, the retention of juvenile physical and behavioral features into adulthood. As compared to the wolf, for example, early domesticated dogs had foreshortened jaws, smaller teeth, and larger, rounded heads in proportion to their body size, with more prominent eyes. Dogs' submissive, attention-seeking behavior toward humans resembled the juvenile wolf deferring to the outranking adults in the pack.

Domesticated animals are, in effect, childlike versions of their wild ancestors. Such neotenous creatures are not only more adapted to but also more attractive to humans. Their appeal inspires care and affection, while not diminishing human ability to use such animals for consumption and other purposes. Konrad Lorenz, in a classic study, showed that similar facial profiles—prominent eyes, large foreheads, shortened noses and jaws, and proportionally large heads—characterize human young as well as those of many other domesticated species, such as dogs, cats, and ducks.[10] To the extent that such animals are neotenous, they resemble human offspring and so tap into responsiveness to our own young. In Stephen Jay Gould's phrase, neotenous creatures trigger "an automatic surge of disarming tenderness."[11] From a child's perspective, neotenous pets and domesticated animals are interspecies peers. The human child sees childlike animals as variants of fellow children.

The term "pet" (from "petty" or small) would not appear until the late 1500s, but thousands of years earlier, well before animal husbandry and widespread domestication of species, children as well as adults began to develop affectionate bonds with those animals who joined the human community. At a 12,000-year-old Natufian site in Israel, one of the oldest agricultural sites yet discovered, archaeologists have unearthed the remains of a boy with his arm around a puppy.[12] In a 7,000-year-old cemetery in southern Scandinavia, dogs were given burial rituals identical with those of humans.[13] The ancient Egyptians, Greeks, and Romans were avid petkeepers. Their dogs, cats, and a surprising variety of other species—pet snakes were particular favorites—lolled about family quarters. On Pompeii's doorways, "Beware of the dog" signs attest to the presence of watchdogs (or at least the pretense of one). Greek and Roman poetry enshrined the faithful canine companion—Argos to Odysseus—as an archetype of devotion.[14] Three thousand years ago, people sailing to what is now Australia took along their dogs, forebears of the Australian dingo.[15]

Petkeeping has been a constant across time and cultures. Anthropologists find petkeeping entrenched in nearly every nonindustrial culture. Affectionate bonds between pastoralists and their cattle, sheep, and goats are reflected in rituals like the initiation ceremony of Dinka youth in southern Sudan. At puberty, each boy is given a special bull as a "brother," to whom he talks and for whom he composes songs.[16] Australian aborigines kept wallabies and opossums in addition to dingoes. Native Americans in North America made pets of deer, wolves, raccoons, bears, turkeys, and a variety of small animals. Pigeons, parrots, and lizards were pets for Polynesians. Francis Galton, Darwin's cousin, collected nineteenth-century travelers' accounts of so-called primitive peoples' fondness for their pet animals. He quotes an English acquaintance traveling in North America, who recounted his difficulties in purchasing a bear cub from a native group: "The red races are fond of pets and treat them kindly; and in purchasing them there is always the unwillingness of the women and children to overcome, rather than any dispute about price."[17]

In the Middle Ages, English courtiers and aristocratic women kept pets as indulged playthings.[18] The great medieval encyclopedia of natural history, *De Animalibus*, compiled in 1258–1262 by the Dominican cleric known as Albert the Great, described *canis* (dog) as "a faithful animal whose love for humans sometimes prompts it to lay down its life for the sake of its master."[19] A 1539 English reference to pets cited "parroquets [parakeets], monkeys, peacocks, and swans" as examples.[20] From the fifteenth through seventeenth centuries, companionship with small animals smacked of pagan worship of animal spirits. Women and men seen talking to their pets risked accusations of witchcraft for consorting with animal "familiars" and perhaps transforming themselves into animals. By the eighteenth century, however, a more sympathetic view of petkeeping emerged, as the Enlightenment challenged the medieval equation of animals with the primitive, "animal instincts" lurking in humans.[21] Petkeeping was spreading from the aristocracy to other classes, and by the middle of the nineteenth century, pets, especially lapdogs, became symbols of bourgeois conspicuous consumption. The historian Kathleen Kete describes this process in nineteenth-century Paris, where coddled canines were both vehicles of class sensibility and "countericons" to what was increasingly perceived as an alienating, dehumanized, scientific age.[22]

In the United States, petkeeping was a marker of middle-class family life as early as the 1820s.[23] For most children then, animals were agricultural products and farm workers as well as companions. In 1880 half of all Americans still lived on farms, and many more were closely tied to the farm economy. Nursery rhymes about milkmaids and gooseherds reflected the daily texture of animal husbandry in children's lives. Horses were a major means of travel and commerce. "Country alphabets" were favorites among English-language picture books of the nineteenth and early twentieth centuries. Farm animals and farm chores were means of teaching the ABC's, as in one lavishly illustrated example from 1885:

A stands for Arabian, with Neptune to guard;
All saddled and bridled, the pet of our yard.
B for the Bees, that fly out here and there,
And bring to the hives the sweet honey with care.
C for the Cows, in the shade of the trees;
They are chewing the cud, and seem quite at their ease.[24]

Both children on farms and children in the cities kept pets. Although precise numbers are lacking, pets were a fixture of the family farm. They were working companions—mousers in the barn, herding and hunting dogs out in the yard. Little sentimentality rounded their brief lives. A dog or cat past its usefulness was "put down" without a fuss. (Today, children living in rural areas still view animals more in terms of their material usefulness for humans than do city or suburban kids.)[25] To judge from children's stories, picture books, and the art of the period, dogs and cats, many of them feral, were underfoot everywhere in the burgeoning cities as well.

The great Industrial Revolution of the nineteenth century was transforming both rural and urban landscapes. A new age of science, of machines and technology, was rapidly replacing agricultural society. Rural populations were shrinking, and work animals such as the draft horse and herd dog were fast becoming obsolete. Many children no longer encountered production animals—cows, pigs, sheep, fowl—as whole living organisms but only as animal parts served up at the dinner table. Wilderness was receding and, with it, the proximity of wild animals. For more and more youngsters living in sprawling industrial cities, animal diversity was draining out of the landscape of growing up.

Today pets remain the primary mode of intense, sustained involvement with animals for most children. In the last half of the twentieth century, the forms and functions of children's ties to animals have narrowed until a single role predominates—"dearly beloved." At the same time, as children are less directly exposed to a diversity of living animals, learning about animals has become one of the cognitive tasks of childhood. Parents teach children the names of animals from stylized drawings in picture books, take the kids to farms to see cows and pigs and to zoos and sea worlds to see living examples of wild species. The television age has brought children images of animals filtered through the syntax of nature shows complete with narrator, background music, slow motion, and commercial breaks. More and more, children encounter both wild animals and farm animals only dimly and at several removes. They come packaged by adults in the wrappings of technology. In North

America and in other industrialized countries, living animals continue to be pervasive in children's lives, but now, increasingly, a narrow band of species serves only as companions and love objects.[26] Pets have become the only nonhumans that continue to share children's daily lives. These dogs and cats, rabbits, guinea pigs, birds, hamsters, snakes, and turtles are ambassadors of "the Others," the animal species wild and tame that are no longer immediately present. For children and adults alike, pets stand in for all the members of the animal kingdom, permitting a distant, ritualized contact with other species. The animals of the human hearth give us the feeling of communion and commerce with the many species that are increasingly remote to us. Pets have come to occupy a shadow world, straddling the boundary between human and animal. A noted ecologist describes pets as "a glimmer of animal ambience, sacredness, otherness" now lost.[27] As pets come to symbolize all of animal nonhumanity, they are more than ever an intimate part of children's daily experience—curled up at their feet for the night, posing in their arms for family portraits, going along on family excursions.

Pets at the Heart of the Family

The late twentieth century brought dramatic changes not only to human contact with animals but to the organization of family life. A number of interrelated trends in North America and other industrialized nations— falling birth rates, rising divorce rates, rising rates of maternal employment, growing economic insecurity—have conspired to deprive families of time and attention for children. Scholarly and popular voices alike decry overscheduled, "hurried children" and their frazzled, insecure parents.[28] In 1979 Christopher Lasch described how the Industrial Revolution had created an image of the family as a "haven in a heartless world," countering a relentlessly ruthless capitalism.[29] In contrast, many writers have depicted the postmodern family at the end of the twentieth century as its own heartless world, riven by violence and cobbled together by bonds too fragile to withstand the combined force of internal and external pressures.[30] Amid the national angst over the lost Eden of domestic tranquillity, pets seem the one uncomplicated family tie. To human sensibilities, the identities of these "companion animals" offer a blessedly simple contrast to our multiple jangling and discordant roles. Their raison d'être, after all, is only to be companions, to give and receive love. Our relationships with our pets fulfill our most ardent fantasy: pure, unconditional, mutually flowing love. In contrast to our messy domesticity, pets can exist for their owners as Platonic ideals of loyalty, affection, and playfulness. Both tensions in contemporary childrearing and a sentimental stance toward pets make them islands of constancy for our children. We can count on these animal companions to dispense affection, relieve childhood isolation, and give our offspring the quality time that we are too exhausted or distracted to provide.

Today pets are ubiquitous in North American and European households. Although precise figures are elusive, organizations such as the American Veterinary Medical Association (AVMA), the Pet Food Institute, and the American Pet Products Manufacturers Association (APPMA) regularly track national trends in pet demographics. In 1996 the APPMA reported that 59 percent of all U.S. households had pets, with 40 to 50 percent having more than one animal. Out of every ten households, three to four had at least one dog, three had at least one cat, and one had freshwater fish. One in twenty households had a small animal, such as a hamster, rabbit, guinea pig, gerbil, mouse, rat, ferret, chinchilla, or hedgehog.[31] Joining the human population in the United States are an estimated 53 million dogs, 59 million cats, 13 million caged birds, 4 million horses, 7.3 million reptiles and amphibians, 12 million small animals such as hamsters and guinea pigs, and 12 million fish tanks.[32] There are more cats and dogs in the United States than there are people in most European countries. Similar high rates of animal ownership exist in Australia and the countries of western Europe. More than half of all households in the European Union are thought to have at least one pet.[33]

Petkeeping is big business. Americans shell out in excess of $8.5 billion annually on dog and cat food, far more than is spent for baby food, plus an estimated $7 billion on veterinary care for dogs, cats, and birds alone.[34] In 1996 dog owners spent an average of $187 and cat owners an average of $147 for veterinary care for their pets.[35] This doesn't include expenditures for the accouterments of pet care—leashes, collars, cages, beds, treats, toys, medications, cat litter, and so on. In recent years the pet care industry has been one of the hottest growth segments of the U.S. economy, rising 15 percent annually. "Premium" products such as gourmet pet food are outpacing "budget" items.[36] Pet cemeteries, pet hotels, pet boutiques for matching outfits, hip replacement surgery for your creaky canine—some view these offshoots of the endlessly branching pet market as neurotic manifestations of "petishism."[37] To others, they eloquently attest to the depth of human investment in those animals singled out for companion status.

The U.S. pet population, like its human counterpart, is becoming more diverse. Dog and cat ownership rates have stabilized in recent years, while caged birds, freshwater fish, small animals such as guinea pigs and hamsters, and reptiles are becoming more common. Domestic ferrets, iguanas, and snakes are increasingly popular as pets, with 800,000 ferrets and nearly a million snakes sharing human quarters.[38]

The penchant for petkeeping is remarkably elastic. Despite their transparent unsuitability for the part, thousands of monkeys, wolves, and large predator cats are smuggled into American homes and drafted as pets. There seems to be a growing hunger for small, helpless creatures dependent on our largesse. The pet-rock craze of the 1970s has given way in the cyberage to the pets of virtual reality. Some 4.5 million Tamagotchi, egg-size computer cyberpets from Japan, have been sold thus far in the United States alone. Once activated, the Tamagotchi (the name comes from the Japanese word for "little egg") beeps its demands from every few seconds to every few hours. The sound soon takes on a plaintive urgency. If not responded to, the "little egg" creature "dies." The Tamagotchis pluck the same chords of devotion, solicitude, irritation, and neglect as living pets wrapped in fur and feathers. Children tote their Tamagotchis in their backpacks to school; once there, they "feed" them surreptitiously in the restroom to quiet their insistent beeping. Or they draft parents or siblings as petsitters during school hours.

"Every Child Needs One"

It seems that Americans of all ages and conditions (as well as their counterparts in other industrialized nations) are besotted with pets, real and
symbolic. Families with children are more likely than any other kind of
household to have pets, despite popular stereotypes that depict pets as
surrogate children for childless couples or company for lonely widows. A
1997 AVMA survey reported that 70 percent of all households with children under six years of age and 78 percent of all households with children over six had pets.[39] Similarly, a 1991 Reader's Digest consumer survey of European households found that dogs and cats are most common
in households with children.[40]

The likelihood of owning a pet appears to increase for children as
they make the transition from preschool to the elementary grades.[41] For
example, between 1985 and 1995 we periodically canvassed families
whose children attended the ten public elementary schools in Lafayette,
Indiana, a midwestern city of about 125,000; each time, approximately
70 percent of families reported having at least one pet, and most of them
had several animals.[42] About 90 percent of the elementary school children participating in studies conducted in California were pet owners.
In Cambridgeshire, England, eight-to-twelve-year-olds lived with a
greater number of pets per family than did teens. By contrast, our studies of families with infants, toddlers, and preschoolers generally find that
between 45 and 60 percent have pets. Advice books for pet owners
wisely caution parents of babies to "think of their dogs as wolves, even if
the dog only weighs five pounds, until they are satisfied that their child
can defend him or herself."[43] And although safety and hygiene are concerns at any age, more vigorous parental monitoring—and more careful
dog training—are important when pets and children live together. Dog
bites, cat scratches, and zoonotic diseases can be health threats. Sixty-
percent of all dog-bite victims are children. In 1994, 4.7 million Americans, most of them children, were bitten, with 800,000 requiring medical attention; experts believe that these figures underreport the true incidence of bites.[44]

Parents also might be vigilant about a small animal's well-being at the hands of a baby or toddler who can't yet resist the impulse to squeeze, pinch, pull, or hit, since observational studies of young children with dogs and cats reveal that the youngsters are more likely than the animals to be rough. When a French research team videotaped two-to-five-year-old children from Besançon with their parents, siblings, and pet dogs at home, the camera captured these young children hitting, pushing, or pulling their dogs about once every six minutes. The toddlers were the roughest. By contrast, the dogs in the study showed great forbearance, almost never growling or nipping.[45]

For most children, aggressive behavior—intentional and unintentional—toward animals tends to decline as the children mature, paralleling decreases in biting, pushing, and hitting other children. Despite some concerns about young children's safety around resident animals and the children's own roughness with small creatures or ability to handle large animals, new parents who already have pets before the advent of children are likely to keep their animals, and many other parents acquire an animal soon after the baby's birth so the two "can grow up together." Overall, at least four in ten children begin life in a family that includes nonhuman members. By the time children are teenagers, at least half are likely to have one or more animals. For example, a census tract survey of households with adolescents in Los Angeles County found pet ownership running at 50 percent.[46]

As one would expect, given the cost and space requirements of keeping animals, pet ownership among families with children varies by income, housing conditions, family composition, and ethnicity. Families with higher incomes or fewer children, living in single-family homes or in rural or suburban areas, are most apt to have pets. In addition, pet ownership may vary by ethnic group, even after ethnic differences in income and housing are taken into account. For example, in one survey of families with adolescents, all from similar neighborhoods and social-class backgrounds, 75 percent of whites, 47 percent of Latinos, 43 percent of Asian Americans, and 37 percent of African Americans had pets.[47]

Piecing together an accurate picture of pet ownership rates and the factors that influence them is difficult. A range of hard-to-pin-down attitudes comes into play in predicting if, when, and which pets are acquired: parents' feelings about their own childhood experiences, their assessments of what they think their children need, the balance of their other responsibilities, and costs. Nonetheless, despite variations stemming from many family and child characteristics, existing demographic data on pet ownership translate into a single startling fact: *for many children in contemporary America, pets are more likely to be part of growing up than are siblings or fathers.* The percentage of children likely to be living with one or more pets sometime between birth and adulthood is estimated to be as high as 90 percent.[48]

These astonishingly high rates become less surprising when we consider parents' motives for getting pets. Mothers and fathers typically report getting a pet "for the children." Most parents, including those who do not have animals, believe that pets are good for children. Sometimes it sounds as if parents are enlisting pets as fur-clad nannies. Surveys offer up recurring themes: pets teach responsibility, provide companionship and love, and help teach a child how to care for others. Many parents view pets as linking their child to the natural environment and teaching them ecological awareness and sensitivity. One father of two wistfully recounted to me his own childhood visits to his grandparents' farm: "I think there is something about this circle of life that we miss out on in being away and isolated from animals, and so having a pet doesn't replace country life, in terms of being closer to nature, but at least it brings a little back; so, in a way, it is a connection."

Parents believe that the lessons pets teach grow more relevant as young children toddle out of infancy toward greater independence and higher expectations.[49] This feeling is most deeply held by adults who themselves had pets as children.[50] In general, petkeeping tends to reproduce itself; children who have pets grow up to be adults who become pet owners.[51] Yet even those with no childhood history of petkeeping often subscribe to the belief that pets are part of the optimal environment for children that the "good parent" should aim to provide. Popular opinion and popular culture conjoin to reinforce the linkage between children and pets, especially dogs and cats. The iconography of advertising pairs a towheaded, freckled young tyke with a Golden Retriever or Lab, as talisman of safety, security, and allrightness.

Pets as Children, Children as Pets

Neoteny brings about a physiological and behavioral resemblance between children and domesticated animals. The association of children and pets has strong historical and intellectual underpinnings as well. The term "pet" itself first applied to the indulged, spoiled child. By the sixteenth century, the word had migrated to other small, childlike creatures such as cats, dogs, and young farm animals.[52] In a worldview that radically separates humans from nonhumans, and rationality from animality, both children and pets straddle this great divide. Each is seen as not quite human and not quite animal. Pets are the humanized animals, the tame ones bracketed off from the wild, bred over generations to exist only in a human milieu. Children are the animal human, the instinctual, untamed substrate that humanity shares with other species. As Leslie Fielder remarked, "Children are uncertain whether they are beasts or men: little animals more like their pets than their parents."[53]

Children's essential animality has sometimes been viewed as problematic; at other times the animal nature of children has been idealized. The equation of child with animal remains.[54] From Freud's perspective, animality governs the infant and young child through the insistent drumbeat of id. The core challenge of socialization is to channel these "animal" urges toward human, civilizing ends. As Georges Bataille asked: "What are children if not animals becoming human?"[55] The Romantic era's notion of children as noble savages put a different cultural spin on the child as animal. As expressed by Jean-Jacques Rousseau, the child is in a state of nature and thereby innocent and good, as are other creatures of the wild, untainted by the selfishness and competition of civilization. Young children initially exist with beasts in a natural harmony. The strictures of human society inevitably wean them from this

Eden. This view saturates Romantic era paintings, which portray plump, ripe children with equally scrumptious young mammals as the bounty of a beneficent nature. A good example is John Thomas Peele's *The Pet* (1853), which features a pampered, ribbon-bedecked cat snuggled in the arms of an angelic little girl, while another cat laps milk at her feet. Another favorite Romantic theme, with echoes that reverberate today, was the exuberant roughhousing that young male humans were assumed to share naturally with animals. In the painting *Children at Play in a Barn*, by Platt Powell Rider (undated), a horse and spotted dog look on as four boys romp around a haycart.[56]

All I Want for Christmas

Although assumptions of children's animality and pets' humanity swirl in the cultural backdrop, parents also react to the messages they get from children themselves. Children put pets high on their wish lists, almost from the age when they can make one. Interviews with children who don't have pets, from preschoolers through adolescents in Montreal, in the Greater San Francisco Bay area, and around Syracuse, New York, reveal a nearly universal yearning for one.[57] Many children report variations on my own childhood experience. When I was about eight and my younger sister five and a half, she took to loud public prayer sessions in the middle of the driveway, a narrow strip of blacktop hemmed in with modest two-family "doubledeckers." She would call upon the Almighty Deity to grant us the little dog that our heartless parents steadfastly refused to get. I was mildly embarrassed but not yet the cynic; a small part of me thought the strategy just might work. We all became true believers when, a few days later, a small blonde creature named Trixie (exactly what we had wordlessly ordered) wandered into the driveway, just as my sister was winding up for another appeal. (Yes, we did get to keep her.)

Children's pleas and parents' conviction that pets are naturally beneficial for their children's development converge to produce disproportionately high rates of pet ownership in families with children. Unfortunately, cute and fluffy baby animals tend to be impulse gifts for children. On the heels of the popular Disney movie *A Hundred and One Dalmatians,* Dalmatian puppies—unsuitable as pets for most young children—appeared in thousands of U.S. households, prompting humane societies to launch a public-relations campaign to discourage the purchases. Bunny rabbits and chicks pop up in families each Easter as regularly as daffodils and with about as long a season. According to many of the humane society professionals I've talked with, a few weeks later, unwanted animals appear at the doorstep of humane shelters.

We Are Family

What happens once pets become part of a human household with children? Given the wide range of species kept as pets, the varied circumstances under which they are kept, and, most of all, the unique dynamics of each family, there is no single or simple answer to this question. One family may keep a guard dog chained outside; another may set a place at the dinner table for their parakeet; a third might decorate the living room with a few goldfish swimming in a bowl. Considering such variability, it's striking that so many children and adults affirm that pets are full-fledged family members. Typical are the responses from a random sample of households in Providence, Rhode Island, contacted in 1985: 80 percent of the pet owners identified their pet as a "very important" member of the household.[58] Many families celebrated the animal's birthday, displayed its picture framed next to those of the human family members, carried the pet's photo in their wallets, and took their pets along to visit relatives and friends. In a 1997 national survey, 66 percent of U.S. dog owners, 54 percent of cat owners, 54 percent of bird owners, and nearly half of all owners of "pocket pets" such as gerbils and guinea pigs gave birthday, Christmas, or "just because I love you" presents to their animals. (One quarter of all fish owners and reptile owners did the same.)

In my interviews with children and their parents, the term "part of the family" is a familiar refrain. In fact most children I've talked with tend to look surprised and somewhat offended at the question, as if I were raising the scandalous possibility that their pet was *not* "family." Children, no less than their elders, use the language of family relationships to talk about their pets. Unlike many adults who sheepishly refer to their pets as "my baby" or "my child," as if confessing to a social failure, children employ the lexicon of family with matter-of-fact aplomb to describe their pets. When we ask children to draw pictures of their family, they invariably color in their pets, often front and center.

When we tune our ears to the pet leitmotif running through families we hear both bits and pieces of familiar melodies and strains of new music. Pets readily get drafted as players in the drama of family dynamics, reflecting within the microcosm of the individual family the human tendency to treat animals as kin. At the same time, bonds with pets are not simply substitutes for human relationships. Pets bring something new into the fabric of the family. This mixture of sameness and difference makes the relationship with pets unique, one that may compensate for a missing or inadequate social tie, may augment qualities already existing in human relationships, or may affect children's development in ways not reducible to the impact of human bonds.

Babyface Pets as Babies

Even before there are offspring, a pet may become the indulged child of a young couple, the practice baby before the real thing comes. Neoteny ensures that the most common pets—dogs, cats, guinea pigs, gerbils, hamsters, birds—retain the same "babyface" cuteness that human babies and young children exude. According to ethologists, this eternal childlike quality is an "innate releasing mechanism," bred by evolution to pull our heartstrings, make us smile, and jump-start our caregiving impulses. In this way, many pets share with human babies and young children the same physiological signals that push "parenting" buttons, and buttress our association of pets with children.

Like older children, animals can feel displaced and jealous (while their owners feel guilty) when the arrival of a human baby abruptly ratchets pets down a notch in the parents' affection hierarchy. As one young mother confessed: "After Mandy was born, I'd say I spend about one tenth as much time with the dog. Before she was born, Foxy was our baby. I do think it's hard for him to accept."[59]

When our first child, Sara, arrived, our large black cat, Max, eloquently played out a similar displacement drama. During the months of my pregnancy, Max's feet seldom touched the ground. With every surge of maternal hormones, I carried, cuddled, and stroked him. Then my husband and I transmogrified overnight into shaky, sleep-deprived new parents, totally absorbed in the new baby. We were grateful for the magic quieting that pacifiers wrought in the middle of the night, but we never seemed to be able to find the wrinkled plastic nipple by the next day. Drowning in disposable baby gear, we shrugged each pacifier off as lost and, every few days, replaced it. Several months later, behind a jumble of boxes in the basement, my husband unearthed a mound of chewed pacifiers, evidence of Max's guerrilla campaign against the intruder. From the first, even before a child is born, pets are sometimes placeholders for "child." Pets can figure in the opening act of family alignment dramas when a couple becomes three, or a trio expands to four.

The Model Kid Brother or Sister

One precociously perceptive ten-year-old girl, Erica, the daughter of a family therapist, clarified the tiers of her family ties to me this way: "First, of course, there's my mother and father. Next comes Igor [her hamster] and Philip [her brother]. And then comes Mozart [the family dog] and Felix [the cat]. Igor is like a sibling, so I put him on the same level as my brother." Many children cast their pets in sibling roles, especially if they have dogs, cats, birds, or other interactive species as pets. In interview studies, seven- and ten-year-olds use the same vocabulary to describe both their pets and their siblings as playmates—"They keep me company; they play games with me."[60] For children without younger brothers or sisters, a pet often serves as the functional equivalent. English eight-to-sixteen-year-olds who are only children or the youngest sibling report owning more pets than their schoolmates.[61] We asked pet-owning parents—90 percent owned dogs, cats, or both—to estimate how much time their five-to-twelve-year-olds regularly spent playing with or caring for family pets. According to these parents, "only" or youngest children, who lacked younger siblings, spent significantly more time playing with and caring for their pets than did children who had younger sibs.[62] In-depth interviews with children suggest that those without siblings or with only older ones often seek out their pets as substitute younger brothers or sisters. At the same time, some animals are eliciting this attention as well; pet dogs themselves direct more of their attention toward a particular child when there are fewer other children in the household.[63]

Studies of siblings depict a leader-follower, teacher-learner pattern, with older children setting the pace for their younger brothers and sisters.[64] Children's play with their pets has qualities in common with this older-younger sib dynamic, as the child becomes the leader, the more mature and accomplished one, in relation to the pet. One mother discerned this dynamic as she mused on their five-year-old dog Holly's relationship with Laura, the younger of two daughters. When Holly was a puppy, she "was Laura's little sister . . . we thought that maybe Holly served a role in our family of being the bad child or the naughty child or the youngest child who doesn't know how to do something. That made Laura feel like she was more competent. There was someone younger than her."

In some ways, however, the quasi-sibling relationship of child and pet is an idealized one for the child. The pet is the younger brother or sister, declawed and defanged of challenge and competition; the relationship is stripped of the tensions and rivalries inherent when two or more human offspring jockey for limited parental time and attention. The pet as younger sibling stakes no claims for reciprocity or privilege. A dog as kid brother or sister distills a sibling substrate of worshipful attention, companionship on demand, and retreat in the face of challenge. Even the youngest child has a one-up position to the animal in the family's hierarchy of power. Perhaps this is one reason why mutual affection and love dominate children's descriptions of their relationships with their pets—"He wants to be with me"; "She purrs when I'm there"—but appear less frequently as themes when children talk about their siblings.[65]

Pets in the Family Drama

Over the last several decades, scholars viewing families under the lens of systems have made new strides in understanding family dynamics. From a systems perspective, families are organic wholes, more than the sum of their constituent individual personalities. Each family member influences and is in turn influenced by every other, as if the family unit were a giant tuning fork, with each individual's movement and feeling reverberating through it. Within each family system nest subsystems based on age and role—the parental subsystem, the sibling subsystem— as well as shifting alliances. Although family systems scholars, with a few exceptions, fail to recognize it, pets, as family members, typically are part of these complex family systems.

Given that a family system is a dense circuitry of emotional currents connecting each family member, pets can, and often do, occupy nodes in that web of connections. In one study, women—usually tapped as reporters on family dynamics—described how their pets, especially dogs, raised family morale. The women endorsed statements like "Our pet helps family members communicate" and "Our pet helps family members relax and unwind at the end of the day."[66] Pets may become part of "triangling," a process in which intense emotions between two persons deflect onto a third person, issue, or, in this case, animal.[67] From interviews with pet-owning military families, Ann Cain describes numerous examples of both adults and children "triangling" pets: a mother is angry at her daughter but yells at the dog instead; a mother talks to her cat so her daughter can overhear, saying things she would not tell her daughter directly; a father is friendlier to the dog than to his son.[68] Parents depict their pets as sensing family tension and actively shifting attention to themselves, by coming up to be petted, even by doing something "silly," to defuse tension. To be sure, dogs, cats, birds, and horses are finely tuned barometers of human feelings, readily reflecting and reacting to the emotional climate. There are even clinical accounts of pets mirroring anorexia, depression, and other disorders in their human owners.[69] Yet the way that some pet owners frame their stories, reading into their pets intentional strategies for peacemaking, attests to the human proclivity for casting pets in the family drama.

Because pets are players on the family stage, human distress easily maps onto them. A scattering of clinical descriptions of adolescent and adult patients describes pathological expressions of displacement of emotion onto pets—intense but anxious caregiving as a substitute for human attachments, and nervous breakdowns after the death of a beloved dog.[70] More typical are expressions of deep emotion—sudden panic when a cat or dog seems to be lost, genuine bereavement and despair when a pet dies, elation at reuniting after time apart.

Pets also can be the coin to express "mine," "hers," "his," and "ours" within the family. As ten-year-old Erica explained to me: "The cat, we don't interact with him as much. He is more with my parents. He jumps on their lap, he sleeps in their bed at night. And then, the guinea pig, he sleeps in my room. I pick him up, I pet him." Her six-year-old brother was adamant that the dog, Mozart, be labeled "ours." When I asked him to describe how he could tell what "your pet Mozart is feeling," he looked stonily back and replied: "Mozart is *not* my pet." Erica rolled her eyes at this and said, "Oh, c'mon, Philip." "No," he explained, "Mozart is *everybody's* pet." It was crucial to get it right—the family dog, embodiment of family cohesion.

Although nearly all families with children and pets incorporate their animals into the dynamics of the family, the precise quality of children's relationships with pets remains elusive. Because research attention has been elsewhere until quite recently, much of children's emotional life with animals is hidden to us. We observe children with their pets, we talk to them about these animals, but we are squinting through a lens adapted to see only human-human bonds. We borrow the vocabulary of human kinship terms—mother, father, brother, sister, grandparent, uncle, aunt—and attempt to map them onto pets. We grope to describe these relationships in terms of "as if" and "like," circling around them with analogy, never quite making contact. The more we listen to children and their parents tell us about their pets, the more we observe the texture of these relationships, the more the simple analogies seem inadequate. A multilayered, complex, and sometimes contradictory love emerges, similar to other family bonds or friendships in some ways, distinct in others.

3

Love on Four Legs

When I first became intrigued by children's attachments to their pets, I set out in typical psychologist fashion to devise a scale to measure the bond. I came up with a series of contrasting descriptions of children and their pets, and asked children to compare themselves with these hypothetical kids. For example, I said: "Some kids talk to their pets. Other kids don't talk to their pets. Which sort of kid are you like?" After the child had made a choice, I followed up with, "Are you a lot like this kid, or just sort of like this kid?" This approach, called a "structured alternative format," is recommended over asking more straightforwardly "Do you talk to your pet?" in order to avoid suggesting to children what they might believe is a desirable response.

I constructed a series of structured alternative questions to tap whether children slept with their pet, believed their pet understood their feelings, liked their pet as much as a good friend, and so on. Next I took the questions out on the road, pilot testing them with groups of preschoolers and elementary school age children. Their reactions were encouraging. I seemed to be tapping familiar and easily understood aspects of life with resident animals. Only one description—"Some children like their pets as much as a good friend, but some children do not like their pets as much as a good friend"—elicited surprising responses. A number of children vehemently disagreed with both descriptions, refusing to select either group of children as "like me." Since the same children had agreed that they talked to, held, played with, and felt understood by their pets, I was puzzled. Finally, one eight-year-old boy, Sam, patiently explained the inadequacy of my question: "Well, I like my dog *better* than a good friend, so I have to answer 'no' to both." (I subsequently amended the description: "Some children like their pets as much as, *or more than*, a good friend.")

The resulting "pet attachment scale" yielded nice round numbers that summed up a child's feelings in a single score. But this scale, like others purporting to quantify attachment to pets, reduces a complex of feelings and behaviors to a few questionnaire items.[1] What does it mean to describe pets as loved ones for children? And how is this love different from human love? We can talk to children and observe them with their pets. Yet children's words, like those of adults, wrap more readily around feelings toward humans. Understanding children's emotional investment in animals is like slowly piecing together a puzzle, knowing that some pieces are still missing.

Description of children's bonds with their pets sets the stage for a further question: What do they mean for kids' growing up? If a child's early relationships are formative, what, if anything, do bonds with pets presage? Perhaps one way to begin is to examine themes—intimate dialogue, nurturing, being in the here-and-now, reassurance, and loss— that emerge from talking with and observing children, their human family members, and their pets. Each theme reveals subtle ways in which children's bonds with their pets both resemble and differ from human family bonds and suggests provocative implications for development.

Intimate Dialogue

Humans of all ages seem drawn to speak to their pets; for example, 66 percent of adult dog owners and 95 percent of bird owners report talking frequently to their animals. This human speech to animals is unlike our occasional outbursts at inanimate objects, as when we mutter at a recalcitrant car motor or hurl invective at a suddenly dimmed computer screen, and also unlike the audible interior monologue of talking to one-self out loud. Talk to animals characteristically takes the form of conver-sation. Much like "motherese," the conversational form of speech moth-ers (and other humans) use toward babies, people speak to their pets in a higher-pitched, soft singsong, often ending an utterance with a rising inflection, as if posing a question, and inserting pauses for imaginary re-plies. Speech tempo slows, and the length of utterances shortens.[2] Hu-mans scaffold both sides of this dialogue, filling in the "take" of a verbal "give and take" on behalf of the nonverbal pet (or baby). Of course, both pets and babies are responding; their body language and nonverbal sounds are highly communicative. Humans seem drawn to translate this nonverbal communication into its verbal equivalent by decoding ges-ture, look, and sound into language.

The use of "motherese" with pets as well as babies challenges one widely accepted explanation for its existence. "Motherese," which Dar-win called "the sweet music of the species,"[3] sounds like a melody de-signed by the evolutionary Earth Mother to promote infants' language development and social engagement. By providing a scaffold for dia-logue long before the baby is able to participate verbally, "motherese" crooners help infants learn to take turns in conversation; they gradually become able to fill in the pauses with their own contribution. The tonal qualities and accompanying nonverbal expressions of "motherese"—alert, bright-eyed, and somewhat exaggerated—highlight distinctive as-pects of language and direct the infant's attention to them. However, adults and children, even many preschoolers, clearly realize that their pets are not candidates for future membership in the human linguistic community. So "motherese" toward animals cannot have arisen to pro-mote animal language acquisition.

Instead, the characteristic speech of children and adults toward their pets is in the service of promoting and affirming intimacy, communicat-ing across species boundaries. Once humans become fully verbal, as early as three years of age, they draw pets across the linguistic barrier separating humans from other species. Through the pet variant of "motherese," called "doggerel" in one study, they make their animals full partners in dialogue.[4] The child is then the animal's interpreter, filling in the nonhuman partner's meaning.

Some qualities of speech to pets, distinctive from speech to babies, support this idea. When adults have been observed talking to their dogs or birds, they place their heads close to the animal's head and invariably stroke, nuzzle, and pet the animal, seemingly compelled to combine touch and talk. Adults lower their voices to a confidential murmur, and their facial muscles relax. With eyes half-closed, a subtle, Mona Lisa–like smile may play across the face. By contrast, adults speaking to babies have more animated, wide-eyed expressions, with tenser facial muscles. Mothers use more words to point out objects when they talk to babies, fewer in "doggerel" to their dogs.[5] Babytalk is less often fused with close physical contact than is talk to pets.[6] Although dialogue with pets in some ways resembles talk to babies, the distinctive features of "petese"–a term I prefer to the canine-limited "doggerel"–reveal it as an affirmation of the bond between animal and human owner.

Even young children appear to use petese for intimate dialogue with their pets in ways similar to older children and adults.[7] Interestingly, when preschoolers watch wild animals around them—birds flying, squirrels scampering up trees—or hold small classroom animals like rabbits, they seldom talk to them.[8] When they do, the talk does not resemble intimate dialogue, which seems reserved for those individual animals who are loved ones.

There also are some distinctive features of children's intimate dialogue with pets that hint at its developmental significance. Young children are more likely than adults to believe that their animals literally understand them. Some preschoolers are adamant that their pets actually can speak back, confusing the child's own ability to speak with that of the animal and conflating talking cartoon animals with their pets. At the same time, even young children often show some awareness of the distinctive properties of animals as sentient, feeling, communicative, but nonlinguistic entities.[9] In describing their dialogues with pets, elementary school children explain how their own verbal contributions differ from the animal's body gestures, barks, growls, whines, purrs, or meows.

Even as pets are enlisted as linguistic partners, children reveal growing understanding of the pretend aspects of the interchange. "Conversing" with pets may help children learn about the distinct communicative abilities of different interactive partners.

What is the intimate dialogue about? Children underscore their bond with greetings ("How're you doing, Buster? Ooh, I guess you're glad to see me!"), commands ("Go get it!"), affectionate endearments ("So, you want your tummy rubbed . . . There's a good girl"), and notes of irritation ("Quit that scratching. You know it's bad"). In many ways, children's talk to pets parallels their talk with human playmates. But one feature of intimate dialogue with pets, less common in conversation with friends—at least until adolescence—keeps surfacing.

Many children report confiding in their pets, who serve as audience for secrets, fears, and angers. One study of seven- and ten-year-olds found that pet-owning children were as likely to talk to their pets about sad, angry, afraid, happy, and secret experiences as with their siblings.[10] Animal silence can be taken as assent, body movement and sound as encouragement. The wide-eyed, silent attentiveness of a dog, cat, or rabbit can seem like a deep pool of limitless understanding. Pets become the uncritical, accepting audience that invites disclosure. The responsiveness of some species of pets, especially dogs, to the human emotional climate reinforces this sense of understanding. For example, there is evidence that puppies reared among frequently smiling humans will mimic the human grin, a facial expression never seen among wild wolves.[11] Many children and their parents have described to me incidents when their dog, cat, bird, or even Vietnamese pot-bellied pig sensed their emotional distress and nuzzled, licked, or just gazed soulfully at them.

As children mature, the tendency to enlist pets as confidants shows no signs of diminishing. Here is a developmental pattern distinct from children's relationships with human family members, from whom children gradually learn to withhold, to guard their secret, private life. Children eventually define themselves as separate and distinct from mother, father, and sibling in processes psychologists have variously de-

scribed as individuation, differentiation, identity achievement, or auton-
omy. Such psychological separation from one's pet, on the other hand, is
never a prerequisite for maturity. Expectations, discipline, values, and
conflicts over means and ends freight human ties; parents are the rule
makers, children the rule testers. Pets are outside all this human complexity. From the child's perspective, they can provide uncomplicated
and unthreatening intimacy.

Although petese-speaking children treat their companion animals as
if they were linguistic partners (even though they know they aren't),
much of children's (and adults') intimate dialogue with pets uses the
language of body, gesture, and tone. Your cat snuggles into your lap as
you watch television, deepening its purrs as you absentmindedly stroke
its fur and rub behind its ears. A five-year-old boy sprawls on the floor to
watch his favorite video, with his head propped up on his dog to create
just the right viewing angle. A teenage girl puts on her coat and hat and
looks expectantly at her dog, who is already at the door, ready for the
walk—a seamless interchange. In dialogues with animals the nonverbal
channel stays fully open, often dominant, sometimes running as an un-
dercurrent. Such multichannel dialogues may help children develop
emotional intelligence, which has only recently taken its place as a worthy field of study alongside cognitive or analytic intelligence.[12] With experience and maturation, children gradually sharpen their skills at mining human facial expressions and body movement for clues to a person's
inner feelings. In human-human communication, says Daniel Goleman,
"the mode of emotions is nonverbal."[13] Yet an estimated 10 percent of all
U.S. children suffer from what has been called "nonverbal illiteracy";
these children can't read nonverbal cues in others, or they use inappropriate or indecipherable nonverbal behavior themselves. Hence, such
children's nonverbal expressions are difficult for others to decode.[14]

The nonverbal communication inherent in child-pet dialogue may
help children hone their ability to pick up cues to the internal states of
other beings from body movements, facial expressions, and voice tone or
pitch. Our interviews contain many examples of children showing off
their expertise as translators of their pet's nonverbal communication.

Eleven-year-old Kate explained that her cat Gina "talks" to her: "Well, not really. You can sort of tell what she's saying, cause she'll jump up, try to push against the porch door and meow until you open it and she'll rub against one of our cabinets until we give her a treat . . . and in the middle of the night, she'll make these sounds, because she doesn't know where anybody is, or she wants someone to come pet her."

There are no empirical studies linking patterns of verbal or nonverbal interaction with pets and children's emotional intelligence. Nor is there detailed observation of how verbal and nonverbal communication occurs between child and pet. However, in several studies, young children who own pets or who are more involved with them tend to show greater emotional sensitivity than comparison children without pets. The pet-involved children express more empathy and are more skilled in predicting how others would feel in different situations.[15]

These findings are not consistent or strong enough to do more than raise possibilities for future researchers. Any association between pets in children's lives and either their concurrent or their subsequent emotional intelligence accommodates several interpretations. Preschoolers typically are on a steep learning curve when it comes to discovering the feelings and thoughts of others. These skills might be sharpened by deciphering animal communication. On the other hand, young children who are already highly empathic might be drawn to the challenge of understanding a different being. Parents may supply an exceptionally caring child with a menagerie of creatures to tend. Nonetheless, the possibility that involvement with pets—and we would need to understand what kinds of involvement—may promote emotional intelligence should stimulate scientific inquiry.

As children deal with the stresses of growing up, the continuing availability of intimate dialogues with pets may provide a nonjudgmental outlet for the uncensored expressions of feelings. An angry or depressed child can always hug a favorite stuffed animal, squeeze a "blankie," or complain to the bedroom walls, but only a pet provides a sentient, feeling audience, one that does not require clear, articulate, and grammatical expression. The niceties of turn-taking, reciprocity, and mutual acknowledgment that make up conversational competence with humans don't apply. For children in the process of language learning, effective communication with humans requires making oneself clear, and this is an imperfectly mastered feat. Dialogues with pets offer a time-out from the anxieties of human interchange. Despite most children's acknowledgment that pets cannot literally comprehend what they are saying, children have the feeling of being heard and being understood. Pets may give children a sense of an especially authentic audience because, as one scholar noted, an "animal does not provoke a divided or 'double-bind' situation . . . since it does not present verbal messages that clash with nonverbal ones."[16] What's more, unlike blankies and stuffed animals, pets never need to be outgrown in the name of "maturity."[17]

"Something to Take Care Of"

When asked to tell us about their pets, children often begin by explaining the ways they take care of them—feeding them, taking dogs for walks, going along with their parents to the vet, cleaning out the cages and litter boxes, giving them baths, and above all, playing with them and giving them attention. Some tasks, like cleanup chores, resemble domestic responsibilities enforced by parents on reluctant youngsters. Children describe other aspects of care—feeding, walking, playing—in different terms. As one seven-year-old boy explained: "I check [my dog's] water dish every morning, to make sure he has enough. If it's low, I fill it. He needs fresh water there." Or this, from a ten-year-old girl: "No table scraps, that's the rule. Spots [the cat] shouldn't have those, even though she really wants them. It's not good for her." Here we see children mindful of the needs of creatures very different from themselves and concerned about meeting those needs. What is remarkable about the theme of nurturing pets is how seldom children employ this vocabulary of caregiving when they talk about other children, parents, siblings, friends, relatives, or teachers.

The image of contemporary childhood in the Unied States and other industrialized countries portrays children on the receiving end of care and nurture. Depending upon one's perspective, that vast undertaking called childrearing—equal parts child protection, safety, stimulation, education, and training—is the province of parents, teachers, communities, government, and society at large. The proper caregivers are grown-ups, whose investments in children ultimately pay off as they mature into caring adults, ready to nurture their own (and others') children. Actual arrangements often fall short of these vaunted ideals, of course, as overburdened parents entrust child care to inexperienced teenagers and underpaid day-care workers.

The view that children are solely recipients of care and adults their care providers is tied to another set of assumptions about the origins of sensitive caregiving. Adults are thought to absorb motivation and skill to nurture by having experienced during childhood the positive benefits of receiving good nurture. In this way, as adults, we care for others in the way we ourselves were cared for.[18]

Cross-cultural studies challenge the notion that nurturing others springs forth in adulthood solely as the outcome of being cared for as children. Many cultures, in India, Africa, South America, and parts of Asia, incorporate sibling caretaking into socialization goals for children. This term refers to children's regular involvement, starting as early as age five or six, in caring for younger brothers and sisters. Such sibling caretaking is quite different from a teenager's occasional help by babysitting for younger siblings or parents' encouragement of firstborns to be kind and gentle with littler ones. John and Beatrice Whiting's pioneering investigations, with their colleagues, of cultural variation in childrearing—in Liberia, Kenya, India, Mexico, the Philippines, Okinawa, and in several small towns in the United States—documented that in the non-Western cultures, older siblings, especially girls, regularly care for infants, toddlers, and younger children more frequently than do fathers or any adults other than mothers.[19] In sibling-caretaking societies, parents viewed nurturing as an important contribution that children can make to the family as well as a skill to be gradually acquired through practice and supervision during childhood. Across cultures, children who spent more time as sibling caretakers, the Whitings found, displayed more empathy and concern for the needs of others and were more skilled and motivated as child nurturers. (The researchers did not assess the caregiving expertise of these children when they later became adults and, presumably, parents.) When average levels of caregiving involvement, skill, and empathic concern were compared across cultures, the U.S. children studied had the lowest levels.

Sibling caretaking patterns around the world show that children can become more nurturing as they mature when they have opportunities, encouragement, and practice in caring for others more needy than themselves.[20] Some thinkers go further, arguing that a basic human need is to nurture others.[21] If we all need to be needed, children, no less than adults, require opportunities to care for others.

In the United States, sibling caretaking lacks cultural support as an important developmental experience that benefits both older and younger child as well as the family. It is illegal to leave children in the care of other children who are under sixteen years of age. Psychologists caution against a "parentified child" whose own developmental needs must inevitably languish while she—usually girls are viewed as most at risk—shoulders responsibility for younger brothers and sisters during nonschool hours.

The absence of sibling caretaking as a widely accepted cultural practice, along with small family size, leaves most children in the United States and other industrialized countries with few outlets to practice nurture. Many parents I've interviewed seem to be intuitively responding to this lack when they explain their hope that pets will bring out the urge to nurture in their children and will give them the experience, while still dependent children, of having some creature dependent upon them. Although children seldom do the lion's share of pet care—parents, especially mothers, take over most of the feeding, walking, litter changing, and cage cleaning—pets remain the primary, and often only, means by which children become caretakers, not just recipients of care.[22]

As we've seen, widespread pet ownership among families with children, combined with declining birth rates, means that in both North

America and western Europe, children are more likely to have pets than younger siblings living with them. Even when younger brothers or sisters are around, taking responsibility for pet care and investing free time in such care are more socially accepted for children than devoting time to care of younger siblings. Pets may be one culturally sanctioned domain of caregiving available for most North American children.

To document this with a nationally representative sample of U.S. families, I hunted through a gold mine of data on daily family life gathered by a University of Michigan team of researchers in 1981.[23] They contacted a representative random sample of Americans four times during that year and each time collected "time use activity records" from each family member. These are minute-by-minute recreations of what each individual did in the preceding twenty-four hours, starting at midnight. This method yields a much more reliable account of what people actually do with their time than notoriously inexact global estimates—how much TV would you say you watch per week?—or one-shot observations.

I examined the records of a randomly selected 200 families who had a father, mother, and at least one child under age seventeen living at home. In this study, as in so many others, the investigators did not ask about pet ownership, although they collected voluminous background information on each family. To uncover the presence of pets, I looked for "pet care" as an activity by any family member over the twenty-four-hour period. This method, missing pets at the vet, gone AWOL, or simply neglected, yielded a conservative underestimate of 76 families with pets. In the same sample, I found 53 families who had a child under three as well as an older child. The activity records drawn from a national sample confirmed that pets are becoming more common in children's home environments than infant or toddler siblings.

Next I compared how much time children with pets at home devoted to "pet care" within a twenty-four-hour period as compared with how much time children with infant or toddler sibs spent on "sibling care" or even "sibling play." Over a twenty-four-hour period during the weekend, pet-owning children spent an average of 10.33 minutes doing pet care, whereas children with baby siblings spent, on average, 2.45 minutes caring for or playing with them. When pets are there, children respond with more caregiving than they do when growing up with baby brothers or sisters—nearly five times as much.

There are many possible reasons for this result. Parents might be reluctant to let their children "practice" caregiving on younger siblings. Baby brothers and sisters trigger all the resentments and conflicts embedded in the term *sibling rivalry.* The cognitive and emotional demands that human babies and toddlers make on their caregivers are far more complex than those posed by pet care. Conversely, caring for a pet is relatively free of conflicts with your charge. The difficulty of the task may more easily match a child's cognitive and emotional abilities. In other words, this is low-risk, accessible caregiving.

Another reason has particular developmental implications for boys. Caring for pets, unlike caring for babies, young children, or other people, is free of the gender-role associations that typecast nurture as an essentially feminine, perhaps quintessentially feminine, enterprise.

Despite contemporary fathers' greater involvement in daily child-rearing and the routines of child care, child nurture remains disproportionately women's work. Mothers do the heavy lifting in this sphere at home, grandmothers tend to be more regular caretakers than grandfathers, and women fill the ranks of day-care providers, babysitters, teachers, and social workers. If we expand the concept of nurture to include meeting the needs of any being who is dependent upon our care—casting the linguistic net wider to encompass care for the infirm elderly, the sick, and those with disabilities requiring assistance— women continue to fill both paid and volunteer positions in overwhelming numbers. As an example, a wife is more likely to take care of her husband's elderly, infirm parents than is their biological or adoptive son, her husband. This disproportionate investment of women in caregiving across the human lifespan is echoed in other cultures. The Whitings found that where sibling caretaking is an important responsibility of childhood, parents assign girls preferentially to child-care duties, although boys often get drafted when there are no daughters. In agrarian societies, parents put boys rather than girls on animal care detail, if both sexes are available.[24]

The gendered quality of nurture toward humans is not lost on even very young children, who both experience and observe human caregiving overwhelmingly from females. In contrast, caring for animals, including pets, does not have this aura of femaleness. Hence we would expect children to view pet care as essentially gender-neutral, as appropriate for boys as for girls.

Seeing pet care as a gender-neutral domain takes on added significance in the light of children's gender-role development. At around eighteen to twenty-four months children begin to consistently label themselves as male or female—I am a boy; I am a girl—and to apply these labels to others. By age three, they understand that such labels are stable: baby boys grow up to be men; adult women were once little girls. By age five, children grasp that changes in outward appearance— boys in dresses, for example—do not change gender identity.[25] Paralleling these developments is understanding of gender-role stereotypes. By age three, most children can sort toys, adult possessions, and even adult tasks by their stereotypical associations: dolls, cooking, and irons go in the "girl" pile; trucks, car repair, and shovels, in the "boy" pile.[26] Grasping one's own gender identity and its associated social stereotypes impels children to behave in ways consistent with gender-role expectations. Girls avoid trucks, boys shun dolls. Young children soon act as "gender police" to reinforce "appropriate" behavior in their peers. For example, four-year-old "guys-in-training" serve as a chorus to admonish a boy who is contentedly feeding a doll in the day-care center "playhouse" area that "boys don't play with dolls."

If young children see the nurturing of humans as essentially female and associate it with the feminine gender role, boys should start to show less interest in caring for babies or younger children, even symbolically through pretend or doll play, as these "little men" take gender-role messages to heart. My colleague Alan Fogel and I observed just such a process. We videotaped two-and-a-half-to-six-year-old boys and girls as they met unfamiliar babies and the babies' mothers in a playroom stocked with toys. In some sessions we asked the mothers to busy themselves with magazines so that we could see how the preschoolers reacted to the crawling babies. In other sessions, we coached the mothers to involve the older children as baby-care "helpers." The mothers would ask the preschoolers to distract their babies with a toy, offer a bottle, or bring over a diaper. Boys and girls under four were equally fascinated with and responsive to the babies and readily complied with the mothers' requests. Among the four-to-six-year-olds, sex differences were emerging, and they were most marked among the oldest preschoolers. The six-year-old boys were less interested in the babies than were any of the other children, in some cases determinedly ignoring infants who crawled after them and tried vainly to engage their attention. In contrast, the four-to-six-year-old girls, bustling about like "little mothers," seemed enamored with the babies and plunged enthusiastically into helping take care of them.[27]

Nurture directed at pets is free of this gendered pattern. Boys who understand their gender identity and have absorbed cultural stereotypes about male and female behaviors are as receptive as girls to the idea of themselves as nurturers of pets. In one study, we questioned a group of four-year-olds and a group of seven-year-olds—half boys and half girls at each age level—about their ideas concerning caring for babies, for young children, for elderly people, and for pets (dogs and cats). To represent possible caregivers, we showed each child line drawings of male and female children, teenagers, young adults, and older adults. When we asked, "Who could take care of a baby?" both the younger and older children picked out drawings of adult females, whom they often labeled "mommies," as best equipped to provide this care. While both four- and seven-year-olds consistently selected teenage or adult females as the most competent caregivers of human infants, young children, or elderly, seven-year-olds showed this female bias more strongly. Only when we asked about care for a dog or a cat did children at both ages choose pictures of males and females as caregivers with about equal frequency.[28]

According to surveys we have conducted with parents, daughters, by the time they are eight years old, are more involved than sons in baby care both inside and outside the home, while boys and girls remain equally involved in pet care. Between ages five and twelve, both boys and girls devote progressively less time to caring for or playing with younger siblings, as school, friends, organized sports, and other activities compete for time. Yet when parents estimated how much nonschool time their children regularly spent on pet care or pet play, no age differences appeared. Parents of fifth-graders who had both younger siblings and pets at home told us that these ten-year-olds—boys and girls equally—spent more time in care of and play with their pets than with their younger brothers or sisters.[29]

Caring for pets is the only outlet for nurturing others that is ubiquitously available for most boys in their homes and does not reflect a suspected diminution of masculine behavior. This makes pet care a potential training ground for learning how to nurture another being who has needs different from one's own. However, we do not know the extent to which nurturing pets in childhood might generalize later to nurturing other humans.[30]

There's also the possibility that nurturing pets sensitizes children to animal-welfare and ecological concerns. In a study of British university students, those who as children had been more involved in caring for pets had more humane attitudes toward both pet and nonpet animals and expressed greater concern for animal-welfare and environmental issues.[31] A cautious conclusion is that caring for pets fulfills an important need in children's lives, especially for boys, whose opportunities to nurture are impoverished. A hypothesis, which we ought to pursue vigorously, is that nurturing pets during childhood *may* contribute later to a more nurturing orientation toward animals and perhaps also humans.

In the Here-and-Now

More than miniature dependents for still-dependent boys and girls, pets are children's playmates, friends, and props as well. Companion animals get dressed up as babies and plopped in carriages, seated as honored tea-party guests, assigned to cover the entire outfield, and enlisted as both story character and audience. The dogs endlessly fetch sticks, catch balls and Frisbees, and show off tricks. They are canine advance scouts on "expeditions" into the wilds of neighborhood parks. The cats curl up on the homework papers and stretch out at the foot of the bed. The rabbits, hamsters, gerbils, and guinea pigs warm laps. The birds and fish animate dark corners of rooms.

In all these ways, pets are living, breathing presences; they go along with and stay beside their child owners. They bear silent witness as children do homework, watch television, play computer games, or laze around daydreaming. One of the most important yet unrecognized functions of pets—from dogs to goldfish—for children may be their *thereness*. (This constant availability may be a major reason why many children bestow the honorific "my best friend" on their pets.) Their animate, responsive proximity makes children feel less alone in a way that toys and games, television or video, even interactive media, cannot. Pets, like all living animals, situate a child in a give-and-take universe of fellow beings.

Spending time with a pet belongs to a category of children's activities that is increasingly endangered—unstructured hours and minutes. A 1998 University of Michigan survey of how children thirteen years old and younger spend their time found that as parents' lives have grown more hectic, their children's free time has shrunk: "Kids are feeling the time crunch, just like parents are," noted one of the study directors, Sandra Hofferth. "They are spending more time in school and preschool. As a result, something has to give at home. What gives is unstructured play—tag, hide-and-seek, board games—all the things that children just do."[32] Hanging out with a pet carves out a time and space in which the child and animal control the agenda. Such "free zones" of time, in contrast to organized sports, household chores, homework, and television viewing—all of which eat into children's discretionary time—can nurture creativity and stimulate young imaginations.[33]

When a child pats a dog, brushes a cat, watches birds at a feeder, or stares at a fish tank—in short, any time a child intersects with the animal world—the child steps off the wheel of human history and time. Child and animal are in the present, in the here and now. As Vicky Mehl, a humane educator in Pennsylvania, remarked to me: "Animals don't bring with them any of the baggage of human relationships. A child can be very upset, but five minutes later, the animal has forgotten."

Reassurance

Another theme that weaves with many variations through children's bonds with their pets is the sense that their animals make them feel less lonely, less afraid, and less anxious. Many children turn to their pets—not just dogs and cats, but hamsters, gerbils, birds, even fish—to make them feel better when they are feeling sad, angry, or afraid. Seventy-nine percent of German fourth-graders in one interview study said they sought out their pets when they were feeling sad.[34] In interviews with Michigan youngsters between ages ten and fourteen, 75 percent indicated that when they were upset, they turned to their pets.[35] Feelings of stress often spike when children are making difficult transitions in their lives—entering a new school, moving from one neighborhood to another, coping with the birth of a new sibling or with an older one's leaving home, or dealing with separations from one or both parents. About three months before they were to enter public school kindergarten, we asked fifty-six five-year-olds, all with pets at home, what they did when they were feeling sad, angry, afraid, happy, or wanted to tell a secret. Forty-two percent of the children spontaneously mentioned turning to their pet—most had dogs or cats—in response to at least one of those feelings. Children who derived greater support from their animal companions in this way were less anxious or withdrawn, according to their mothers and fathers.[36] From preschool years into adolescence, children seem to use their pets as calming time-outs and restorers of equilibrium.

A useful way to think about the role of pets in such circumstances is as providers of social support. Because social scientists traditionally have reserved supportive functions to other humans, we're only now recognizing pets as contributing to their owners' feelings of being loved, cared for, esteemed, and interconnected. Both adults and children who feel isolated and disconnected from others, who have no one to whom they can turn for material assistance or a friendly shoulder to cry on, and who have no one who needs them suffer from more physical, psychological, and emotional ailments. Social support is implicated in everything from adults' recovery from stroke, cancer, and heart attacks to children's risk of abuse and their success in school. Both adults and children who have human social support weather stress more successfully than their isolated counterparts.[37]

The ways in which pets reassure children echo many aspects of human social support. At a minimum, pets are a familiar presence, and they may communicate a sense of connection, a message that an acknowledgment, if not an effusive welcome, awaits the child's return home. Some aspects of pet support may make it even more effective than the human variety. Pet support is free of the complexities and ambivalence of much human support, with its norms of reciprocity, conflicting demands, or burnout when a shoulder has been cried on once too often. In this respect, pets are a refuge from the strains of human society.[38] More "on call" than many human sources, pets may be the most easily renewable fount of reassurance. When elementary school age children rated all their ties that bind—friends, parents, and pets—their pets got the top prize as most likely to last "no matter what" and "even if you get mad at each other."[39] In another study, third-grade pet owners ranked their dogs in their "top five important relationships." These children considered their dogs more important sources of comfort when ill or when scared than "a best friend" and of equal importance to their mothers or fathers.[40]

A primary function of human social support is to communicate a sense that others love, value, and care about you. Pets—perhaps especially highly interactive ones like dogs—clearly fulfill that role for many children. We know little about how affirmation from pets might be linked to the support children receive from parents, friends, or other adults. Would pet support compensate in part for lack of human support? There are hints of such a compensatory role. Children in so-called latchkey or self-care arrangements report feeling less afraid and more comfortable when they are not entirely home alone, but with a pet.[41] Abused children, as well as battered women, often derive solace and comfort from their pets.[42] These findings should prompt exploration of children's feelings of support from their pets when their parents divorce, when a parent or sibling becomes seriously ill or dies, when children move to new communities, or when other major events upset the equilibrium of children's lives.

The reassurance that children get from pets may mirror rather than compensate for supportive experiences with parents and other significant humans. Nancy Bodmer queried 752 German-speaking Swiss teenagers between twelve and sixteen years of age on their feelings of well-being, indexed by their endorsement of statements like "My future looks good." Those teens who owned pets and reported playing with them in the previous week—a very crude measure of the child's bond—had more family support, getting along better with their parents and spending more time with their families, than their counterparts without pets or with pets they had not played with recently.[43] A child's sense of support from a pet's presence or behavior may be a consequence, not a cause, of the child's social skills, empathy, or social adjustment. We need more research to clarify the connection between support from important humans, such as parents, other relatives, friends, and teachers, and important animals in a child's life.

Loss

An estimated 80 to 90 percent of America's children first confront the loss of a loved one when a pet dies, disappears, or is abandoned.[44] Children in modern, industrialized societies rarely witness human births or deaths; these events are shut away from young eyes in the specialized institutions of hospital, nursing home, funeral parlor, and cemetery. Only with pets and occasionally, small wild animals, like birds, squirrels, chipmunks, and rabbits, are children likely to encounter the essential dramas that bracket life.[45] Seeing a litter of pups come into the world or finding a goldfish floating belly-up on the water's surface brings children up against the momentousness of the beginning and end of life.

In modern, industrialized societies, pets are the only attachments that most children are likely to lose while still in childhood. Even quite young children are aware of their animals' mortality and worry about pet safety and health. Because children often see themselves as attachment figures for their pets—"he really depends on me"—young pet owners sometimes sound like fearful parents, anxious if their animal is out wandering around, or concerned for its safety while the child is in school and unavailable to take care of it.[46]

Preschooler logic likens death to sleep and insists that the dead can "wake up" or "come down from heaven." Young children are vulnerable to magical thinking, believing their "bad" thoughts or passing rages have destroyed the animals they love. Only gradually do children absorb the full import of death's message. Experiencing a pet's death is one of the few places where that message rings with all its emotional resonance. Virginia Morrow, a British sociologist, recorded this exchange between ten-year-olds Max and David: "*Max:* Well, when they die, its kind of like a family member dying, so you get all sad. *David:* I can't remember what it's like when a fish dies. *Max:* It's not that bad when a fish dies, but when a hamster dies . . . but when I was really young I cried when my fish died."[47]

An animal's death can evoke a child's spiritual questions, not just a search for facts. As Max and David discovered, new emotional territories of grief, mourning, and commemoration open. For some children, an animal's death can be a way to access other losses in their lives. One school psychologist I spoke with called pets "metaphors for loss." "When an animal dies," he said, "it brings up all kinds of losses, even moving to a new home."[48]

A runaway Spot or runover Fido forces parents to wrestle with how to explain what "dead" is, how to answer where Spot has gone or what sort of funeral Fido would have wished. A therapist friend of mine, Sandra Diskin, remembered how, upon discovering her five-year-old's turtle was dead, she prepared to break the news: "Armed with the idea of a deity of turtles and where his afterlife would be, I waited for our young boy to come home from school. When he walked in the front door I said simply, 'Ralph died,' and waited for our long talk to ensue. He said, 'Oh . . . What's to eat?' Later, when he was older, we did pick up on that long talk."[49] The writer Christopher Manes recalled his awkward wrestling with the mysteries of life and death when his five-year-old daughter's pet rabbit died and she asked what had happened to it: "I answered awkwardly that her animal had gone to 'rabbit heaven' or 'pet heaven' or something of the sort. It struck me later that I had once had a very similar conversation with my father when I was a boy, and no doubt his father before him . . . The words that passed between my daughter and me were less a conversation than an ancient ceremony, one perhaps critical to becoming a fully conscious human being."[50]

Less sensitive parents than Manes employ subterfuges to hide the reality of death. They return from euthanizing Fido to describe the dog's new home with a loving farm family. They obfuscate Fluffy's fate with euphemisms like "gone to sleep" or "put down," frightening and confusing literal-minded youngsters.[51] Some parents, uncomfortable with their child's or their own grief, immediately install a replacement. This invalidates the child's loss and short-circuits opportunity to talk about it.[52] Sometimes even conscientious, responsive parents struggle to find a balance between trivialization and overreaction. When pets die or disappear, the parents' (and child's) reaction throws into relief the complicated ways in which bonds with pets are like and unlike human bonds.[53]

For one group of children, loving an animal and losing it are tightly intertwined, even foreordained. The bond these children forge with the animal fuses elements that seem contradictory—the animal as both subject and object, something both to love and to use. Nowhere is the mix more complicated and fascinating than in 4-H "production" animal projects. In the cavernous pig barn at the local county fair near my home, Sally, a slight ten-year-old, introduced me to her three not-so-little pigs—Curly Tail ("he's a character"), Wilbur ("she's named for my favorite character from *Charlotte's Web*"), and Whacker ("he's always whacking his tail"). In a few moments, Sally explains, she will bring them into the judging pen. And then? I ask. She shrugs. She'll sell Whacker at auction tomorrow, right after the fair. Wilbur and Curly Tail will go to the state fair in a few weeks to be sold there. Sally's mother, looking on, chuckles at Sally's description of each pig, but then grows serious: "These are market animals. We tell them that at the beginning. But even so, on the auction day, you'll have trouble, you'll shed tears, I know I will. They *do* get attached."

"You Will Lose What You Care About"

Brian is a strapping eighteen-year-old whose worn jeans, boots, and John Deere cap seem molded to him. He swings with absentminded ease over the steel wire enclosures of the two pens that hold his five pigs—three Yorkshires and two Hampshires. He gives each one a last-minute check and a pat. In a few moments he'll lead them down a narrow corridor between the long rows of pens into the judging ring at the county 4-H fair. There, an intensive four months of daily feeding, weighing, and "walking"—nudging them along with a stick for about a mile of daily exercise—will come down to no more than three minutes of maneuvering his pigs back and forth in front of four judges as several hundred fellow 4-H'ers and their families look on from the stands. In the lull before the judging, Brian, his older sister, Crystal, his mother and father, and several friends slouch around, chatting comfortably. This is Brian's eighth annual 4-H pig project at the fair; the pig barn is almost a second home.

Brian bought ten four-month-old piglets in April, four months ago, at a cost of $100 to $300 each. He met half of the cost with money he'd earned mowing lawns, and his father picked up the rest of the bill. From April until July, Brian got up every morning at five to walk the pigs before school and before the sun's heat. (The Yorkshires are albino and sunburn easily.) Every evening at nine, he would walk them again. He estimates he spent two to three hours a day caring for them. "Some are smart," he points to two albino Yorkshires; "within the first two weeks, they know who is feeding them. They follow you. They become friends; they get really attached to you."

Two weeks before the fair, he selected the five "best"—"You're looking to have a muscular, lean animal by fair time," he explained to me. The other five went directly to slaughter. Tomorrow, after the judging, all but one of the remaining five will go to "pool," or slaughter at market price. A farmer has agreed to buy the remaining pig from Brian.

He doesn't give the pigs names: "Females do that. I don't care about names." He did give his pigs names the first few years, when he was ten and eleven years old, but that was long ago. Crystal, who recently graduated from many years of pig projects to 4-H judging, chimes in: "I used to give the pigs names too. When you give them names you get too attached. You had to tell yourself they'd be gone."

Brian and Crystal's mother and father spent their teen years with 4-H animal projects as well. They call themselves a "4-H family." Brian's mother remembered what she had got out of her 4-H animal projects. "It's something to care for, that's alive and breathing," she said. "You get to love and care for them; you learn responsibility. When I had my calves, I broke them to walk behind the tractor, as if they were tame. I brushed them and washed them. They like being brushed. When you rub calves under their necks, the calves stretch out their necks, 'asking' to be rubbed some more." She described the animal production projects, like Brian's, as part of growing up. "You learn that everyone will lose what you care about. That is why we took our children, even when they were small, to funeral parlors, so that they would understand."

Brian's family has a 2,000-acre farm on the southern edge of Lafayette. It's one of the largest family-owned spreads around. The farm used to have hogs, but switched to cattle because profit margins were too narrow. Brian helps out on the farm, as Crystal did before she went off to college. Brian wants to be a farmer, but his mother, a nurse, says he needs to have a trade, another option in case farming doesn't work out.

Another veteran 4-H'er, eighteen-year-old Ryan, has brought six sheep to show at the fair. Ryan, like Brian, is part of a farm family with a long history in 4-H animal projects. He too dreams of making a living as a farmer, but sees little chance of that really happening. His older brother will inherit the 3,000-acre farm; only one child can. His brother won "reserve grand champion sheep" a few years ago. Ryan utters the words "reserve grand champion" in a hushed voice tinged with awe. As he looks over his six sheep, it's clear he doesn't see grand champion material in any of them. He points out to me the heaviest, which he has selected for auction, where he'll get a better price per pound than at "pool."

I ask him to describe the "pool," which takes place the morning after the judging of animals finishes. He tells me how "they" come and back up trucks to the barn, pick up the animals and throw them in the truck, and take them to be butchered. Some winners bring their animals down and put them on the truck, but some young kids get too upset to do that. He gestures to the adjacent pen where ten-year-old Tony and eight-year-old Bethany, children of the hired hand living on Ryan's farm, crouch over two sheep, stroking their coats. Bethany is cradling the head of one of the sheep in her arms, as she plants kisses on its forehead.

Bethany introduces me to Dorsey, her Dorset sheep, and Speck, a crossbred. Tony's and Bethany's mother fills me in on the background of the project. It began five months before, when they paid $250, $125 for each sheep. She explained how they were chosen for meat content, since the judges will feel the sheep to see how much meat versus fat is on them. Tony goes over to Speck and demonstrates by pinching along the back of the sheep in imitation of the judge's assessment. What are Tony and Bethany getting out of this experience? According to their mother, they are "learning to take care of something else, even though they know there will be the end, here. They'll look forward to next year, getting more lambs."

As Bethany, Brian, Crystal, and Ryan talk about their pig, sheep, and cattle projects, you can hear them wrestling with the powerful pull of attachment to animals entrusted to their care pitted against the need to turn the animals into meat products. These 4-H'ers, most of them children, grandchildren, or neighbors of farmers whose way of life they will not inherit, confront the hard truth that the bottle-fed calf who gazes after you with big brown eyes, the one you brush every day and lead around by a halter, the one who lets you laze on its back, will abruptly become cuts of beef. These animal projects seem like rites of passage, repeated harsh lessons in which children coddle, cuddle, and care for a baby animal, and then, in its maturity, abruptly sever those ties. The next year, the process begins all over again. Protective psychological mechanisms take hold like wild vines around the intensity of their attachment and slowly smother it.

I spoke one afternoon with twenty-year-old Amanda, who grew up on her parents' hog farm and is a veteran of ten years of pig projects: "At auction it's hard. You walk out of the ring after you know how much money you're going to get [for the animal]. Then they take your pig away. They take it right out of the ring. You don't see what happens past the ring. A lot of parents tell their children the pig goes to another farm, instead of to market. As you get older, it's easier to understand. But as a little kid, it's hard to understand. This pig, or any animal, you've grown so attached to, you're never going to see it again. I remember my first or second year, as a little kid, crying because I walked in when they were taking the pigs out, loading them up to take them to market. I told everyone I smashed my hand, that's why I was crying. But I was really crying because they were taking my pigs away. Even now, it's hard. You try to disattach yourself. We won't name our pigs anymore. If you name them, it means, it's actually . . . you know, happening." Amanda's voice trails off on a sad note. A few minutes later in our conversation, she explains: "It's something you have to learn how to do, to understand the whole cycle, how they *have* to go to market. It teaches you about life, that things aren't always going to be there but you should enjoy them while they are there. Life has to go on, after. But still, it's always hard."

Raising a pig or heifer for the 4-H fair teaches an animal husbandry code of conduct. Lavish care and attention on these animals, but remember they are not pets. At the same time, don't reduce them to walking stalks of corn or tractors, agricultural objects without sensation or feelings. The children must learn an ethic of care and welfare for animals that are bred only to die for human purposes. Alongside the necessity of killing these animals lies the responsibility to care for them properly. The goal is to learn to *care for* and *care about* the animals, even to recognize an animal's personality and delight in its quirky behavior, but then to be able to have this same animal killed and turned into its monetary value without regret.

Many children and teens involved in 4-H with whom I talked use various distancing strategies to make the attaching and "disattaching" less wrenching. The most common is not naming the animals. As Amanda's younger sister said: "A lot of kids give names when they're younger. But then as they get older they realize if I don't name this pig, it's not a real thing. One year you decide not to name it, and you hope it's easier that year." Another distancing strategy that parents and 4-H leaders encourage is to focus on the competition and on the money that selling the animals bring. I spoke with Latisha, a thirteen-year-old, a few months after the county fair. She recalled the red Angus heifer she had raised and shown in the ring: "I cried because I wasn't used to giving up my animals. I'm like, 'I don't want them to die!' but"—Latisha's voice switched from sad to perky—"now I have money for college! When I got the money, I felt pretty good."

4-H leaders, judges, parents, and recent participants all emphasize a list of "positives" to be gained from animal production projects, ranging from responsibility, planning, family involvement, and camaraderie to, as one county extension agent in Georgia put it, "more about physiology than [children] will ever get in a classroom."[54] However, they skirt the issues that youngsters like Amanda, Latisha, and Brian grapple with—how to reconcile emotional attachment to an animal cared for almost since birth with the exigencies of turning that animal into meat products.

4-H production projects have plenty of critics, though, notably, not among former participants. Animal rights organizations such as People for the Ethical Treatment of Animals, or PETA, indict these projects as murdering not just animals, but children's empathy for animal suffering as well. A few shrill voices even depict 4-H pig, sheep, and cattle projects as training grounds to produce future killers, although there is no evidence for this claim. Activist groups such as Maryland-based Friends of the Pig "rescue" 4-H animals from the chopping block by purchasing them at fairs. PETA organizes information booths at 4-H fairs to win over hearts and minds to vegetarianism and, in their view, to save children's souls. Predictably, 4-H participants, veterans, and leaders adamantly disagree. In surveys conducted by 4-H organizations, the overwhelming majority of youngsters who complete what 4-H prefers to call "animal science" projects report greater, not less, understanding of and respect for animals.[55]

These 4-H projects do not steel young hearts with a callous "love for sale" message. Neither are the projects simply animal science learning in a fun package of friendly competition and family togetherness. These youngsters shower loving attention on sheep, heifers, pigs, and goats for the day of both a blue ribbon and the animals' slaughter.

Intimate dialogue, here-and-now presence, nurturance, reassurance, and loss: these aspects of children's bonds with their pets do not exhaust their complexity. Each aspect highlights a distinct facet of pets as loved ones. Intimate dialogue with pets, like children's friendships with their peers, reflects a sense of partnership and companionship. "Here-and-now" signals the immediate, in-the-present, time-out quality of engagement with animals, a feature increasingly absent from human ties. Nurturance casts children as "proto-parents" or caregivers of pets, while reassurance shifts the feeling of being cared for to the child. Unique among the array of children's ties to others, loving an animal is a "flexible alliance," within which children can alternately—or even simultaneously—experience sharing, caring, giving, receiving, being, and losing, even destroying.[56]

4

Learning from Animals

The Pine Village Elementary School hugs the ragged edge of cornfields hunkered down in drifts of snow. Wind whips across the squat 1970s brick building to the water tower across the road and the ramshackle post office, café, and general store clustered at the intersection. Inside, there's a warm, musty school smell tinged, as I approach the first-grade classroom, with aromas of cat, gerbil, and guinea pig. I've come to observe a classroom infused with animal presence. A row of small cages lines one wall—a newt, two guinea pigs balled together in a furry lump, two gerbils, a turtle, and a pair of hamsters. In the middle of the room under a desk, a floppy-eared black and white rabbit pads about an ample cage. Two goldfish circle in a large aquarium propped against the opposite wall. A mottled gray cat wanders in and out, and around the children.

These animals are what Linda Stillabower, the teacher, calls the classroom "critters," and she organizes virtually all the children's learning around them. On the day I'm there, each child is choosing an animal species to be the subject of a report. The room bustles with purposeful activity as the fifteen six-year-olds jump up and rummage through stacks of picture books about animals. The children have only five minutes to gather up materials on the animals they've chosen. At the same time, several of the children are eager to show me the living animals in their classroom. One girl is elbowing another for the floor; both spill over with stories about how each animal came to live in the classroom. The children also want me to know about the ones no longer there, like a second rabbit whom the children discovered cold and lifeless one morning when they returned to school after vacation. They show me how to pick up the hamsters and how to transfer the gerbils carefully from their cage to a small basket used to carry them around the room. The children's air of expertise is so convincing that I quickly forget I'm speaking to six-year-olds. These first-graders have amassed an astonishing store of information about this little slice of the animal kingdom.

As Linda explains the daily schedule to me, it's clear that the classroom animals function as more than living biology lessons. Each child takes a turn as "critter helper"—designated feeder, cage cleaner, and general caretaker—for a two-week period. Some children jump into the role, while others drag their feet, especially at the mess of cage cleaning and kitty litter, and then Linda supervises more closely. In Linda's view, the "helper" rotation teaches responsibility and boosts confidence as children see that what they do really matters to the welfare of the animals.

I settle in a corner of the room as the children launch into a half-hour of "tech time"—three children at the computers using educational software, the others looking through books. The atmosphere is relaxed, so different from my first-grade stay-in-your-bolted-down-chair memories. A few children sprawl on the floor; others perch on top of desks or move around the classroom from one learning center to another. The cat meanders through the maze of small bodies. While I'm there, no child focuses attention on the cat, but there's an incidental, indirect flow between it and the children. As the cat glides by, a small hand darts out to give a few pats or a hug. Casey, the smallest girl in the class, pulls the cat onto her lap as she looks at a book, her eyes never leaving the page, and as she releases her hand to turn the page, the cat slides off. Someone has opened the rabbit cage, and the rabbit is making a tentative foray across the room. DJ, a shy, slight boy, shoots a look of alarm from rabbit to cat to Linda, who quickly reassures him, "It's OK. They're fine." His reaction reminds me of many examples I've seen of children as young as three years old spontaneously showing concern for animal well-being.[1]

Later in the afternoon, Linda gathers the children in a circle to talk. Knowing of my interest, she invites them to tell me about each of the classroom animals. Her words send a spark of energy through the circle. A "let-me-tell-it" light gleams in each pair of eyes. Arms shoot into the air. One child picks up after another the well-worn pieces of each animal's biography. The children tell of small, brief lives rounded with perilous adventure—how the gerbils got out of the cage one day and no one could find them, the time the rabbits were shaking so hard, and no one knew why. Their stories were like the classic fairy tales of lost, almost eaten, fallen-under-a-spell children rescued in the eleventh hour. Did the misfortunes of these small mammals, reptiles, birds, and fish in their classroom mirror the children's own anxieties? When the gerbils were tucked safely back into their cage, did the children register their own sense of "found" after "lost"?

Unlike fairy tales, some of the children's stories about the classroom animals ended unhappily. A hamster sickened and slowly faded; some fish floated to the top of the aquarium one morning. The past fall had seen several animals die. "We had a bad winter," Linda explains. She had recently added some new animals to the classroom and talked with the children about plans to get a second rabbit. One boy launched into a narrative about a large and very vocal parrot who had been a class resident before the winter break. "Yes, he was just too noisy, wasn't he, children," Linda chimed in. On went the talk of deaths, losses, and replacements with (it seemed to me) a matter-of-fact, even slightly hard edge. Animals die, and frequently too, or they become too troublesome, like the parrot, and then they can be replaced. Perhaps the emotional punch of these animal deaths and losses had been bleached out over months of discussion and drawings and pet funerals. Or maybe I was hearing from these first-graders the stirrings of a contradictory mix of sentiment and utilitarianism—what Paul Shepard calls the "paradox of frenetic emotion and casual dismissal"—that he and others argue is the cultural undergirding of petkeeping.[2] On the other hand, these six-year-olds may already be veterans of animal loss and replacement. Many of them come from hardscrabble rural poverty. A few live on small working farms, and all but one child have pets at home.

After the children have left for the day, Linda acknowledges with a sheepish grin that some of the other teachers at the school do not share her enthusiasm for "critters"; a few have complained about a kitty litter smell. Typical of preschool and elementary school teachers who do incorporate animals into their classroom, Linda is convinced of the direct and indirect ways in which animals enriched children's learning. She describes the attention-grabbing way they taught children about the natural world, the homey atmosphere the animals lent the classroom, the opportunities they gave children to be caregivers, even the recurrent cycles of birth, sickness, and death they enacted. These themes echoed the way parents talk about how pets contribute to their children's lives.

Yet children's ties to their pets at home or in the neighborhood may differ in interesting ways from encounters with animals in classrooms, zoos, or animal parks. Children form emotional bonds with pets in ways that parallel important human relationships. Companion animals become assimilated into the framework of intimate ties within the family. By contrast, in a classroom, zoo, or nature center, animals, even the same species kept as household pets, are no longer companions, confidants, and loved ones—in other words, *intimates;* they become objects of inquiry. Animals in schools, zoos, or nature parks fall under the umbrella of scientific scrutiny. They become information, facts to know. John Berger, in his much-quoted essay "Why Look at Animals?" bemoans this shift: "Animals [in zoos] are always the observed. The fact that they can observe us has lost all significance. They are objects of our ever-extending knowledge. What we know about them is an index of our power, and thus an index of what separates us from them. The more we know, the further away they are."[3]

As one year after another clicks by, schooling often increasingly renders animals, plants, indeed all phenomena, into content to be analyzed and understood apart from the texture of daily experience, rather than embedded within it. This process reaches its apogee by high school, when living animals serve only as raw material for biology experiments and science projects. Yet observing animals need not diminish their immediacy. As animal behavior captures youthful interest, as children study animal habits and are amused by animal "antics," this process can underscore animals' integrity as living beings. Children experience animals in classrooms, zoos, and nature parks, even in high school biology classes, as intellectual puzzles, to be sure, but also as other feeling, thinking, and behaving beings who pose the potentiality of relationships.[4] Wherever children encounter animals—in the backyard, on the vacant lot, beside the creek, in the drainpipe—they raise questions about animal welfare, humane treatment of other species, and environmental conservation. Involvement with animal life, whether inside or outside school walls, has the potential to confront children's moral sensibilities and prompt them to consider their own place as humans within the ecosystem.

Zoos, aquariums, and nature parks draw millions of children and their families annually, more than to any professional sports event. Over 135 million Americans visit over a hundred U.S. zoos, and 10 million more visit the thirty-five most popular aquariums each year. Yet observations of zoo visitor behavior seldom focus on what children are doing.[5] Although animals reside in many classrooms, only a few accounts consider what impact these creatures might be having on children.[6] No one even knows how frequently teachers furnish classrooms with living animals, much less what species are likely to be included and how they are used by teachers. The inclusion or omission of live animals as part of the learning environment seems particularly unremarked—the enthusiasm of some teachers and principals in preschools, day-care centers, or elementary schools, the indifference or even distaste of others.[7] Teacher reports occasionally surface in early education trade journals. In one account, Pat MacIsaac and Susan King, two preschool teachers in Ypsilanti, Michigan, describe their three- and four-year-old students' encounter with death in the lifeless form of Sophie, the class guinea pig. The teachers recorded the children's spontaneous comments about

Sophie—"She could be just asleep"; "She wasn't doin' nothin'"—and her burial—"Could Sophie feel the dirt?"—and used them later at "circle time" to help the children understand the finality of death.[8]

Teachers I've talked with who have classroom pets describe similar teachable moments raised by animal deaths, births, or illnesses. Typically, teachers of young children emphasize the same broad array of benefits that parents talk about in getting pets for their children—how contact with animals provides love and comfort, promotes responsibility and nurturance, and teaches appreciation for nature. Educators who incorporate living animals into their classrooms identify other benefits geared to the developmental challenges that young children face—mastering impulse control, refining language skills, and stimulating moral concern. Teachers also talk about how the presence of animals exposes children to the complexity of different life forms, each with a distinct "story line" of development. Animals are living demonstrations of diverse ways of eating, reproducing, communicating, and perceiving—some similar to, others different from, human behavior.[9]

When I spoke with Meridyth McLaren, whose class at a university preschool includes her beagle puppy, Lucy, a turtle, and a guinea pig, she stressed how the animals helped the children to modulate the intensity of their behavior: "The smaller ones love her [the guinea pig] a lot, and it's not that they are trying to hurt her but sometimes they want to hug her and squeeze her and so we have to remind them about gentle touches. We get the turtle out, just for [the children] to practice keeping an eye on the pet because the turtle will run, and you don't want him to get stepped on. [They practice] just being careful, being gentle."

I often stop to watch Meridyth's children in the playground behind their preschool. On fine days, there's a happy blur of waving arms and jumping feet, with Lucy the beagle whizzing around them. Playing with Lucy, some of the children get especially excited, shrieking and jumping up and down, carried along in the boisterousness of rough-and-tumble play. Meridyth and her teaching assistants become more vigilant then, reminding the children how small Lucy is and that they must be careful not to get too rough with her. An internal struggle between heightened arousal and "chilling out" seems to play across the children's faces and bodies. I see one little boy, who has skidded to a halt in midchase after Lucy, unconsciously clench and unclench his fists as he listens to Meridyth's admonitions. Small classroom pets, like Lucy the beagle, the turtle, or the guinea pig, often evoke an interesting duality. They excite young children, who want to touch and squeeze and chase *right now*. At the same time, the vulnerability of these small animals demands that these heightened impulses be held in check. In this mix of excitement and adult-supported restraint, young children rehearse the rhythms of urgency and control. Classroom animals' combination of arousing appeal and dependence may help young children as they struggle to command their emotional swings, a process developmentalists call self-regulation.[10]

Several children in Meridyth's class have language delays or disabilities; a special education teacher, Sally Mohler, assists them. One little girl, very slow in language development, had been taught sign language by her mother, who was a hearing interpreter for the deaf. As a result, the child had started in the class that fall with a vocabulary of 300 signs. Gradually, though, over the next six months her hands had fallen silent. Sally explains: "We see that happen. About age three they get more sophisticated, and they do not see other people in their environment signing. They don't want to stick out. We weren't seeing her use the signs. When she saw the dog, however, running on the playground, darting under the bushes, going in and out of view, that was such a novel, exciting event, that this propelled her. She discarded all those inhibitions, and very excitedly signed and tried to say, 'puppy.' When the puppy would disappear, she would come up, 'Where is puppy?' using her signs and speech approximations."

Meridyth had similar observations about several other children in her class who were acquiring English as a second language: "Some of [these] children . . . are all of a sudden saying, 'Lucy,' 'puppy,' 'dog.' So we are seeing a lot of interest in her, a lot of language coming out of these children who don't speak much English on their own." Hubert Montagner, a French psychologist who has been studying animals in classrooms over the past decade, has found that when children speak about animals, especially their pets, their vocabulary is richer and their speech more grammatical than when they talk about other subjects.[11]

Animals do more than elicit language. Children with classroom pets often act as their moral agents, especially in dealings with the world outside the classroom.[12] Meridyth's class shares a playground with an adjacent group of three-year-olds: "The children in our classroom worry about the children in the other classroom, that they will chase [Lucy]. The children in that classroom know that they are not supposed to chase her. So if the other children chase her, they tell them, 'Don't chase Lucy! Don't pick her up!' They are pretty protective of her."

The search for classroom animals brings us to many preschools and day-care centers. In kindergartens and the early grades, living animals are frequently in attendance. By third grade, however, animals become less common, and once children reach middle school or junior high, resident animals are a rarity, except for an occasional special education class. "Animal-focused" educational packages show the same pattern. For example, the Pets and Me curriculum developed at the University of Pennsylvania and the Animal Awareness Club, from the San Francisco SPCA, offer preschool and elementary school teachers resources to convey natural history and biology, to integrate humane education into the curriculum, or simply to organize basic skills instruction around animal themes.[13] Animals also dominate picture books, early readers, and CD-ROMs for the younger set; crowded subgenres with an educational bent include how to take care of your pet, basic facts about fauna, habits of wild and domestic animals, endangered species, and dealing with pet death. Resources thin out as reading levels rise, so that by high school, except for biology classes, living animals have largely disappeared. Animals almost never figure as topics of study in their own right. Even rarer is the use of animals to structure teaching of other subjects, like math concepts, spelling, vocabulary building, or writing.

Why do animals in all their forms fade from classrooms and educational materials as children get older? Several assumptions run like invisible threads through educational practice involving animals. The first, which we've encountered before, is that young children and animals naturally go together. Math concepts or letter discriminations wrapped in feathers and fur are seen as intrinsically appealing to young children before the "age of reason," traditionally pegged at the seventh birthday. The pull of animals is assumed to be time-limited, strongest for pre-schoolers and children in the early grades. The whys and wherefores of this assumption are rarely examined. Many teachers fall back on a "natural" attraction, the old equation of the childlike animal and the animal-like child. Some, like Sally Mohler, pinpoint how young children often "lock on" to the novel movements of animals. Still others contend that young children experience animals as other selves, beings who speak to the child's nascent sense of self with a powerful immediacy.[14]

A second assumption about what animals might teach children in classrooms stems from Piagetian theory and what's called "developmentally appropriate practices." Young children learn best when they explore and manipulate concrete, tangible objects. Out of such active engagement with the "thingness" of the world, children gradually distill abstract principles and relationships. For example, water play helps preschoolers to understand the concept of conservation of liquid quantity. The child, as kiddie experimenter, pours water from a squat, wide container into a tall, narrow one and back again, slowly realizing that the *amount* of water, an abstraction not directly observable, remains the same even though the water level rises and falls in differently shaped containers. Since the "thingness" of the world includes animals, they take their place alongside other interesting objects—trucks, blocks, Leggos—for the child to explore in the quest for their logical properties. In this view, observing living animals helps young children to develop logical reasoning skills and understanding of biological principles, such as maturation and metamorphosis. Animals serve as vivid examples that make abstract concepts concrete for young children, but lose their utility and appeal as formal reasoning powers expand.

A contrasting perspective argues that children's thinking at all ages remains grounded in sensory experience. The most effective teaching, even for teens and young adults, engages all the senses. As James

Schrock, a college biology instructor, put it: "Seeing a real spider is more information-laden than seeing a movie of it, than a color photo, than a black-and-white photo, than a written description . . . while Johnny may drift off during the spider photo or film on bee dances, everyone wakes up when you bring around a real brown recluse [spider] or visit a real honeybee colony."[15]

Contemporary accounts of cognitive development describe thinking more broadly than the manipulation of abstract symbols. As children develop, they are refining *practical intelligence,* the application of reasoning to varied real-world problems. Many of these problems engage our thinking about animals. Do animals have rights? What do we believe and do about environmental issues? A contextual take on the development of thinking maintains that animals have the potency to stimulate children's thinking beyond early childhood into adolescence.[16]

We need to examine closely what and how animals may be teaching young children, both in classrooms and outside them. This will lead us to reevaluate what the absence of animals might mean for older children. Living animals invite children to wrestle with fundamental questions in ways that are distinct from their other experiences. How are living beings different from inanimate objects? How do I know other minds? What is personal identity, and how does it endure despite radical transformations of appearance? How should I treat humans, animals, and things? For what and whom am I responsible? Do environmental issues engage my moral concern and action? Since such questions linger to perplex adult minds, animal presence—in homes, schools, and elsewhere—should continue to enrich the ways older children and adolescents learn.

How Are Living Beings Different from Objects?

To appreciate how contact with animals can illuminate this question, we first need a brief digression into a baby's mind. Infants come into the world hardwired to be captivated by movement. Still damp from the womb, a newborn will jerkily track a slow-moving object; by four months, the eyes will follow movement in a smooth tracking motion. A young infant, watching things move through space, is conducting a visual fact-finding investigation about the coherence of objects—look how all the parts move together—and the properties of objects—see how some bump and push others into motion.[17] In this way, every baby recaps Christopher Columbus' journey into an unknown world. The great scholar of perceptual development Eleanor Gibson describes learning as discovering the *affordances* of objects, the "what-can-I-do-with-this?" of things.[18] Infants make a core distinction early, though precisely when is debated: the movement of living beings contrasts with the movement of inanimate objects. Seven-month-old infants register a surprised expression if they see inanimate objects move without any force being applied to them, but not when people do.[19] Cognitive psychologists have interpreted these differential reactions as evidence that a "naive theory of physics"—what objects are like—and "a naive theory of biology"— what living beings are like—are taking shape before the first year is up. In this baby version of biology, living beings, in contrast to inanimate objects such as stuffed bears, are coherent entities whose autonomous movements are powered by an inner force. What has life has a fundamentally different affordance, to use Gibson's term, from an inanimate thing.

Once babies can grab hold of objects, devouring their properties with their eyes, ears, hands, and mouths, and then crawl, walk, and run in, around, under, and above them, they have a full set of perceptual and motor tools ready for world exploration, at least on foot. Consider the cognitively enriching qualities of animals to children at this point. Here are living beings who present complex affordances distinct from both inanimate objects and humans. A dog, for example, is packed densely with interesting movements, sounds, smells, and opportunities to touch—a living being, but different from the other living beings the infant encounters. A stuffed dog can be dragged, pummeled, and thrown until its trajectories etch themselves into the baby's memory circuitry. A living dog, turtle, spider, or snake, on the other hand, moves on its own in indeterminate, arresting ways. Each creature presents a new vitality, a distinct form of aliveness, for the child to consider.

Animal movement conveys an even richer message when babies themselves go on the move. Crawling and walking infants master the cognitive challenges of planning and executing routes in order to avoid painful bumps into furniture. The mobile baby is constructing mental maps of landmarks. How much more of a brain teaser is adapting one's own movements to another moving being! As an infant paddles after a cat, the baby is continually recalibrating—*I* am *here, it* is *there, I* can go *there*—a dynamic shifting of perspective, a sense of self moving in relation to another moving self. Of course, babies also have such experiences with humans. However, experiencing the self in relation to living, moving, *nonhuman* selves is different, both more complex and at times more predictable. It is richer, because animals embody different repertoires of movement from humans. Snakes slither on the ground; cats leap and pounce on four paws; horses trot, canter, and gallop. It is simpler, because those animals typically kept as pets in homes and classrooms have more predictable repertoires of movements and sounds than do humans. In fact we tend to package animal behavior for children (and perhaps for ourselves as well) into highly simplified, signature routines: as in "Old MacDonald Had a Farm," dogs go "woof, woof," cats go "meow, meow," and cows go "moo," the vocal complexity of their real counterparts ignored. In this way, children acquire a shorthand for distinctive ways of being.

Even one-year-olds respond to animals as a "third way" of being—unlike either other humans or inanimate objects. Aline and Robert Kidd, known for their observations of children and their pets, recorded how infants and toddlers, ranging from six to thirty months of age, behaved toward their pet dogs or cats as compared with a "lifelike" battery-operated toy dog and toy cat that the Kidds had brought for the children. The toy dog walked, wagged its tail, sat upright, and "barked," while the toy cat "meowed" when its back was stroked and "purred" when petted on its head. The babies smiled, held, followed, and made sounds to the live animals, especially their dogs, more than to the toy ones. The living animals, again dogs more than cats, in turn responded to the children—nuzzling the babies in answer to hearing their names called, rolling over for a tummy rub, or licking the babies' faces. For the Kidds, it is not movement or novelty that engages young children with living animals, since in their observations, infants and toddlers preferred their familiar pets to novel mechanical toy animals. Rather, the reciprocal interaction of living animal with child, the give-and-take of two beings aware of each other, sustains attention.[20]

Babies also react distinctively to unfamiliar living animals, not just their own pets. Two researchers from the University of Montreal videotaped nine-month-old infants and their mothers in a playroom as each baby encountered one of three novel events: a live dwarf rabbit; an attractive wooden turtle that moved, made noises, and flashed lights; or an unfamiliar young woman. Babies who saw the rabbit quickly left their mothers' side to approach and touch the animal, but infants who met the female stranger held back, staying close to their mothers while looking and smiling at the woman from a distance. Babies were not treating the rabbit as equivalent to an interesting toy, since they looked more often and longer at the rabbit than at the moving wooden turtle. The live rabbit had more drawing power than person or thing; on seeing the animal, the babies were least interested in their mothers and most drawn to explore this new presence. The live rabbit was not just more attractive, but a different sort of being—a living, breathing creature, autonomous, moving, indeterminate, and possessed of what the researchers called "agency."[21] In other words, the babies seemed to understand that this rabbit, an animal they had never seen before, was another being with a soul.[22]

Nine-month-olds typically react to unfamiliar adults with wary appraisal from the safety of a caregiver's arms. On the other hand, novel animals don't inspire the same caution. Instead, they captivate attention. How can we account for this? Environmental influences are implausible. It's more likely that, as the biophilia hypothesis suggests, humans are innately interested in other living things, predisposed to respond to them attentively and as one living being to another. Added to this is the

neoteny of dogs, cats, and domestic animals coupled with the playfulness and curiosity of human young, which draws them toward such animals. This early engagement with animals whenever they are encountered may be the reason why words for different animals—*dog, cat,
duck, horse, bear, bird,* and *cow*—appear among the first fifty words that
most toddlers in the United States say. In fact in one study more children included the words *dog* and *cat* in their initial productive vocabulary than *juice, milk,* or *ball.* Indeed, more children said these animal
names than any other words except *mama* and *daddy* or their equivalents.[23] Children learning other languages, including sign language, as
well as children without pets show the same precocious use of animal
words.[24]

Experiencing animal beings helps children clarify the ways in which
animals are similar to and yet different from themselves. Preschoolers
engage animals as other subjectivities, other beings or selves, with the
core properties that the children themselves share with other living beings—being autonomous, coherent agents of their actions, having intentions, and feeling emotions. Like the children themselves, animals behave intentionally, and their behaviors map onto feelings. But for each
species, a different code unlocks the import of animal behavior.[25] What
does it mean, how does the animal feel, when a porcupine's quills stand
on end, a dog's ears flatten against its head, or a cat swishes its tail? The
movements of small animals take place at the child's eye level; animal
bodies seem within the grasp of small fingers. Most pets and almost all
classroom animals come child-sized, making them ideal tutors in multiple ways of being, while the human shapes of parents, teachers, and
older brothers and sisters loom large overhead.

Different animal species elicit contrasting reactions from young children. In one study, researchers brought some live animals—a Mexican
red-legged tarantula, a two-and-a-half-month-old English angora rabbit,
a mature cockatiel, and a five-year-old female golden retriever dog—as
well as two realistic stuffed plush animals—a dog and a bird—on separate days to a day-care classroom of two-to-four-year-olds and a kindergarten class of five- and six-year-olds in Alberta, Canada. While the chil-

dren ignored the stuffed animals—80 percent never even looked at them—the live animals were a powerful stimulus. Each animal attracted the children in a distinct way. For example, only 10 percent of the children touched the tarantula (which was on the floor in a terrarium), but 74 percent touched the dog, who was in a sit-stay position. Twenty-one percent kissed the dog. Over two-thirds talked to the bird, but only 16 percent talked to the rabbit, and none spoke to the tarantula. Each live animal evoked its own mix of looking, approaching, touching, and talking from the children. Almost all the children talked *to each other* about the spider, bird, and dog.[26] Living animals engage attention on two levels—directly and indirectly—through the questions and conversations they jump-start in children.

These two levels were apparent during a series of observations that Laura Richards, a student of mine, conducted in Linda Stillabower's first-grade classroom. Over a four-month period Laura visited the class twice a week, each time for an hour during unstructured, "free play" time, to record the children's spontaneous reactions to the guinea pigs, gerbils, hamsters, rabbit, newt, hedgehog, and fish who shared their room. What she saw fell into four categories: "interactive" (looking at, holding, hugging, carrying, talking to an animal); "nurturing" (for example, feeding, giving fresh water, cleaning out a cage, brushing); "learning" (talking about animal characteristics, behaviors, and needs—for example, a child exclaiming that the hedgehog has just uncurled, another child explaining that a newt cannot be trained like a dog); and "social glue" (animals as the focus of children's interactions with each other—for example, two girls talking with each other about how to divide up the job of cleaning out the rabbit cage). On average, during a single hour visit, Laura observed 46 instances of interactive behaviors, 29 of nurturing, 19 of learning, and 21 of social glue. The affordances of different animals drew different reactions. Children held, carried, and hugged the guinea pig with long gray and white silky fur and a high-pitched squeak much more often than the shorthaired albino guinea pig. The hamster cage became the focus of intense interest in early April when the children found a litter of pups had been born. The large, soft rabbit who often hopped freely among the children evoked the most looks, pats, and cuddles.

Laura's observations were a single snapshot of a single classroom, which itself is unusual in the plethora of animals it contains and in the teacher's encouragement of children's interest in them. However, this preliminary investigation confirms that a variety of classroom animals engage children's curiosity, encourage their nurturing, and offer social opportunities both directly with the animals and with other children around an animal focus.

One winter afternoon I watched how children reacted to meeting unfamiliar animals, when some zoo animals visited the children's reading room of the local library in my town. Over a hundred children, from infants asleep in their strollers to ten-year-olds, crowded with their mothers and a smattering of fathers and grandparents into a large circle on the floor as DeeDee Long, education director of the local zoo, unveiled Calypso, a magnificent white plumed parrot. As Calypso emerged from its hooded cage, a collective intake of breath swept the room. The children's faces (and those of many adults) took on what I have come to recognize as the "new animal encounter" look—eyes widened, face flushed, mouth open and smiling, an excited "will-you-look-at-that!" expression. As Calypso perched on a stick, DeeDee instructed the children: "Put your thumb and pinkie finger together, like this," demonstrating with her fingers. "How does your pinkie feel? Smooth and dry?" As the children nodded, she continued: "Your tongue is wet, right? But this is how Calypso's tongue feels, like your pinkie." Later, she passed around the circle of straining hands, inviting the children to touch the spiny coat of an African pygmy hedgehog, the cool smooth skin of a boa constrictor, and the soft fur of a slow loris, a rare subprimate, each time asking: "How does it feel?"

Under DeeDee's guidance, these children accessed each animal through touch, through the feel of its body. The tactile sensations each animal produced opened a window into imagining another way of being—my body, its body. Many educators tend to undervalue and hence underuse the sense of touch, particularly as children get older. Yet knowing from touch remains an important channel for information, long past the infant and toddler years. As children felt each animal at the library demonstration, questions tumbled out: "What does the hedgehog like to eat?" "Can you make its spines stick out?" "How can he knock over rocks with such a little nose?" Beginning with the look and the feel of a creature, the children were delving deeper into its characteristics and behavior.

This picture of children's thinking is quite different from the one presented by Piaget—that children younger than seven cannot grasp the difference between living and nonliving things, much less the finer distinction between thing, human, and animal.[27] We now know that Piaget severely underestimated young children's remarkably early sensitivity to varied ways of being alive. Whether it's with pets at home, pigeons in a city square, or squirrels in a park, there is an infantile substrate of cognitive and emotional responsiveness to animal beings as living presences. On this foundation, children build more elaborate understandings—how different species move, eat, sleep, hide, eliminate waste, and reproduce; how each grows and develops, some through simple enlargement and subtle shaping, as the kitten elongates into a cat, others through dramatic transformation like the metamorphosis of caterpillar into butterfly.

Recent research on cognitive development depicts children as much more biologically savvy than did Piaget. Children as young as three attribute to animals biological properties—an animal has a heart, has a brain, grows from smaller to bigger, can have babies—as well as mental ones—can think, can want something, can know something—and refuse to assign such properties to inanimate objects such as airplanes. From early childhood, *animal* is what psychologist Susan Carey calls an "ontologically basic category." By this, she means that even three-year-olds consider animals to be fundamentally different sorts of things from artifacts or inanimate objects, even those that look remarkably like animals. For example, in one study, five-year-olds, when told that people had made a stuffed dog that looked and acted exactly like a real dog, nevertheless insisted that the stuffed dog could not turn into a real dog.[28]

However, young children's concept of animal is not identical with adults'. Children under age ten generally do not classify people as animals or consider both animals and plants to be subsumed under the overarching category of "living things." In this sense, young children's concept of animal is more restrictive than that of older children. In part, this narrower understanding may reflect the shifting uses of the terms "animal" and "human" that children hear. These words are often used as contrasts—animals as distinct from humans—obscuring the fact that humans are also animals.

Reasoning about animal biology begins by generalizing from humans. Young children are swayed by how similar an animal looks to a human. For example, preschoolers, when queried about a mechanical monkey and a worm, are likely to say that the toy monkey, not the living worm, has a heart, brain, and other biological characteristics. By contrast, seven-year-olds comprehend that a worm, not a mechanical monkey, has a biology.[29] Gradually, children are filling in the outlines of their "naive theory of biology"—how animals and plants are both similar and different; what the defining characteristics of mammals, reptiles, and fish are; and how other animal species are like and unlike humans.

Psychological research has spun a rough narrative of how such ideas become elaborated and increasingly accurate as children get older.[30] The general pattern of cognitive maturation refines ideas in many domains. As brain maturation, schooling, and daily experience intertwine, biological knowledge expands. Might living in proximity to animals, and to plants and natural environments, stimulate understanding of biological principles? What does even the occasional observation of living animals do for children's understanding of the living world? These questions have attracted little investigation.

A small, exploratory study in Japan raises the possibility that young children who care for pet animals make strides in biological knowledge. Kayoko Inagaki from Chiba University interviewed eighteen kindergarteners who had been taking daily care of goldfish at home, most for over a year. Compared to their schoolmates without goldfish-care experience, these children not only knew more about routine care of goldfish—"How many times is a goldfish fed a day?"—but also more about their unobservable properties—"Does a goldfish have a heart?"—the hidden biology of animals that young children have trouble comprehending. The goldfish raisers also reasoned about unfamiliar animals using analogies from caring for the fish. When asked "Can we keep a baby frog the same size forever?" one child replied: "No we can't, because the frog will grow bigger as my goldfish got bigger." The experience of caring for the goldfish enabled the children to link pet care to consequences for the fish, using cause-and-effect reasoning. When asked "What will happen if we feed the goldfish ten times a day?" half the children who had raised goldfish predicted correctly that they would die, and went on to explain the connection between overfeeding and harm to the animals. None of the comparison children could explain the consequences of overfeeding, or even understood that food ten times a day would be excessive.[31]

Wherever they meet animals, children make more than cognitive distinctions among humans, animals, and objects. They laugh, clap their hands, shriek, worry, and yelp in fear. They are stopped cold in their tracks by the slither of a garden snake, they shrink back at the advance of a turtle, they stare intently as a caterpillar crawls from one hand to another. This emotional engagement fuels curiosity and fascination with nature; like any powerful motivator, it is a catalyst for learning.

As Inagaki puts it, a living animal presents "inherently occurring variations in its critical parameters."[32] Simply put, animals are predictably unpredictable. Piaget pointed out that learning is triggered by cognitive incongruity, novel information that challenges well-worn beliefs. Animals confront children with cognitive incongruity by virtue of being living beings—no two goldfish or rabbits exactly alike, no single animal ever reacting precisely the same way. Caring for living beings, even just observing them, involves indeterminacy.

When we watch children in classrooms with animals, at zoos, in parks, and on beaches, we see many ways in which living animals embody biology lessons, with a concreteness and immediacy that has the potential to make them effective teachers, especially of thorny biological concepts like biorhythms or sonar navigation.[33] In the library visit I described earlier, the hedgehog stimulated children to discuss what it meant to be nocturnal ("When you go to bed, he gets up and has breakfast"), the boa constrictor gave rise to a brief but spellbinding explanation of how to dispatch prey by constriction, and the slow loris made children ponder what it meant to be an endangered species.

When children care for animals that they care about, their motivation to understand deepens. Inagaki contrasted the biological knowledge of the goldfish-raising children to a group of Japanese six-year-olds who were assigned by their teachers to care for classroom rabbits and ducks over the course of a school year. The teachers closely monitored the children to ensure that they followed prescribed care procedures. By year's end, the children had gained a lot of factual and procedural knowledge about the rabbits and ducks; for example, they knew that ducks lay eggs but rabbits do not, and they knew what each species should be fed. But unlike the kindergarteners who raised goldfish at home as their own pets, the first-graders who tended rabbits and ducks as a school assignment could not explain *why* certain food was good or bad for those animals; could not make inferences to other, unfamiliar species; and could not reason about the consequences of improper care. Given these results, classroom animals may be more effective teaching tools when children can choose actively to participate in their care, rather than as part of a top-down curriculum in which teachers set out pet-care tasks for children to complete.

The visceral immediacy of animals, bonds with pets, and identification with animal characters often blinds children to seeing animals on their own terms. Children's wholehearted involvement with animals leads to strong likes and dislikes for different species. Abetted by stories and cartoons filled with humanoid animal characters, children readily divide the animal world into "good" and "bad" creatures. Dogs, cats, horses, rabbits, dolphins, panda bears, and chimps top the "best-liked" list, "peopled" with cuddly pets, wild mammals endowed with childlike features, and animal heroes of film and television. Rats, spiders, cockroaches, wasps, crocodiles, and wolves, that unfairly maligned villain of fairy tales, fill the ranks of disliked creatures, which children under ten describe as "yucky," "slimy," and "scary."[34] Every whale becomes a Free Willy, every lion a King, and every vulture a plotting enemy.

Animal characters resonate for children precisely because young children's sense of self is bound up with their animal encounters. This very immediacy can cause children to misread the meaning of wild animal behavior. A humane educator told me how children who had seen the movie *Pocahontas*—in which a hummingbird character attacks people—believed that the purpose of a hummingbird's long, pointy beak was for pecking children's eyes out.[35] In a similar way, attachment to pets, by casting animals in human roles, can obscure their real natures. When parents and children insist that "Fido is just like a person," they are overriding canine species membership. Young children, in part because they are more invested in their pets and other animals, in part because they are less cognitively adept in taking the perspective of others, are less sensitive than teenagers or adults to the actual needs of animals or to environmental issues.[36]

Widespread misconceptions about animals and ecological ignorance persist through childhood into adolescence and beyond. When Stephen Kellert of Yale University queried 267 second- through eleventh-graders throughout Connecticut, he found that 55 percent identified a whale as a fish, 79 percent believed that veal came from a lamb, and the majority indicted animal predation as "wrong." African-American children living in large cities had the lowest knowledge scores, while children in rural areas were the most knowledgeable. These findings suggest that when children grow up around animals, they are likely to absorb more accurate knowledge about them.[37]

Contact with animals may also help children address issues at the core of figuring out themselves and the selves hidden within others. How do I stay the same even though I too am transformed as I grow? How is my mind related to my actions? How do I know and understand other minds?

Animals and the Theory of Mind

All this most children know by their third birthday: mental "things," such as dreams or ideas, are different from other objects—you can't touch or pick up an idea. "Things" in the mind stand for their tangible equivalents in the world; when I think about a dog, my thought corresponds to a real dog. Desires and beliefs link predictably (though imperfectly) to action. If you're convinced you hid the keys under that flowerpot, that's where you'll go to retrieve them. Eighteen-month-olds, seeing a person repeatedly hammer just to the left and right of a nail, interpret this behavior as "trying but failing" to hit the nail.[38] These toddlers are working backward from behavior to unseen desires and intentions. In short, they are developing, according to cognitive psychologists, a "theory of mind." A four-year-old's theory of mind even encompasses predicting action on the basis of false beliefs. Show a four-year-old a box marked in big letters "CANDY," and then untie the ribbons to reveal, not candy, but pencils inside. (Preschoolers love this trick.) Then invite in another person who has not seen the interior of the box. Our four-year-old will predict that this newcomer will believe that the box contains candy, even though the child has seen the ruse. Children younger than four often confuse their own beliefs with those of others, thinking that the person somehow must know about the pencils inside the box.

Developing a theory of mind is key to living in an ordered social universe in which our own behavior and that of other people become more transparent to us. Autistic children have great difficulty with every facet of the theory of mind, struggling over these ideas more than do other children of similar intelligence.[39] Given the importance of theory of mind, it's striking how little we know about what shapes these ideas. Theory-of-mind studies assume that we turn our wondering gaze only upon human minds. For example, Robert Siegler, a prominent cognitive psychologist, states as self-evident: "we do not attribute purposes or beliefs to cars, trees, or most other animals."[40] Yet while the existence of animal minds is controversial for adults, children readily approach animals as minded actors, individuals with intentions and desires whose actions are intelligible from their mental states.

Animals have certain qualities that may make them especially effective conveyors of theory-of-mind ideas. Imagine a dog who goes to the front door, gazes fixedly at the doorknob, whimpers, and scratches at the door, looking back at her owner, say an eight-year-old boy, and back at the door again. After a few moments she leaves the door and comes up to the boy, whose eyes are still glued to the computer screen. After fixed doggy stares and more whimpering, the boy finally looks up. Back to the door the canine runs, now with more urgency. Is there any doubt that we can infer a mental state—she wants to go outside, she really *needs* to go outside—from these behaviors?

Paradoxically, the animals with whom children are most likely to be spending time present both simpler and more complex puzzles about other minds than do humans. Animal minds are simpler to read than those of humans because we can connect the dots from animal behaviors to corresponding mental states with more assurance. Our dog doesn't go to the door and scratch just to tease us or to trick us into thinking she really wants to go out when in fact she doesn't. Animal behaviors convey authentic, pure data about mental states unmuddied by pretense, metaphor, deception, or irony. This makes reading the thoughts and feelings of animals easier for children than reading those of other humans.

In other ways, animal minds are more opaque than human ones. We can't decode how an animal is feeling by reading its face for happy, sad, or angry expressions. Instead, each animal's behavior requires its own lexicon. What does it mean when the rabbit is trembling, when the cat's fur stands on end, or when the dog's tail is between its legs? Because animals behave in decidedly nonhuman ways, children's attempts to guess at their internal states are frequently foiled. Generalizing from their own minds and those of other humans, children (as well as adults) often make inaccurate guesses, treating animal minds anthropomorphically.[41]

A turtle slides into his shell, and a child exclaims: "She's shy; she wants everybody to go away!" A particularly comely cat drapes himself on the easy chair. "Look how he wants to be admired!" we say.

The distinct subjectivities of animals challenge children to take non-human perspectives, to step with human feet into animal paws, claws, gills, shells. Young children generally tend to attribute their own desires to another person. For example, a three-year-old who likes chocolate will claim that another little girl does too, even when told that chocolate makes the other girl sick. Children younger than five struggle with grasping other minds, particularly when those minds appear to have desires or ideas that conflict with the child's own.[42] The very differentness of animal species brings children sharply up against the limits of such egocentric thinking. Skilled adults can help children appreciate the contrast of self and other across species. At the library, DeeDee asked the children: "Do you like to eat bugs?" and they all shouted back a resounding "NO!" She countered: "Well, the hedgehog likes to eat bugs." "How do *you* hear?" she queried, and after the children called out, "with our ears!," she invited them to search for ears on Victor, the boa constrictor. "So how does he hear?" A few of the older children knew: by feeling vibrations.

Understanding animal minds and feelings is not just an intellectual exercise in deciphering a radically different subjectivity. The sensitivity with which children can do this is basic to their humane regard for animals. Attunement to animal bodies and minds speaks to how well children can feel with and for animals and their environments. Nurturing humane attitudes in children seems ever more pressing given widespread human callousness toward companion and domestic animals, the elimination of hundreds of species and endangerment of many more, and the wholesale destruction of fragile ecosystems sustaining plant and animal species. The biophilia hypothesis suggests that children's striking interest in animals can take on many forms shaped by culture and society. On the one hand, a child may embrace other living beings and their environments under the mantle of moral concern; on the other, animals may evoke fear, dislike, and the urge to destroy and dominate.[43] Not infrequently, positive and negative attitudes commingle.

At least nine distinct orientations toward animals have been documented in children as well as adults. Three types of attitudes toward animals tend to increase as children get older—appreciation for the ecology of wild species and their habitats, moral concern for proper treatment of animals, and a "naturalistic" enjoyment of wildlife and the outdoors. Correspondingly, dislike, fear, or avoidance of animals, need to dominate and control them, and interest in animals primarily for their material benefits to humans all decline with advancing age. Within these broad age trends, children who have direct experience with living animals show the highest ecological, moral, and naturalistic attitudes and the lowest avoidance, dominance, and exploitation views.[44] These findings support many teachers, humane society professionals, and zoo educators, who believe that contact with animals is an ideal opportunity to convey respect, appreciation, and humane regard for animals.

How Should I Treat Animals?

Theories of how children's moral sensibilities develop offer differing accounts of this process, but all exclude children's experiences with animals from discussion. Children's treatment of animals raises no moral issues, caring for animals leaves no moral residue, and the ethical treatment of humans does not impinge on that of animals. According to Piaget, the egocentric perspective of "preoperational" children—under the age of seven—leads them to assume that their own desires coincide with those of others. Slowly, young children shift from an egocentric to one-among-many stance, a process Piaget called decentration. This occurs through the give-and-take of play with other children, each of whom is equally intent on his or her own agenda. When two preschoolers tug on opposite ends of the same shiny red truck, each confronts the undeniable reality of another, opposing will. Gradually children learn that theirs is just one of many competing interests to be adjudicated, raising issues of turns, sharing, fairness, and rules. Treating others as you would have them treat yourself becomes an extension of the morality of fairness. In this account, play with other children mixed with cognitive maturation is the catalyst for moral reasoning applied to children's human relationships.

From a psychoanalytic perspective, conscience develops as the superego, embodied in parental figures, especially the father, muffles the selfish drumbeat of id, the "I want" of instinct. Piagetian and psychoanalytic traditions disagree about the underlying dynamic, but they arrive at a similar endpoint: young children must learn to curb their unruly impulses and develop consideration for others. Childhood harbors a natural albeit unintentional cruelty, outgrown by the need to adapt to a world of competing egos and held in check by careful teaching and social sanctions. An insistent self embarks on life's journey and only gradually relinquishes "me-hood" for (human) community membership.

An alternative view begins with humans as inherently social creatures, innately vibrating to other human currents. This view suggests that the milk of human kindness flows early and unbidden even in the very young. Both empathy—vicariously sharing in the emotions of another—and sympathy—feeling *for* another's sorrow and pain—sprout within the earliest relationships that children form. A toddler's brow furrows as he grimaces in distress at the sight of a playground companion falling off the swing; an eighteen-month-old girl offers her precious blankie as solace to her sad-faced, sniffling mother. By age three, a rudimentary moral compass elevates universal principles, such as "Don't harm others," above social conventions, such as "Use a fork and knife to eat" or "Wear a smock for painting."[45] From this perspective, children begin life as socially connected, socially aware beings who over time extend and elaborate an already moral sensibility.

Both accounts of moral development—from outside in and from inside out—are anthropocentric. Children's relationships with animals receive scant attention either as influences on or as consequences of moral development. Given this state of affairs, it's curious that some assessments of children's moral thinking tap attitudes toward animal welfare,

if only tangentially, as if implying but not explicitly recognizing a link between concern for people and concern for other living beings. A twenty-
two-item scale widely used to measure children's empathy toward other
children includes several items about treatment of animals, for example:
"It makes me sad to see an animal get hurt."[46] An index of children's in-
clinations to be of service to others mentions kindness toward animals.[47]
To demonstrate that watching models of helpfulness would encourage
children's readiness to help those in need, one study had first-graders
watch an episode of the television show *Lassie,* in which Jeff rescues one
of Lassie's puppies, and then measured the children's willingness to
help puppies in distress.[48] In these examples, research on moral development gives an occasional, glancing nod toward children's views about
animals, but never incorporates them into a full account of childhood
morality.

Precisely because children accept animals as other living beings,
they raise issues of just, fair, right, and kind conduct. When we expand
our vision of moral issues to include relationships with animals, the result is a richer, more complex description of children's moral thought
and behavior. Children are alive to the moral implications of human
treatment of animals. At the same time, because children are awash in
contradictory cultural messages about the moral standing of animals,
children's thinking about moral questions with respect to animals is
complex and particularly fascinating. The roots of an ethic of animal
treatment and concern are laid down in the tender years. Even preschoolers are beginning to wrestle with questions of protection of natural habitats, animal rights, use of animals in scientific research, and mistreatment of animals. Robert Coles, reflecting on how experiences with
animals can build a child's moral intelligence, recounted how he inter-
vened to prevent his young son from playing too roughly with their dog:
"The dog in his own way was a teacher, one who had helped all of us
come to terms with the meaning of understanding: to put oneself in another's shoes, to see and feel things as he, she, or it does."[49]

As a child's moral framework consolidates, the morality of relationships with animals and the natural environment stands alongside the

morality of human relationships. When children are asked to reflect on the moral dimensions of their engagement with animals and nature, their responses show they have been wrestling with these issues all along. For example, Peter Kahn's interviews with African-American first-, third-, and fifth-graders in inner-city Houston revealed them to be acutely sensitive to issues of environmental protection and animal welfare. They were just as troubled about environmental degradation as were children their age living in the Amazon region of Brazil or in the Prince William Sound region of Alaska about the time of a serious oil spill there. Said one Houston child: "[I care about animals because] those are animals that everyone must take care of . . . Because God put the animals on earth for people too, like for pet stores. To keep and take care of them."[50]

At the same time, children's attitudes about animals are often morally ambiguous and even contradictory. Expressions of concern coexist with "squish that yucky bug" reactions. Childhood biophilia is often unsophisticated and misguided. Misled by their emotional identification with animals, children sometimes inappropriately humanize their pets and stereotype wild animals. Still, a resilient core of engagement persists. Within it, children are figuring out what living and nonliving things are like, how humans and animals differ, what it feels like to be a particular animal, and perhaps even what it means to be another human being.

5

The Healing Lick

The road begins in the baking heart of Brooklyn, in a shimmering mirage of overflowing garbage cans, rusty iron grid gates, and graffiti. The asphalt-and-concrete landscape lends a grayish hue to the scraggly weeds and saplings poking through the cracked sidewalks. Our car glides through miles of crumbling, boarded-up tenements, bare lots gleaming with glass shards. Gradually the landscape opens up, as I move north out of the city. Like a black-and-white movie slowly saturating with color, my visual field fills with green—green roadside grasses, a green canopy of trees. An hour and a half later, I pull off the highway and drive along lanes from a storybook landscape—white picket fences, horse pastures, gently rolling fields—to a set of jaunty green-and-white signposts: Green Chimneys. I pass the large vegetable gardens, the composting and recycling center, and now I see the red barns of the "lower" and "upper" farms.

This is the bus route, I realize. The bus transports mothers, grandmothers, sisters, and occasionally fathers from inner-city New York neighborhoods to the countryside, to see their children on visiting day once each month. I imagine quiet descending on the bus as it slides into the leafy landscape, the collective breath of these women slowing and deepening as they inhale the country smells. Or perhaps the women anxiously ask themselves: How will my child greet me? How will he be, since the last time? The children able to make home visits travel this way, too, when they return to Green Chimneys from a stay with their families in the city. Do the children feel more at peace, safer in the pristine rural environment? Or do they feel more at home in the city, which is, after all, their real home?

For these children, Green Chimneys Children's Services, a residential treatment facility for severely emotionally disturbed children, is literally the end of the line. More than three-quarters of the 100 residents are African-American boys between the ages of six and twenty-one. Many of them have spent time in psychiatric facilities without much improvement. Many come from a tangled knot of family pathology, a lethal mix of child abuse and neglect, family violence, drug dependency, and poverty. Some have witnessed deadly assaults. A few have already killed another human being.

Green Chimneys looks like a bucolic farm grafted onto a summer camp, nestled among the rolling hills and manicured pastures of Putnam County in New York State. In reality, it is a living experiment in the healing potential of connectedness with animals and nature for our most troubled youngsters.[1] At Green Chimneys, as at a small but growing number of other treatment centers around the country, animals are the essential vocabulary of the therapeutic milieu. Each living unit (the children live in dorms with "counselors," much like summer camp) has its resident dogs. Each classroom has its menagerie of small animals—rabbits, guinea pigs, and turtles are common—and dog "classmates." The pet dogs and cats of staff members wander in and out of administration buildings. In a corner of the office of Dr. Samuel B. Ross, the founder and, until his recent retirement, executive director of Green Chimneys, a majestic plumed parrot presides in a large cage.

The soul of "animal-assisted therapy" is the 150-acre farm. At the "lower" farm, tucked just behind the dorms, classrooms, and dining hall, horses are groomed, fed, exercised, and ridden. The "upper" farm is the "Old MacDonald" song come to life—a few goats, sheep, pigs, cows, ducks, chickens, and rabbits. Here, once school and therapy sessions are over, children can choose to come to help care for the animals. (They get paid for their labor in a "learn and earn" program.) A child might "adopt" a particular animal for a 4-H project or just choose one to call "mine." One corner of the upper farm houses a shed with the imposing name "wildlife rehabilitation center." People living in the surrounding communities who find injured animals along roadsides or in the woods bring them here to be nursed back to health and, if all goes well, released. Today a hawk hobbles unevenly along his perch, tilted off balance by one bandaged wing.

"Animals Don't Read the Chart"

The philosophy of treatment at Green Chimneys is deceptively simple. Animals provide a living connection for children so lost in depression and anxiety that other humans—adults or peers—are too threatening to reach them. At night, the dogs in the residence dorms are silent keepers of children's secrets. In the classroom, the small furry animals give contact comfort. The horses and farm animals ask no questions, make no verbal demands. As one of the social workers told me, "Animals don't read the child's chart. They don't care about his history."

The animal connection then becomes a stepping stone to rebuilding ties to humans. Animal contact opens small fissures in the armor of defenses inside which the small child cowers. Through the cracks, the child's "issues" bubble up. This darkness made visible becomes an opportunity for therapeutic intervention. A therapist on the staff described this example to me: "Bobby had been sad, angry, and withdrawn as a result of the loss of his mother's love and attention but was having difficulty expressing it. He began taking out his anger on the dorm dog by teasing and hitting it. There was also some sexualized touching. This provided an outlet, although an inappropriate one, for his feelings and opened up discussion of his real feelings of loss and abandonment by his mother."

Even at a residential facility like Green Chimneys, therapists are available to children only for brief periods during the day. The animals become "therapists on call." Gerald Mallon, a clinical social worker who has studied hundreds of children in treatment at Green Chimneys, sees them using the animals and human therapists in similar ways—to confide secrets in the assurance that confidentiality will be maintained, to relieve feelings of sadness or anger, and to learn new ways of coping, especially through learning to care for others. The resident dorm dogs are wells into which all of a child's "badness" can be poured. The dogs are always listening, unconditionally accepting, and, to some children, even making astute replies. One child explained to Mallon: "Well, like if I did something wrong, I'll tell [the dog] I didn't really mean it. It makes me feel good because I know that he probably understands. Because he's a good listener. When I tell him something, he does it. When I'm sad I say, 'Why does this happen to me? Why am I here? Why can't I just go home and live with my family?' It makes me feel better because I'm talking to somebody. He's around all of the time and he's never too busy to listen. At least he listens to me."[2]

Another child provided a translation of canine therapeutic feedback: "She understands me. When she says no, she walks away. When she says yes, she puts her paw on me and looks at me with those big brown eyes, and then I pet her on her ear."[3] Children tell Mallon of their conversations with farm animals as well: "I talk to the goats and cows. Mary Jo [a goat] is the best listener; she does motions that mean yes and no to me—she really does!"[4]

When pangs of homesickness strike, the children describe their urge "to go AWOL," as they put it. Then waves of sadness or anger flood in, and feel-better sessions with animals can be scheduled on demand, twenty-four hours a day. On one of my visits, twelve-year-old Nancy, who had been at Green Chimneys for a year and a half, laid out the way it works: "If you are feeling upset one day you could go up to the farm and you could talk to any animal, 'cause you can really trust them. I mean they can't talk or anything, so you could tell a secret." Her words reminded me of Donald Winnicott's description of therapy as a "holding environment," a nonjudgmental haven to safely contain threatening feelings.[5] For Nancy and the other children who spoke to me about how the animals were helping them, pigs, sheep, and rabbits were functioning as holding environments.

Animal conversations, unlike those with human therapists, typically involve touch—holding, stroking, petting, and grooming—particularly when the animal is small, soft, furry, and placid. The comfort of soft touch is a theme that both staff and children return to again and again. I spent one windy April afternoon talking with Suze Brooks, a clinical psychologist at Green Chimneys: "I have chosen ferrets, guinea pigs, and rabbits for my office because they are very mushy-gushy, and they can sit on your lap. Better yet, the ones I like are the ones that lie on your chest, because our children haven't been touched enough in healthy ways, and they need that clean, good, physical touch that we all need as human beings. Animals can provide that kind of second chance to be held and nurtured in that way." Always available, all-understanding, sensitive to each inchoate feeling, a warm, enveloping soft presence—the animal as "the good parent." Brooks hopes that children who've never had what Winnicott calls "good enough parenting" can be reparented through connecting to the solid mass and liquid eyes of a cow, through sleeping curled up with a dog, through burying their fingers deep in a sheep's wool.

A farm is a place where birth and infant care are on daily display. On one of my visits, two goat kids, eleven lambs, and chicks too numerous to count were living at the farm. As Nancy was guiding me around, she was fascinated with the birth process, a tantalizing mystery just out of reach, because, as she explained, the babies had been born late at night or in the morning when she'd been in school. The babies *are* irresistible. Nancy, the other children, and any adult around, including me, simply have to pick them up and cuddle them. But as soon as anyone does, a mother goat or sheep or chicken issues a determined squawk or bleat, reassured only when her young are safely returned to her side. Nancy stares at this "good mothering" in silence. Sometimes a child closed to the past will be shaken by these examples of animals caring for their young and moved to connect to his or her own more impoverished experiences. Lisa Ross, the intake coordinator at Green Chimneys, finds that some of the best opportunities for diagnosis occur when she takes a prospective child resident to visit the farm. She recalled a withdrawn, frightened boy who sat immobile and frozen during the initial intake interview. When Lisa suggested, "How about a walk?" and showed the boy the farm animals, he stood transfixed by the solicitude of a mother rabbit for her babies. "My mother never took care of me like that!" he blurted out.

Teaching a new repertoire of nurture to children who have themselves never experienced good care is a cornerstone of the Green Chimneys therapeutic approach. The child watches good parenting by animals and then tries on the good-parent role by caring for animals, who seem to evoke a nurturing instinct from children armored against members of their own species. As the animal thrives or suffers under the child's care, feedback is immediate and clear. Staff are there to elaborate the lesson. Lisa Ross's beloved Scottie, Molly, is a fixture in one of the classrooms. Eight-year-old Tina, entrusted with the coveted job of Molly's morning walk, repeatedly yanked and pulled her along on the leash. "Tina," Lisa said, "I see you pulling the dog's leash. I know that you don't want to hurt Molly. But you know, dogs really understand, so you have to talk to the dog, not only pull the dog. Say, 'Molly, I want you to come.' Or, 'Come! Sit!' Instead of just pushing, you have to communicate just like we have to do with each other. If I just pulled on your arm, would you know what I was asking you?" As Tina shakes her head, Lisa continues: "Animals are the same way. They have certain words they understand." Thus began Tina's lesson in substituting words for force.

A social worker told me about a boy who had brought back to Green Chimneys a wounded pigeon that he had found on the curb in the city during a visit home. He named the pigeon Lucky, explaining that the bird was lucky to be found and rescued. Because this child had shown so little empathy toward other children, the social worker interpreted his words as a positive step. She felt the child identified with the pigeon and would like to be "rescued" himself. The phrase "lucky to be found and rescued" resonated for me. This most unlucky boy nonetheless believed that a lost creature was lucky to come into the orbit of his care. He saw himself for the first time as a competent, reliable caregiver.

Bonding with animals, caring for them, and being nurtured in return by them are all experiences that open children to loss. Some animals inevitably become sick and die. When a beloved animal dies, the whole Green Chimneys campus mourns. But for children whose brief histories are peppered with losses—mothers swept away by AIDS or crack, disappeared fathers, older siblings incarcerated—an animal's death is weighted down with the unmourned, the grief shut away. The death of Daisy was one such event. For years, the refrain to anyone who visited Green Chimneys was: "Have you seen Daisy? You must visit Daisy." On each of my previous visits, children had dragged me to the upper farm to gaze upon a 500-pound immobile mass of porkflesh splayed out on a pile of hay. It seemed to be eternally sleeping it off. This was Daisy, an unlikely candidate for most-beloved animal. When Daisy died, staff and children joined in weeping. As the children talked about Daisy, they began to recall other losses, buried deeply because they were too painful to talk about.

In any residential institution, issues of power and powerlessness crackle beneath the surface. Rules and medications tightly circumscribe life for a severely emotionally disturbed child. By necessity Green Chimneys' children exercise little control over their own lives and perhaps even less over their own impulses. In their families these children often occupy the bottom rung of a ruthless hierarchy of coercion.

No wonder the horses are favorite animals for many of the children. Big and powerful, they symbolize freedom and flight, but also control. Up on the horse, the child towers over the adults who rule his life. To command the horse, the child must give respect, learn how to speak to the horse and how to listen to it. Riding lessons become a laboratory in how to transmute power into partnership.

The animals are potent symbols, at times almost like actors taking on the roles of the children, mirroring their experiences. Injured hawks at the wildlife rehabilitation center are living lessons that just as damaged wings may heal and birds fly back into the wild, the damaged child ultimately can undergo repair and return to his or her family. For this reason, a graduation ritual for a child ready to leave Green Chimneys is the release of a rehabilitated bird as a symbol of healing and freedom for both.[6]

Animals as Healers

The Green Chimneys philosophy draws on thousands of years of human-companion animal bonding. The idea of animals as healing agents is equally ancient. In fact the earliest and most pervasive human system of spiritual beliefs—found throughout the world in all hunter-gatherer societies and in many agricultural ones as well—was animism. Central to animism is the belief that animals have spirits or souls, which can cause illness and even death when offended or can help and protect as "guardian spirits." The spiritual leader, or shaman, through ritual, out-of-body trance states can contact these animal spirits. The shaman then talks to the animals in their languages, recovering a primordial but lost human ability. He (most shamans are males) can even transform himself into an animal. Shamanistic healing powers derived from this fusion of human with guardian animal spirit, or animal "familiar."[7]

Vestiges of animism infused the premodern world. In pharaonic Egypt, dog-headed Anubis was physician to the gods. Dog and snake companions flanked images of the Mesopotamian healing goddess, Gula. These animals also were sacred emblems of the Greek gods of healing and medicine. (The snake imagery persists in the caduceus, the modern symbol of medicine.) Sufferers made pilgrimage to Epidaurus, the shrine of Asclepius, son of Apollo, god of medicine. As they slept, the god, in the guise of a dog, would visit them and bestow restorative licks on the injured parts of their anatomy. (Dogs specially trained to lick the visitors were kept on the premises.) Tablets at Epidaurus recount the cure: "Thudson of Hermione, a blind boy, had his eyes licked in the daytime by one of the dogs about the temple, and departed cured."[8] In 100 A.D. the Roman Pliny wrote: "As touching the pretty little dogs that our dainty dames make so much of . . . if they be ever and anon kept close unto the stomach, they ease the pain thereof."[9] Pliny's views about the curative powers of lapdogs were so widespread and enduring that fourteen hundred years later, physicians in Elizabethan England were still extolling little dogs' ability to absorb disease when clasped to the bosoms of suffering ladies.[10]

In medieval Europe, the association of animals with healing persisted. Saints Francis, Christopher, and Bernard, known for their healing powers, were often depicted in communion with animals. The thirteenth-century cult of Guinefort elevated a greyhound of that name to sainthood, and pilgrims traveled to the dog's grave seeking miraculous cures for their sick children.[11] Although the idea of living animals who healed was anathema to Christian dogma, medieval medicine relied on animal parts for its cures. A thirteenth-century encyclopedia of natural history advised those suffering from chronic cough to drink a broth of boiled elephant meat, water, salt, and fennel. A meal of deer's brains was the treatment of choice for bone fractures. Cotton soaked in a mixture of sour wine and fresh ass's manure would stop a nosebleed.[12]

In the late eighteenth century, a Quaker group in England, the Society of Friends, established what most consider the first therapeutic environment utilizing animal and nature contact. Developed as an alternative to the punishment and restraint typical in mental institutions of the time, the York Retreat had a distinctly noninstitutional ambience—courtyards, gardens, and small animals such as rabbits and chickens. The philosophy, radical for its day, was to "normalize" patients by allowing them to wear their own clothes instead of standard-issue uniforms and encouraging them to focus on daily plant and animal care. William Tuke, the progressive founder of York Retreat, believed that as patients cared for small animals, the animals' dependence would elicit greater self-control and responsibility in the disordered minds of their caretakers. Caring for animals and tending gardens would draw patients' attention outward, away from their own inward distress, toward engagement in the world.

The use of guide dogs to assist the blind and handicapped gained ground in the nineteenth century. The French government indirectly subsidized the practice by taxing guide dogs at a lower rate than pets.[13] When Florence Nightingale, in her *Notes on Nursing* (1860), observed that "a small pet animal is often an excellent companion for the sick," she was reflecting a growing belief in the ameliorating effects of nature on an increasingly urban and industrialized population.[14] The Bethel institution, founded in Bielefeld, Germany, in 1867, was part of the same ethos. Its working farms, riding center, and host of small animals were the context for the treatment, first of epileptics, then of individuals suffering from a broad variety of physical and mental disorders. Other, scattered efforts to develop analogous programs began in the first half of the twentieth century. For example, in 1944 the U.S. Army Air Convalescent Center in Pawling, New York, incorporated dogs, horses, and farm animals to "humanize" the therapeutic environment.[15] However, none of these centers ever put this theory of the curative properties of nature, and especially animal contact, to the test. The programs remained historical curiosities. In any case, they focused on the treatment of adults and so never included children.

Levinson and Jingles

The use of animal contact in the treatment of children in psychic pain has a surprisingly brief history. The father of the movement—for it remains more a movement than a science—was Boris Levinson, a child psychoanalyst, who came to New York City in 1923 as a teenage immigrant from Lithuania. Eventually he became professor of psychology at Yeshiva University and spent his adult life treating severely withdrawn, autistic children at the Blueberry Treatment Center in Brooklyn, not far from the mean streets that many of Green Chimneys' children call home.

Levinson's success in treating children with his "co-therapist," his dog Jingles, made him a passionate crusader for the use of animals to unlock a child's troubles and stimulate positive change. Levinson recounts the now-famous episode in which he accidentally stumbled upon this "eureka!" experience. Jingles was at his customary spot curled up at

Levinson's feet while he was writing up case notes at his desk. A distraught mother unexpectedly appeared at the office door several hours early, with her little boy. He was severely withdrawn, repeated therapy had been unsuccessful, and she had been urged to hospitalize him. When the door opened, Jingles, a friendly, outgoing dog, bounded up and licked the child, who, instead of shrinking back, began to pet and cuddle the dog. Rather than banish Jingles, as Levinson usually did when a patient session began, the doctor impulsively decided to let the dog stay while he talked to the mother and observed the child. At the end of the session, the boy declared that he wanted to come back and play with Jingles. Over the next few sessions, the boy was engrossed with Jingles, ignoring Levinson and talking only to the dog. As Levinson also began speaking to Jingles, the animal became the medium through which therapist and child started to converse. Levinson said: "Eventually, some of the affection elicited by the dog spilled over on to me and I was consciously included in the play . . . Some of the credit for the eventual rehabilitation must go to Jingles, who was a most willing co-therapist."[16]

From then on, Jingles' therapeutic role steadily expanded as Levinson tested a variety of techniques. The dog's presence seemed to make other wary children's first visits to the therapy room less threatening; the friendly dog gave the office, with food and water dishes and canine toys scattered around, a more homey, welcoming presence. Levinson mined each child's responses to Jingles for diagnostic insights. The animal was playing much the same role as toys or drawings do in conventional play therapy. As a living toy-playmate, Jingles nuzzled for attention and responded eagerly to affection or overtures to play, capturing the child's interest more effectively and eliciting a wider range of responses than toy play. Jingles, of course, went about just being a dog, therapy or no therapy—shedding fur, taking a nap, licking his genitals, slopping up water from his dish. How children responded to this essential dogginess gave Levinson clues to the hidden, internal battles being fought. For example, Levinson watched as one child, who was having difficulties with toilet training and was afraid of dirt and obsessively clean, reacted to the messiness of Jingles' shedding hair and spilled water dish. The child liked to feed the dog little tidbits of food in his dish, play with the shed fur that had drifted to the floor, and then wash Jingles' dishes over and over again.

Levinson reported the case of another little boy whose mother punished him for masturbating, which she saw as a sign that her "innocent" small son would slip into degeneracy. The boy continued to masturbate in secret, overwhelmed by guilt. When Jingles plopped down in the middle of the office and contentedly licked his penis, the boy gazed in a mixture of apprehension and fascination. How would the doctor react? Levinson credited his nonchalant acceptance of a dog just being a dog as giving permission for the boy to accept his own sexuality.

Children invariably compared themselves to Jingles as they were drawn into bonding with the dog, observed Levinson. They would say to themselves: Here is a dog who urinates, defecates, and masturbates in public and yet is loved and accepted. Despite all my "badness," why can't I?

The way children played with Jingles revealed for Levinson the interplay of aggression and passivity. He interpreted aggressive play—which he monitored carefully and never allowed to hurt the dog—as a projection of the child's angry feelings toward parents or the therapist. The ideal opportunity for revealing the child's troubles was what Levinson called "ambulatory therapy," that is, taking the dog for a walk. Everything about the dog walk offered up interpretations. How does the child react to other people, traffic, stores? Does the child hold the leash firmly or just drop it? How does the child respond to the dog's urination and defecation, or to the approach of another dog? On display were responsibility, mastery, impulse control, fear, and withdrawal.

For those children so severely disturbed that they must be separated from their families and hospitalized, Levinson speculated that animals might humanize the institutional setting. Their steady presence, the reassuring sameness of their limited repertoire of habits, might be a source of continuity and structure amid the high turnover of human aides. Having a pet to hold, cuddle, and love would distract a child from preoccupation with inner demons. Giving children responsibility for the care of a creature more helpless than themselves was a vote of confidence that they could be trusted. Green Chimneys would become a living laboratory for many of Levinson's ideas.

Levinson's 1969 book, *Pet-Oriented Child Psychotherapy,* became a bible for a small but growing band of true believers who filled his mailbox with testimonials. One therapist, Jon Geis, wrote to Levinson about the success of his feline "colleagues": Charlie, a seven-year-old multicolored cat with a mantle of white down his front; and Gunther, less than one year old, sleek and cream-colored, both of humble alley origins. Geis would use the cats for imaginary conversations when a child felt unable to talk directly to him: "Let's suppose, Billy, that Gunther there could talk. What do you think he'd say about you? Probably he'd say that you're a friendly boy who is scaring himself when really there is nothing to be scared of." Another technique was addressing the cats directly about a child's problems: "Fellahs, JoAnne here seems, in my view, to be on a sit-down strike against her parents . . . Though she hasn't said this, that seems to be my guess."[17]

In the academic community, few were persuaded. At the 1961 meeting of the American Psychological Association, where Levinson presented his findings that Jingles established connections with autistic children who had previously been unresponsive, several therapists derisively asked whether Jingles got a share of his fees.

Steadily, however, clinical evidence has mounted that animals like Jingles and Gunther can be an effective part of therapy with deeply troubled children, for whom other approaches may have been unsuccessful. Kevin, a three-year-old prenatally exposed to cocaine and heroin, was uncommunicative, resisted human touch, could not walk, and habitually flew into uncontrollable rages. He impassively rejected rewards for "good behavior" that worked for other children—food, toys, music. Then, on a trip to the beach, the sight of a seagull ignited a first glimmer of expression. When the family soon afterward acquired a cockatiel, at the therapist's suggestion, his mother used a visit to the bird as a reward for bathtime completed without flailing and kicking. Kevin's tantrums began to subside. Within weeks he said his first word: *bird.* Soon afterward he was given a trained therapy dog and immediately reached out to stroke it. In each subsequent therapy session, the dog waited for the little boy a bit farther away, and by the eleventh session, Kevin walked unaided halfway across the room to greet the dog.[18]

Bethsabee Sees a Dove

Perhaps the most vivid documentation has come from a transformation captured on videotape by Ange Condoret, a French veterinarian. He was filming an experiment in bringing together animals and preschool children with emotional and physical disabilities. The animals included Polo, the four-year-old half-terrier owned by the preschool director, a resident cat, and an assortment of small caged animals. Among the most severely ill children in the class was Bethsabee, a three-and-a-half-year-old girl whose autism had locked her in a narrow world of inanimate objects. Her attention fixed only on paper, boxes, and blocks, which she held with rigid, extended arms. Toward the teachers, children, or animals in the classroom, she flicked only oblique, fleeting glances. She could not bear to be touched. Grimaces constantly distorted her mouth and eyes, and unintelligible hissing, clacking, and clicking noises were her only sounds. For a year Bethsabee remained impervious to Polo, who had quickly settled into his role as the focus of attention and play for most of the other children. She took no notice of the resident cat, who was willingly held and petted by the children.

Then, one day, a dove, one of the small animals kept in the classroom, suddenly took flight in front of her. Condoret's videotape captured the moment that a curtain lifted, and Bethsabee looked directly at the bird, her face and body softened, and, for the first time in her life, she smiled. Her arms made awkward flying motions in imitation of the bird. Each time the dove flew, the smile returned. Bethsabee made new sounds as if trying to communicate with the bird. The flight of the dove seemed to unlock Bethsabee's soul, frozen by an unspeakable infancy spent tied to a bed and drugged. She gradually touched, stroked, and finally, kissed the bird.

Encouraged by this, the teacher brought Polo close to Bethsabee. This time she patted the dog and soon was searching him out and following him with her gaze. She started to watch the teacher play with Polo and tried to imitate her. She began holding the teacher's hand, imitating speech sounds, and one day she joined a circle of other children in "Ring around the Rosie." Her speech sounds slowly approximated words. Soon afterward she spoke: "Mommie."[19]

Therapy on a Horse

While Dr. Condoret was recording this transformation of Bethsabee, others were exploring an expanded role for animals as therapy for children with physical handicaps. The idea of using horses to rehabilitate people with disabilities is only about fifty years old. When Liz Hartel, a Danish woman whose legs were paralyzed by the polio she had contracted nine years earlier, won a silver medal in grand-prix dressage in the 1952 Olympics, her feat jump-started programs in therapeutic horseback riding, first in England and then in North America. Some programs, inspired by Hartel's accomplishment, focused on using specially adapted saddles, reins, and stirrups to teach riding or cartdriving skills. Others developed equine-assisted psychotherapy, in which emotional and educational goals supplement riding skills. A third type emerged: hippotherapy, which does not aim to teach riding skills, but rather to give an immobilized person greater freedom of movement.[20] In the 1960s Mary Woolverton, a social worker and dedicated horsewoman, developed an equine-assisted psychotherapy program in Colorado for Vietnam veterans who were amputees. Her results—new feelings of mastery and freedom for the wheelchair bound, greater self-confidence, increased head and trunk control, improved self-esteem— were similar to those reported by other programs scattered around the country.[21]

Efforts to help children with severe physical disabilities gained momentum. Clinical evidence suggested that after horseback-riding therapy, children with spastic cerebral palsy improved in postural control, weight bearing, and balance and reported less fear of movement.[22] A summer program designed by Natalie Bieber in North Haven, Connecticut, illustrates the approach.[23] Each Friday she brought her horse Shadow, a large black mare, along with a small palomino pony, to the playground of the Village School, where forty-two children with severe physical handicaps were in a separate unit. Many were quadriplegic and nonverbal; some also had mental and emotional impairments. The children's disabilities were too severe for mainstreaming or even special education classes within the school.

Shadow was big and sturdily built, large enough to accommodate several riders. She had what Bieber called "impeccable manners." The pony was small enough for children to groom and stroke from a wheelchair. Both animals had lustrous coats and luxuriant long manes that begged to be touched. They were gentle horses, unruffled by the parade of riders, an unfamiliar playground, or the noises of the fire station across the street. On each visit the children learned how to groom, feed, and saddle the horses. The pony, attached to a wide, stable cart, gave some children rides around the playground, while others took turns riding Shadow, most with a backrider firmly balancing them, often with volunteers walking on either side.

With forty-two children and just two horses, actual riding time was limited, so "off-horse" times were devoted to a horsey curriculum. Children practiced walking and trotting like a horse at an indoor obstacle course, they worked on speech sounds to talk to the horse with the right commands, and they measured the horse's height and girth for a math lesson.

At the end of the five-week program, Bieber documented gains in motor control, self-confidence, and zest for life for all but a few children. Typical was a child she called "T," a fourteen-year-old boy with severe cerebral palsy, quadriplegic, and nonverbal. He lived in a residential institution, where he required continual custodial care. His sharp mind made him acutely aware of his condition; he felt like a prisoner trapped inside a useless body. On the horse, with the therapist as a backrider, T's uncontrollable movements subsided, and for the first time he could gaze down and around from a lofty height, rather than craning up at adults from his wheelchair. The riding sessions helped him gain more head and trunk control. He smiled and laughed for the first time. A poster of a horse soon hung over his bed.

Another boy, whom she called "D," also had cerebral palsy but was severely retarded as well. He used simple sign language as a very limited tool of expression. Soon after the program ended, news of Shadow's death reached the children. When Bieber visited them without her beloved horse, D ran over, put his arm around her, and signed the two words *horse* and *sad.*

More recently, therapeutic riding programs have been tried with children and teenagers who have cognitive or emotional disabilities but not necessarily physical ones. The rationale is that the challenge of controlling a 1,000-pound snorting creature both concentrates the mind and, when successfully met, stokes the dampened fires of pride. I watched this process one frosty morning in a huge indoor ring lined with horsestalls. Nine third- and fourth-graders were there, all diagnosed with emotional and learning disabilities—attention deficit disorder, problems controlling impulsivity, language delays. Other troubles dogged them—one boy's grandmother had committed suicide shortly before the program began. Every Friday for eight weeks they came to learn about horses and, most important, to learn to ride them. The curriculum focused on individualized goals: for one child, articulating words more clearly; for another, applying math concepts; for all, focusing attention and following through on tasks.

On the day of my visit, seven weeks had passed, and by now each child was sitting comfortably astride a horse, but each face belied intense concentration. In the middle of the ring, the instructor spelled out the exercise—lead the horse in a trot straight down the side of the ring, passing over a riser and negotiating the animal through two goalposts, turn left and trot the horse down the middle of the ring over more risers, and then turn right and trot down the other side of the ring, over risers and through goalposts to the end of the course. All this must be done while maintaining a "two-point position," slightly raised off the saddle, leaning forward, with thighs gripping the horse's flanks. This riding sequence poses the type of challenge these children consistently fail to meet in their classrooms—following a series of complex instructions. As each child took a turn, the single-minded focus was apparent. One boy, Shilo, with a permanent furrow on his brow, seemed apprehensive as he started down the ring. He was having trouble staying in two-point position and gripping the reins. The instructor kept shouting out like a cheerleader: "Don't look down! Look straight ahead! Remember, what comes next?" I heard Shilo muttering from atop the horse, "I can't," but he continued. As Shilo and horse neared the end of the course, the horse broke into a trot, spurred on by an adult "guider" who was leading the horse by a rope. Shilo's tensed face suddenly dissolved into a grin.

Dolphin Rides and Horse Whispering

A more unusual and controversial variation of therapy involving animals took place at the Miami Seaquarium, where the Dolphin Human Therapy Program has treated over 700 children with severe multiple disabilities from 1988 to 1996. Here therapists attempted to increase children's verbal and motor abilities by training them in a pool of warm water, with a dorsal ride on a dolphin as reward. David Nathanson, director of the program, and other proponents of such therapy argue that dolphins are ideal attention-holding and rewarding animals because of their high intelligence, interest, and cooperativeness. Nathanson claims that warm water reduces stress, makes children more ready to learn, and buoys movement.[24]

Critics point out the absence of any carefully controlled studies, with control groups, to document these claims.[25] Animal-welfare organizations oppose the use of dolphins or any other wild animal for therapy, as both unsafe for children and exploitative of the animals. Maureen Fredrickson, of the Delta Society, cautions against what she sees as a dangerous trend to view dolphins as smart, friendly healers who swim: "Remember, a dolphin having a bad day can easily kill someone."

The mystique of what appear to be magical animal cures can lure desperate parents to try untested and potentially harmful encounters. Programs claiming to heal troubled teens through "horse whispering" are the latest fad. "It's a bandwagon," notes Frederickson, "There are no professional or educational guidelines. Even twenty years working with horses doesn't make you a child behaviorist."[26]

From Levinson's accounts to dramatic clinical cases, such as those of Bethsabee, Kevin, T, and D, skeptics have zeroed in on the so-called evidence as no more than a pile of unscientific anecdotes offered up by clinicians whose love for pets clouds their judgment. Levinson's own writings, alternately circumspect and effusive, may have inadvertently contributed to the climate of doubt. He cautioned that pets were no panacea for the pain of growing up and warned that simply supplying a pet for a disturbed child, in contrast to involving the animal in a carefully planned therapeutic intervention, actually might cause harm.[27] Levinson recognized that pet-facilitated therapy did not work for every child. At the same time, he waxed on about pets as a link "in the golden chain leading to good mental health," ignoring objections by other respected child therapists, like Selma Fraiberg, that children might bond with animals as a defense against expressing feelings toward humans, transferring affection away from humans onto animals.[28] Couldn't children form a pathological tie to an animal, as a substitute for humans, not a bridge to them? Such children would be exquisitely sensitive and caring to their pets, but cold and formal toward parents, siblings, or other children. Does a therapeutic breakthrough mediated by animal contact always spill over to human relationships, as it did for Bethsabee? Or might it be "bracketed off," independent of or even harmful to reconnecting with people, as Fraiberg cautioned?

Many questions persisted. To some degree they reflected the usual reluctance of tradition to embrace unorthodox therapies. A basic problem was the difficulty in drawing general lessons from single cases, however stunning in their transformative narratives. On closer examination, further complexities emerged from them. Bethsabee had been unresponsive to the dog and cat and other classroom pets for nearly a year. Why was the flight of the dove her breakthrough animal experience? Other therapists described how autistic children ignored some dogs, yet suddenly responded to others. Aaron Katcher, a pediatric psychiatrist who has pioneered therapeutic interventions with animals, recounted the case of a severely autistic boy who stonewalled one well-trained dog for two therapeutic sessions. Then Buster, a "hyperactive" adolescent dog from a local humane shelter, bounded into session three, at first meeting the same indifference. When the fourth session began, however, the boy suddenly said his first words—"Buster, Sit!"—and began to play ball with the dog. As therapy continued, the boy played appropriately with Buster, gave him food rewards, and sought out the dog for comfort. Why one dog "worked" where the other failed is unclear.[29]

Not every contact of child with animal ignites a spark. Bieber described a seventeen-year-old autistic boy, fascinated by electronic gadgets, and a twelve-year-old girl with spina bifida and severe emotional problems, both of whom remained impassive to Bieber's horse Shadow and to the pony cart. The spotlight, understandably, has been on the dramatic breakthroughs wrought by animal contact and away from the indifference of some children. In every animal-based therapy, however sensitive, some children don't respond or may even worsen. As Bethsabee's case shows, a particular animal species or particular individual animal, and no other, suddenly clicks, like a key that turns the lock. The sensational cases tend to obscure the mysteries of this process. Enthusiastic therapists often ignore the "misses" in order to highlight the "hits." Ultimately the effectiveness of any therapy may depend on a complex nexus of many singularities—the individual therapist, individual animal, individual treatment, individual family, and individual child.

Clinical case evaluations often report more positive results than standardized tests. Consider a recent questionnaire assessment of self-concept changes in a group of twenty-three adolescents with disabilities who completed an eight-week, sixteen-hour therapeutic riding program. On average, the youngsters reported fewer behavior problems after the program, but in other areas of self-concept, including acceptance of their physical appearance, their popularity with other youngsters, and their overall happiness, children's feelings did not improve.

Were the pet-brokered miracles reported by Levinson, Geis, and other therapists reliable? Can they be reproduced systematically? To demonstrate the effectiveness of "pet-facilitated psychotherapy," the term coined by Levinson, in comparison to other approaches, research was needed. What was it about Jingles, Gunther, or other animal "co-therapists" that made them effective? Equally important, what is the edifice of human therapeutic skills built around the animal that successfully links animal contact to psychological growth?

Therapists who use animals, often their own beloved pets, may feel better and be more effective because their animals are around. I see Boris Levinson at his desk with Jingles curled up at his feet. With his dog there, he was more relaxed, more attentive, more open to a child's distress. The idea of animal contact as helping the healers is not new. Many animal visitation programs in nursing homes and hospitals report increases in staff morale and well-being. However, a few staff members complain about the extra work involved in accommodating animals, express concern about sanitation and allergies, and just don't "get" the benefits of animal contact.[30] Therapists who believe in the psychological benefits of animals in their own lives are most likely to be effective in using them as aids to help children in treatment.

A few researchers have risen to the challenge of empirically evaluating the effects of animals on children with physical, mental, and emotional disabilities, designing studies to document more rigorously what happens during animal-assisted therapy and why.

The Companionable Zoo

Chinchillas, rabbits, guinea pigs, iguanas, turtles, doves, finches, cockatiels, goats, and Vietnamese pot-bellied pigs—over 100 animals in all—share quarters at the "Zoo," a building on the grounds of the Devereux School, a residential facility in Philadelphia for boys with severe conduct disorder and attention deficit hyperactive disorder. These children have such difficulty controlling their aggressive impulses that they often have to be physically restrained. They have problems following rules and are impervious to the usual rewards and punishments effective with other children. Not surprisingly, destructive behavior at home and at school litters their brief histories.

Aaron Katcher, who developed the Zoo, designed a "crossover" experiment to test the claim that involvement with his menagerie of animals would have curative powers. He randomly assigned fifteen boys, all between twelve and fifteen years old, to six months of Companionable Zoo involvement, and fifteen to an Outward Bound nature education program, which lacked any sustained animal contact. At the end of the six months, the two groups crossed over: the boys who had been at the Zoo now began Outward Bound, while the boys in that program started coming to the Zoo.

The Zoo program itself consisted of five hours weekly of classes. At first the boys learned how to hold and care for the animals. Once they had mastered the biology, characteristics, and care requirements of one animal, they could adopt it as a pet and give it a name. After that, each child could earn "skill cards" by learning more about his animal—how to weigh it, how to chart its growth, how to breed it, how to show it to other children and adults, how to take it on field trips to rehabilitation hospitals and special education classes. There also were campouts, ecology lessons, and field trips to a state park, a veterinarian, and a pet store. Two cardinal rules reigned at the Zoo: speak softly and be gentle with the animals, and respect the animals and each other.

After the first six months the results were dramatic. On the basis of the boys' histories, the Zoo staff had expected that these boys would have to be physically restrained thirty-five times over the six-month program. Remarkably, not a single incident happened. While these children continued to struggle with aggression in their dorms, classes, and other activities, when they entered the animal kingdom of the Zoo, they calmed down. They could focus their attention and keep themselves from racing, grabbing, hitting, and pushing. As a result, they learned a great deal about animal behavior and care, as the records of skill cards earned and their scores on a knowledge exam after six months showed. The boys loved the Zoo experience, competing with each other for a chance to go. Attendance, which was voluntary at both programs, averaged 89 percent at the Zoo and 64 percent at Outward Bound.

Behaviors at the Zoo—nurturing, affection, play, lowered aggression, peer cooperation, accepting responsibility, teaching others, respecting adult authority—were in sharp contrast to the boys' problematic profiles. Although every boy had been hospitalized as "out of control," not a single instance of cruelty or carelessness toward the animals occurred. The boys readily obeyed rules enforced in the name of animal care—for example, "We have to clean up after each animal so they have a clean place to live"—even as they rebelled against "do's and don'ts" for getting along with people. By the end of the six months, episodes of out-of-control behavior in the dorm residences began to decline. According to their regular teachers, "Zoo boys" were significantly less aggressive in the classroom than boys in the comparison program. These were signs that improvements were generalizing from the Zoo to other contexts.[31]

For the boys in Outward Bound, aggression did not diminish, and their rate of physical restraint held steady. When the groups switched, the symptoms of the former "Zoo boys" began to mount, raising concerns that the benefits of the Zoo experience might not endure once the program had ended. However, longer-lasting effects were linked to individual variation in responsiveness to the program. Throughout the year of the Zoo study, teachers in the boys' regular classrooms periodically evaluated their in-class conduct. Boys whom the Zoo personnel had independently evaluated as high performers there—lots of learning about animal characteristics, high motivation, and gentle, respectful behavior toward the animals—steadily declined in classroom aggression and other disruptive problems. Boys rated as minimally engaged at the Zoo were seen by teachers as steadily increasing in classroom disruption. By year's end, six months after the Zoo experiment had ended, those boys who had been most successful at the Zoo showed significantly less "classroom behavioral pathology" than did boys who had performed poorly.[32] These findings underscore the importance of investigating variability among intervention participants, not just contrasting a therapeutic intervention group as a whole with their controls.

Katcher has concluded that sustained contact with animals in a structured learning program like the Zoo can increase focused attention in children with attention deficit disorder as effectively as medications such as Ritalin. In the nine years since the Companionable Zoo was first evaluated, the model has been extended to children with developmental disorders such as autism, severe emotional problems, and learning disabilities. Animal-assisted therapy promises a natural alternative to reliance on addictive and potentially harmful drugs to control children's behavior.[33] The Companionable Zoo evaluation is the kind of research needed to give scientific underpinning to the work of dedicated therapists who see firsthand the healing power of animals but have yet to convince skeptics. However, there still are remarkably few experimental or even well-detailed observational studies of animal-assisted therapy with children.

The Companionable Zoo study contrasted what happens when severely hyperactive boys are in an intensive animal care program as compared to an environment without any direct animal contact. The results don't shed light on what *aspects* of an animal-based therapeutic program are most effective. As with any complex intervention involving the creation of a therapeutic milieu, it is difficult if not impossible to tease out the relative contribution of cognitive challenge, perceptual novelty, opportunities to nurture, or other elements.

Different components of programs may be more effective with children who have varying temperaments or who are at different developmental stages. Establishing bonds with individual animals addresses young children's need to establish a safe relationship within which they can be nurtured. Learning how to be an "expert" animal caretaker may strike a deeper chord in later childhood and early adolescence, when task mastery, or what Erik Erikson called "a sense of industry," assumes more importance.[34]

Animal contact might work best when retrofitted to a child's particular problem. For example, abused children who have disturbed attachment bonds might benefit more from those aspects of a program centered around being nurtured and learning new ways to nurture. The living laboratories of Green Chimneys and the Companionable Zoo, as well as other therapeutic programs, pose more questions than they answer: What works? With what children does it work best? How does it work?[35]

Researchers are beginning to provide a more nuanced description of the process as animal-assisted therapy unfolds. Jennifer Limond, a psychologist at the University of Southampton, England, and her colleagues videotaped eight children with Down's syndrome while each child was in a therapy session with a friendly seven-year-old neutered male black Labrador dog. In effect, Limond created an analogue of Levinson's sessions with Jingles. To ensure that children were not just responding to the *idea* of a dog or to the novelty of the situation, she also filmed each child in an identical therapy session, but with a stuffed dog of the same size and appearance as the real one.

In therapy sessions with the real dog as compared with the toy one, children were more attentive to the animal and more responsive to the therapist, less distracted by noise or other people outside the therapy room, and more positively interested and enthusiastic. The children, all of whom had severe learning disabilities and limited language, were twice as likely to engage the therapist in conversation about the real dog as about the toy dog.[36] The "hook" of a friendly dog in these therapy sessions parallels Levinson's accounts of Jingles' appeal.

Evidence is growing that groups of children with emotional, physical, and mental disabilities who get animal-assisted therapy, on average, improve and function better than other, similar children who do not. But the average child exists only in the virtual reality of statistical analysis. Rigorously conducted case studies are well suited to explore individual differences in children's progress. Here, research seeks to understand a single child's unique experience more fully. Case studies aim for depth, not breadth. Such case studies are more objective when conducted by trained observers without a stake in the outcome. This excludes the pet-owning therapist, who may be predisposed to look for positive results.

Brenda Bryant, a child therapist and professor of child development at the University of California at Davis, went to Green Chimneys with such a case study in mind. She brought in trained observers from her university to "shadow" one eight-year-old boy, whom she called "Lewis," all day every day from July through mid-September. When the observations started, Lewis had been at Green Chimneys for twelve weeks. Like most of the other children there, he had a history of highly aggressive behavior, both toward others and toward himself. He had made suicide attempts, was hyperactive and learning disabled, and, not surprisingly, could not function in a conventional school setting.

The observers followed Lewis as he went from his dorm to school classes, to meals, to therapy, and to the farm, keeping a running record of the quality of his behavior toward others: Was he angry and aggressive? Did he withdraw, avoiding the greetings of other children and adults, turning away from invitations to play? Or did he show positive social skills, like taking turns, joining in conversation, or simply smiling and talking? The results were clear: when Lewis was in the company of animals—dorm dogs or farm animals alike—in contrast to only other children or adults, his behavior was most sociable, least aggressive, and least withdrawn.[37] In this boy at least, animals brought out the best.

Bryant's case study doesn't tell us *why* Lewis became less self-involved, less disruptive, and more appropriately outgoing toward people when he was with animals. Plausible ideas come from recurrent themes in interviews with Green Chimneys children and staff, and echo Levinson's case histories. The unconditional love that Lewis felt from the contact comfort of the animals was not only intensely rewarding but also a novel emotional experience. As in the Companionable Zoo, animal contact both calmed him and captured his attention, drawing him out more effectively than other people could. Another possibility is that other children and adults saw Lewis as a more appealing social companion whenever he was with an animal. The presence of animals in Lewis' company may have exerted a benign magnetic pull on other people.

Animal Halos

Animals tend to bring out the best not only in children with disabilities, but in the people who interact with them. A major problem for children with disabilities of various kinds—physical, emotional, mental—is that other children and adults often avoid them. Even in "inclusive" classrooms where children with disabilities are "mainstreamed" with typically developing children, inclusion is usually only name-deep. When free play comes, the children without disabilities congregate together, self-segregating themselves and excluding those with handicaps. At the grocery store, in the mall, on the playground, eyes are studiously averted. A spastic child with uncontrollable, jerky movements and a twisted expression is not a conventionally "pleasant" sight. Negative attitudes toward people with disabilities show up in children as young as age five.[38]

Something remarkable happens when a service dog, a large soulful-eyed Lab or Rin Tin Tin–lookalike, accompanies a wheelchair-bound child. In one study, researchers trailed three girls and two boys, each between ten and fifteen years old, in a wheelchair and using a trained service dog.[39] As the youngsters navigated their wheelchairs and their dogs through school corridors and shopping-mall lanes, the researchers recorded the "social acknowledgments"—friendly glances, smiles, and conversations—that schoolmates and passersby at the mall directed at the children. The investigators next counted the social acknowledgments that five other wheelchair-bound youngsters, matched for age, sex, and disability but without service dogs, received. None of the participants in the study knew that they were being observed.

The results were striking: at school, half of all those who passed by the wheelchair-bound children with dogs sent friendly glances their way, compared to only 20 percent of those walking past children without dogs. More than a quarter of the passersby in the school corridor directed friendly conversation at a youngster in a wheelchair when a dog was in tow. Usually they included the dog in the conversation, and sometimes they stopped to talk initially just to the dog alone. The wheelchair-bound boys and girls without assistance dogs glided through the school corridors as if encased in a transparent shell; only 9 percent of children or adults walking by stopped for conversation. At the mall, the same pattern held. About a quarter of all those strolling past smiled at child and dog together; not a single child without a dog got a smile.[40]

We could discount any halo effect from the dog's presence by arguing that more sociable and appealing youngsters with disabilities acquire assistance dogs. This study can't rule out such an interpretation. However, other evidence points to the animal and suggests that even less interactive species than dogs can reduce isolation for children with disabilities. Fiona Innes, as a graduate student at Purdue University, observed a preschool girl who, as a result of a stroke, had moderate mental retardation and multiple physical disabilities. The little girl was mainstreamed into a classroom with preschoolers without disabilities. Over several months, Innes observed that each time she took the classroom guinea pig out of its cage and plopped it next to the little girl, twice as many classmates came up to talk and play as when the girl had no animal.[41]

The presence of a dog, guinea pig, or other companion animal seems to make looking at a person with a disability more acceptable; it's no longer a rude stare, but a sociable approach to someone's cute pet. The term used by writers on this subject—"social lubrication"—is apt.[42] A friendly dog oils the creaky gears of first meetings. The animal can be a noncontroversial focus of conversation. Ironically, the simple juxtaposition of a human with a disability—too often viewed as not fully human—and a dog, small pet, or domestic animal humanizes people with disabilities. The handicap recedes into the background, while the person comes to the foreground as more attractive, approachable, and pleasant.

Benign animal presence envelops humans in a positive halo. Randall Lockwood ingeniously demonstrated this when he showed undergraduate psychology students a series of line drawings of pairs or trios of adults.[43] In each drawing the scene was purposely ambiguous, a stimulus to encourage the student to "read" identities, relationships, and plot into the picture. Half the students saw pictures with a small but critical addition, a line drawing of a dog or cat depicted next to, but not interacting with, any people. Students rated the drawings of adults shown with a dog or cat as happier, bolder, friendlier, wealthier, more intelligent, and more generous than their exact duplicates without the animal. When people were pictured with animals, students described them as less lazy, worried, or sad. The animal halo effect worked for pet-owning students and non–pet owners alike, even for those who had been bitten by a dog or severely scratched by a cat. Later variations on this study, using color photographs and asking somewhat different questions, confirmed the same general findings.[44]

Fiona Innes showed that the animal halo works for young children much as it does for adults. She showed three-to-five-year-olds pairs of color photographs of same-sex classmates in wheelchairs. In each pair, one photo depicted a child alone, while the other showed the same child sitting next to a medium-sized female mixed-breed dog with black and brown markings. When asked "Which child do you like best?" children consistently preferred the photographs with the dog. When asked about ways they could help the wheelchair-bound child, boys responded with more ideas when they saw a child with a dog.[45]

Social lubrication and animal halo effects may be operating in treatment programs for children like Lewis, who have severe emotional disabilities, and for children with physical handicaps, like T and D in Bieber's riding program. In addition to the direct benefits that animals dispense as they lick, nuzzle, and cuddle children, animal presence seems to draw in human contact, replacing avoidance with friendly overtures. Why?

A Calming Presence

Aaron Katcher observed it in the slowing down of the hyperactive boys in his Companionable Zoo study. Green Chimneys' children return to the feeling again and again. "When I'm with the animals, it makes me feel peaceful," one eight-year-old boy there told me. Levinson described Jingles as creating a less threatening, more welcoming environment in the therapy room.

A child goes to a neighborhood friend's house. The friend's father greets her at the door, accompanied by a small, friendly dog. The parent, trailed by the dog, escorts the young visitor to the living room and invites the child to take a seat. He places a child-size blood-pressure cuff on her arm and asks her to rest quietly in the chair for a few minutes and then to read aloud from a book of children's poetry. The little girl reads one passage while the dog is in the room sitting nearby, and then another passage, after the dog has left.

The father, James Lynch, a professor at the University of Maryland, is a member of a research team documenting blood-pressure changes in children in the presence of a friendly dog. Studies with adults show that reading aloud to someone, even an old friend, ratchets up anxiety; during reading, blood-pressure rates rise from their resting levels. For these children—their ages ranged from nine to sixteen years—reading poetry is a rather recent and, for many, shaky achievement, and so might be expected to produce at least as much anxiety, if not more, as in adults.

As predicted, the children's blood-pressure rates rose when they began to read aloud. The dog's proximity didn't prevent that, but it did reduce the amount of the gain. In the dog's presence, the heart rates of children resting in the chair were lower than those of children resting without the dog there. The dog produced both a calming effect under mild stress and a deepening of relaxation when, supposedly, children should be at ease anyway.

Dog-induced relaxation lingered after the animal had gone. Half the children in the study read aloud, first with the dog present and then again when the dog had left the room. The other children reversed the sequence—reading aloud first alone, then with the dog. The children who read with the dog first showed a carryover effect. When reading with the dog, their blood pressure was lower, and it stayed lower when they read aloud again after the dog had gone.[46]

Only one other small-scale study documents the physiological effects of friendly animal presence on children.[47] In the initial study, only thirty-six children participated, and most of them were friends of the researchers' children. The animal connections in the children's lives are unknown. None of these children was in therapy or had any identified physical or psychological problems. We don't have blood-pressure data on dog-induced relaxation in children debilitated by overwhelming anxiety and stress, as are most of the children at Green Chimneys or at the Companionable Zoo. A mild relaxation effect may not be strong enough to moderate the impact of very high distress. If Suze Brooks at Green Chimneys is right, the tactile comfort of holding a rabbit, guinea pig, or cat might induce a greater drop in blood pressure than the nearby presence of a friendly dog. Perhaps a child's own pet would enhance the relaxation effect. Conversely, fear or dislike of animals—or of the particular species used to induce relaxation—might have the opposite effect, increasing distress.[48]

Although this blood-pressure study raises many questions, its results converge with therapists' observations and the testimony of highly anxious children themselves. The findings suggest that what has already been shown to be good for children in treatment may also be good for "typically developing" children. The deep connection that so many children feel with their pets, as well as the lure that animals, tame and wild, hold for children may stem in part from combined relaxation and attentiveness that occur even when just watching or in the presence of other species. This relaxed-while-attentive mode resembles what researchers on infancy call the "quiet alert" state of arousal, when babies—neither fussy nor drowsy—optimally learn from the sensory stimulation around them.[49]

The biophilia hypothesis helps explain why animals might induce such a quiet, alert state. Throughout evolution, human beings and other animal species have been mutually dependent; the survival of *Homo sapiens* has depended fundamentally upon alert and careful monitoring of animal and plant life. Human beings became attuned to the rhythms of the animal life around them. Animals became sentinels, their behavior the coinage of safety and danger. Hawks drawing lazy patterns in the sunlit air signaled that all was well; the sudden squawking flight of birds in a dark, lowering sky threatened peril. In this way, calm, friendly animal presence became associated with safety and induced relaxation in humans. To Aaron Katcher, there are two key properties of benign animals in nature scenes: Heraclitean motion, always changing yet always the same, and an association with psychological comfort and safety.[50] Horses and cows grazing in a field, waterfowl swimming in a pond, even waves lapping the shore or fire flickering in the fireplace capture our attention, while reassuring us that all is right with the world.

Biophilia addresses the calm that distressed and out-of-control children report as well as the focused attention seen in children with emotional and cognitive impairments. Watching animals at peace may create a coupling of decreased arousal with sustained attention and alertness, opening the troubled child to new possibilities of learning and growth. The child can then experience unconditional love and models of good nurturing, practice caring sensitively for another, and assume mastery tempered with respect. The biophilia hypothesis also helps clarify the phenomenon of social lubrication. Friendly animal presence, because of its evolutionary association with safety, bathes in a warmer glow the ambiguous, the unfamiliar, and the potentially disturbing impact that individuals with disabilities may have on first encounter.

However, evidence for social lubrication, halo effects, relaxation response, and heightened attention all appear to depend upon the continued presence of animals. There is little evidence that these effects persist for more than a short time in the absence of the animals. If therapeutic benefits of animal contact require "maintenance doses," children's ready access to animals and natural settings becomes more important.[51]

Biophilia may shed light on why certain animals seem to trigger speech in autistic children, such as Bethsabee and Kevin. Even as we insist that language is uniquely human, we are drawn to share our language with animals. Our evolutionary heritage of attunement to animals led early humans to place themselves imaginatively within animal skins and animal minds. The hunter-gatherer world of the African savannah, the environment of evolutionary adaptedness, is long gone; but if the biophilia hypothesis is correct, children and adults retain the "old ways" engraved in their genes. We are all predisposed to respond to friendly animals as sentinels of safety and as partners in dialogue.

The biophilia instinct is an amorphous one, shaped by culture and socialization into diverse forms. Coupled with the biophilia instinct is an equal emphasis on how human environments shape our engagement with animals. Our natures tend us toward biophilia, as heightened interest in animals, while our environments shape the forms this interest takes. For example, some of the boys at the Companionable Zoo had histories of cruelty toward animals, but what they learned redirected a destructive fascination with animals toward desire to care for them.

Therapeutic programs like Green Chimneys and the Companionable Zoo may work because they build on the foundation of biophilia—intrinsic interest in animals and the calming effect of animal presence. Upon this foundation they overlay a structure of moral lessons in nurturing and being nurtured, to direct this interest into positive regard for animals and, through such regard, to the child's own ability to heal.

6

Animal Selves

The year was 1955. A young psychologist from Tufts University, Evelyn Goodenough Pitcher, visiting the Gesell Nursery School in New Haven, Connecticut, asked four-year-old Colin: "Tell me a story. What could your story be about?" Colin started to recount Hansel and Gretel, his favorite bedtime tale, but Pitcher pressed him: "Now I'd like a story that is your very own, one that nobody else told you, that you made up all by yourself." Colin obliged: "This is about a pussy cat. She found milk all over the barn. She went for a walk and met a bear, and she did something. She found a cannon, and it was loaded and she fired at the bear, and that's the end of my story." Then it was three-year-old Dulcy's turn: "Once there was a little pussy. He went outside. One time, I had pussy cat, and somebody taked it. My daddy will bring one again."[1]

The stories that Colin and Dulcy told were two of the 360 that Pitcher collected over a three-year period from 70 girls and 67 boys ranging from two to nearly six years of age. She and her Yale colleague, Ernst Prelinger, were digging for what they called the "personal internal wealth" within each child, the "constellations of thoughts, images, wishes and fears" that make up children's imaginations.[2] Pitcher and Prelinger saw each story as a child's "implicit map" of the world and of the self. For them, a story's characters and events revealed how the child was representing different facets of self and others. The "story line" reflected the child's attempts to thread these facets into a coherent whole.

These first narratives are peppered with animals of all kinds—pets, especially dogs and cats; domestic animals such as cows and horses; wild wolves, bears, lions, insects; and fantastical animals, like the "mosisaur," in five-year-old Kent's story, a "type of dinosaur that lives in the sea."[3] Eighty-five percent of the stories of the five-year olds, 80 percent of those told by three-year-olds, and 65 percent of those told by two- and four-year-olds have animal characters. There are friendly bears and mad, biting ones, little boys trapped in lions' mouths, "little doggies" run over by trains, a little pig who gets a "real ballet suit" for Christmas. Animals express anger, aggression, excitement, fear, sadness, happiness, being "good," and being "bad."

The young children telling these stories were not typical, even of their time and place. They were attending private, "progressive" preschools and came from white middle-class and upper-middle-class backgrounds. But the animal themes running through their stories crop up in the dreams, play, and stories of other children in different circumstances.

Animal Play

On April 26, 1949, Raymond was seven years and four months old. On this day a team of psychologists from the University of Kansas, led by Roger Barker and Herbert Wright, carried out a project never before or since attempted; to observe and exhaustively record a single child's every moment, from wake-up to slumber. (Their account would fill 423 print pages.) At 5:30 P.M., Raymond was out with his pals, Clifford and Stewart, playing with an old crate they'd found: "When Stewart came back around the crate, Raymond reached out at him, growled very gutturally, and said: 'I'm a big gorilla.' Growling very ferociously, he stamped around the 'cage' with his arms hanging loosely. He reached out with slow, gross movements."[4] By day's end, Raymond and his friends had become not only gorillas, but monkeys and horses-with-

riders as well. Animal play fueled the three boys' pretend games alongside "chase" and "cops and robbers."

From 1924 to 1927, the psychoanalyst Susan Isaacs documented
play themes as she observed the two-and-a-half-to-eight-year-olds attending her school in Cambridge, England. The children's make-believe
frequently incorporated resident animals as props, as when Dan,
Duncan, Frank, and Priscilla enlisted the class puppy as "baby" for the
"family." The wildlife around the children also inspired them; for example, after watching a young robin, the children began hopping and
"flying," asking their teacher to catch them.[5]

Echoes of the Kansas boys and the Cambridge children can be
heard on jungle gyms, at school recess, in playgrounds—almost any-
where that children's pretend play has the freedom to wander off in its
own direction. At a neighborhood "pocket park," a little girl squats in the
middle of a sandbox, affects a plaintive "meow," and swishes her phan-
tom tail. A three-year-old boy at a local day-care center hunkers down in
a corner, buries his head under his arms, and calls out: "Look, I'm a turtle." At the water's edge, along a glorious expanse of Cape Cod beach, a
trio of six-year-olds races behind a retreating flock of seagulls, their
flapping wings mirrored in the flapping arms of the children. Some pen-
guins waddle along the edge of the artificial pool that is their home behind the glass at the New England Aquarium. On the other side of the
glass, a gaggle of children crowds and jostles. Some rock penguin-style
on their toes and stick out their elbows at right angles to mimic penguin
wings. In front of the lion cages at the Lincoln Park Zoo in Chicago, a
boy swivels with a roar toward his startled younger sister, driving her
into the arms of their grandmother.

Dragons and Monsters

Stuffed animals, animal make-believe, animal stories, and imaginary animal companions figure prominently in children's imagination, especially
during the preschool and early elementary school years. In one study, 40

percent of children under five reported dreaming about animals, in contrast to less than 10 percent of children between nine and twelve years of age.[6] Louise Bates Ames described the typical contents of children's dreams based on the recollections of 100 New Haven children from babyhood to age sixteen. Four-year-olds "dream of animals, especially wolves"; five-year-olds have nightmares, in which "animals, especially wolves and bears, chase the child and domestic animals, especially dogs, hurt him or his dog." By age seven, nightmares become uncommon, and animal themes give way to dreams about friends, family, and what Ames called "ordinary things."[7]

Contemporary dream researchers like David Foulkes record children's dreams immediately after they occur by waking children periodically as they sleep. This method, more reliable than parents' reports or children's delayed recollections, also uncovers the predominance of animals in preschoolers' dreams. Foulkes collected dream narratives filled with what he calls "the same menagerie found in fairy tales, cartoons, and children's stories." However, unlike Ames, he found relatively few frightening images of animals, in fact few nightmares overall. The dream animals of young children were drawn mostly from unthreatening domesticated farm animals—cows, sheep, pigs, horses—or familiar and unaggressive wild animals—frogs, birds, deer.[8]

Some animals play a prominent role in children's waking fears as well. Like animals in dreams, fears of animals peak during the preschool years and then gradually decline. These fears likewise change in character. Young children are often wary, startled, or made afraid by the sudden movements, loud noises, or unexpected behaviors of dogs, cats, birds, squirrels, and other common animals. In a 1935 study of children's fears, New York City parents of toddlers and preschoolers spent three weeks making daily records of what seemed to make their youngsters afraid. Amid notations of tears at the doctor's office, wariness at unfamiliar objects or strangers, and fear of the dark were these animal encounters: a small dog on a leash, squirrels in the park, a spider crawling up the child's arm, a turtle wiggling in a child's hand, a horse shaking its head vigorously as the child passed, and a cat jumping up into the child's crib. In all, 38 percent of the children showed fear in an encounter with a living animal.[9]

In the same study, the investigators watched each child's reactions first to a large, stolid collie and then to a small, frisky terrier. Most of the preschoolers showed some fear of both dogs, especially when they made sudden movements. (Because of this, the terrier was more frightening than the quieter collie.) Often, mixed with fear were fascination and curiosity, as if these animals introduced the children to novel, exciting, but possibly dangerous beings.

For five-to-twelve-year olds, other concerns—dying, being hurt, getting along at school, fears of kidnappers, earthquakes—begin to crowd out fears of animals. Still, in the 1935 "fear" study, 18 percent of children in this age range stated that their biggest fear was of wild creatures, such as lions, tigers, and wolves.[10] Only 7 of the 398 children reported an actual frightening encounter with any animal.

Dramatic evidence of the salience of animals in children's fearful imaginations comes from the responses of 570 elementary school children in rural Michigan to the request: "Write down all the things you are afraid of." They recorded their thoughts in 1945, the last year of a world war that had been going on for as long as most of these children could remember. Yet, with most of their fathers away fighting and the newsreels, radio, and newspapers full of war, only 3 percent of the children mentioned any fears related to the world conflict. Instead, scary bears, cows with horns, bucking horses, biting dogs, mean elephants, and biting tigers dominated their lists of fears, with all other scary things a distant second.[11]

These assessments of children's fears are quite dated, with the most detailed investigations over fifty years old. Would today's youngsters be too burdened by images of drive-by shootings, schoolyards sprayed with bullets, and the unending mayhem on their big and little screens to think about lions, tigers, or unfamiliar dogs? Recent studies, across several countries, reveal the persistence of animal fears. In 1999, for example, Australian fifth-graders found thirty-two different kinds of animals fear-arousing. Most were animals that the children had never encountered as a real or even potential threat—lions, tigers, bears, and crocodiles.[12] "Top ten" lists of fears of U.S. elementary school children and adolescents, compiled through periodic surveys during the 1980s and 1990s, regularly include snakes, sharks, and spiders.[13] Contemporary observations of young children with both familiar and novel animals read much like reports from the 1930s and 1940s; children's fascination teeters between fear and delight.[14]

"Seeing" Animals

Children also "see" animals in Rorschach inkblots more readily than do adults. Bees, cats, ducks, chickens, horses, dogs, bears, rats, spiders, butterflies, and birds slowly swim into focus. Here's B. T., a ten-year-old boy, responding to a series of inkblots: I.: "Some kind of ghost or witch . . . no, no, no, a cat, a cat, a cat. With his glaring teeth." II.: "Looks like two dogs kissing each other." III. "To me, looks like two monkeys, doesn't it? IV: "That to me looks like a bear skin." V.: "This one looks very much like a bat."[15] In a study of 650 children from ages two to ten, half of all the inkblot interpretations involved animal images. After age ten, animal imagery emerging out of inkblots gradually subsides, but adults typically describe animals in Rorschach inkblots at least a quarter of the time.

To psychoanalyst Leopold Bellak, this childhood propensity to see creatures in amorphous blobs and to dream about animals held the key to uncover children's inner conflicts and to gain insight into a child's most important relationships. "We had reason to assume," he explained," that animals might be preferred identification figures from three years to possibly ten."[16] With that in mind, in 1949 he and his wife and colleague, Sonya, designed the CAT, or Children's Apperception Test, a projective test for children. Projective tests, then the rage among psychoanalytically oriented scholars, were ambiguous pictures, which, like inkblots, encouraged the viewer to "read into" or project onto them desires, fears, or wishes that were presumably too threatening to express directly. In wide use at the time were projective measures like the TAT, the Thematic Apperception Test, which consisted of drawings of adults in pairs or trios—their facial expressions neutral, the setting unclear, their relationship open to interpretation.

The CAT, a kiddie version of the TAT, was a series of ten cartoon animal drawings; for each picture, the child was invited to "tell a story." In one drawing, a puppy is splayed face down across the lap of an adult dog, whose raised paw hovers over the puppy's rump. A toilet, lid up, sits in the background. Another drawing depicts a monkey tea party—two adult monkeys delicately balance their teacups as they sit on a sofa, under a framed portrait of a bonneted monkey, while a third adult monkey, perched on a hassock, converses with a baby monkey. A kangaroo "mom," with joey in pouch, hops across a third picture. She clutches her flowered straw hat against the wind, her pocketbook flying behind, while a young kangaroo pedals a tricycle alongside.

Each drawing cast its animal characters in scenes designed to evoke the classic dramas of a child's inner life. As the Bellaks explained, the puppy-and-dog picture gives rise to stories of "crime and punishment" set against a backdrop of toilet training or masturbation themes; the monkey gathering reveals a child's feelings about fitting into the family constellation; and the kangaroos on the move typically elicit stories of sibling rivalry or concern about the origin of babies. Versions of the CAT soon appeared in France, Italy, Germany, Spain, Japan, and India. In the 1950s other scholars with a psychoanalytic bent began mining children's associations to a wide array of animal pictures and concurred that children seemed less "blocked" when they used animal pictures as a springboard for stories. Their stories seemed "meatier," riper for psychoanalytic interpretation.[17]

To some psychologists, animal figures were so effective in bypassing resistance to disclosing sensitive material that they should be used with adults as well, to access their deeper recesses of personality. Two psychiatric social workers at Mt. Sinai Hospital in New York City began asking adult psychiatric patients to draw animals in an effort to uncover what they called their patients' "animal or primary impulses"—the childish substrate buried within the adult psyche.[18] Gerald Blum developed the Blacky pictures, a set of twelve cartoon depictions of a small black dog, Blacky, and his canine family—Mama, Papa, and Tippy, a sibling dog of indeterminate sex and age. For Blum, "the canine medium, thanks to Disney cartoons and comic strips, still preserves sufficient reality for subjects to identify themselves freely with the cartoon figures and project their innermost feelings. It seems almost as if the animal cartoons appeal directly to the residues of childish, pre-logical thinking in adults."[19]

Beastly Tales

This equation of animals with childish thinking in adults and children's thinking in general persists in animal-saturated stories, media, toys, even wallpaper, created for children (and often for the simultaneous amusement of grownups). Adult humor signals its playful, childlike quality through *New Yorker* and *Far Side* cartoons in which animals wryly comment on or act out human foibles. Fairy tales—Little Red Riding Hood, the Three Little Pigs, Goldilocks and the Three Bears, the Ugly Duckling—have many more animals than fairies in them. Contemporary children's literature, movies, videos, cartoons, commercials, toys, and CD-ROMs create more animal worlds. They supply ready-made animal characters like Big Bird, Curious George, Babar the Elephant, Mickey Mouse, Donald Duck, Ninja Turtles, Barney, and Pokémon creatures. By one estimate, at least half the characters in Sunday comic strips are animals.[20] Looking for educational software to help get your preschooler ready for kindergarten, polish your first-grader's reading skills, or stimulate your second-grader's math concepts? The odds are that Reader Rabbit, a Bugs Bunny–lookalike cartoon character; CJ Frog and his sidekick, Edison, a cartoon fly sporting a green bowler hat; Bailey, a cat with glasses and an askew baseball cap; Casey Cat; and Kisha Koala will host your child's computer-based learning.[21]

A cursory glance down the shelves of any well-stocked children's library or bookstore makes it evident that animals guide a young child's first encounters with books. Historically, as English-language children's literature shifted, in the late nineteenth century, from didactic moral instruction, with heavy doses of biblical quotations, to stories designed to entertain, not just instruct youngsters, both children and animals moved from the periphery to center stage.[22] Today, seven of the top ten all-time best-selling children's books in the United States are about animals; *The Pokey Little Puppy* (1942) and *The Tale of Peter Rabbit* (1902) top the list.[23] When Kathryn Norcross Black, a psychologist at Purdue University, examined 100 randomly selected picture books published from 1988 to 1992, she could find only 11 that did *not* mention animals. Most featured animals as central characters, with over fifteen species playing major roles. In more than 40 percent of these books, the nonhuman protagonists lived thoroughly human lives; they sported dresses and suits, ate porridge, and slept under snug comforters.[24] Animals are the topic of three out of five picture books, according to a 1994 survey of preschools in and around Pretoria, South Africa. When the teachers in those preschools chose their young charges' ten favorite books, all ten featured animals, usually humanized or fantasy creatures, as main characters.[25]

Inventories of early readers, school textbooks, and literature for children show a similar pattern. In a random sample of U.S. children's books published between 1916 and 1950, three-quarters had animal characters.[26] As the reading level gets more difficult and the target audience older, animals appear more realistically, and overall their presence slightly declines. Even so, nearly a third of the stories in fourth-grade school readers published in the United States from 1900 to 1970 have animal characters, and half of them are the main protagonists.[27] The most widely used third-grade reading texts feature stories about children's relationships with animals, usually pets, nearly as often as children's ties with parents.[28] When third-graders heard stories with animal characters and identical stories with human characters substituted for the animals, three-quarters of the children preferred the animal stories.[29]

In a random scan of books garnering the Newbery Medal, the most prestigious award in children's literature, animal themes crop up most of the time. There is the 1927 best book, a paean to the eponymous *Smoky the Cowhorse,* whose cowpoke author, Will James, leads off with: "To my way of thinking there's something wrong, or missing, with any person who hasn't got a soft spot in their heart for an animal of some kind."[30] Marguerite Henry's *King of the Wind,* the winner in 1949, retells the legend of a great Arabian stallion. *It's Like This, Cat,* the 1964 choice, describes a New York City boy's coming-of-age through his bond with an adopted stray tomcat named Cat. (As the boy, Dave, says, "I know he's a cat, he knows he's a cat, and his name is Cat. Even if you call him Admiral John Paul Jones, he won't come when you call, and he won't lick your hand, see?").[31] In 1970 the award went to *Sounder,* the story of a great coon dog with a booming voice who shares the travails of a African-American boy and his poor sharecropper family. In *Julie of the Wolves,* the 1973 winner, a young Inuit girl, lost on the vast North Slope of Alaska, is adopted by wolves whom she comes to love as a family.[32] *The Midwife's Apprentice,* the 1996 winner, tells of Beetle, a homeless waif in fourteenth-century England, who saves a cat from drowning, and girl and cat find solace in each other's company.[33]

A survey of Caldecott Medal books, the most honored picture books for young children, gives the impression that prereaders yearn for, if they don't already inhabit, an animal world. In little Johnny's rescue and rearing of a bear cub, *The Biggest Bear* (1953) inveighs against hunting. In *Sam, Bangs, and Moonshine* (1967), the animals of little Samantha's overripe imagination, what her father calls her "moonshine"—a fierce lion and a baby kangaroo—endanger her real, old, wise cat, Bangs. *The Girl Who Loved Wild Horses* was the 1979 selection, and *Fables,* a humorous update of Aesop, took the prize in 1981. *Smoky Night,* the 1995 winner, depicts the terror of Los Angeles racial rioting through the eyes of little Daniel, whose beloved yellow tabbycat, Jasmine, may be lost in the fires raging around them.[34]

Over the last hundred years, with few exceptions, the best-selling, best-loved children's books feature animal characters, from *Black Beauty* (1877) to *The Tale of Peter Rabbit* (1902), to *Winnie the Pooh* (1926), to *Stuart Little* (1945), to *Charlotte's Web* (1952), to *Old Yeller*

(1956). Today a gaggle of anthropomorphized, neotenous animal stand-ins for children, what one critic decried as "the bubonic plague of children's publishing," join these animal literary heroes.[35] There are Russell Hoban's Frances, the irrepressible badger; Arthur the aardvark; Curious George, the monkey always getting into mischief; the rabbit of *Good Night Moon;* Clifford, the big red dog; Franklin the turtle; and many more. Children's books now come packaged with matching stuffed animals and ancillary *tchotchkes,* like notebooks, keychains, pocketbooks and party goods. Consumer products for children, from McDonald's Happy Meals to Saturday morning cartoons, are awash in animalia. As we've already seen, children's own imaginations—in dreams, play, stories, and fears—teem with animal life, particularly in early childhood. Are the media responding to children's "natural" interest in animals? Or are kids unwitting consumers being manipulated by savvy marketing?

Popular culture and media clearly shape children's (as well as adults') symbolic life. The Mouseketeers of my childhood are no longer around to keep Mickey's name on the lips of today's children. The advertising juggernaut of movie-book-toy-game-funmeal tie-ins spurs cravings for Ninja Turtles one year, Pokémon the next. Stuffed animals, now ubiquitous "archetypal toys," landed on children's beds only after the teddy bear craze started in 1906 and edged out the drums, popguns, trumpets, and rocking horses emblematic of nineteenth-century childhood.[36]

Stuffed bears first appeared as a Christmas novelty item that Morris Michtom, a toy manufacturer, concocted after seeing a 1902 *Washington Post* cartoon of then President Teddy Roosevelt, an avid hunter, sparing a black grizzly. (After an unsuccessful hunting expedition in Mississippi, local hosts tried to ensure the president his kill by presenting him with a tied-up, rather mangy black bear. The president refused to dispatch the captive animal, deeming such an act unsportsmanlike.) "Teddy" bears swiftly became an icon of childhood. In 1907 Steiff, the German toy manufacturer, sold over a million in Europe. Parents adopted the custom of photographing their children holding teddies.

Within a few decades, a Garden of Eden full of soft, plush creatures proliferated.[37]

This animalization of children's culture has deepened over the last century. It parallels changing societal views of nature and animals—from wild threats against civilizing humanity to carriers of humanity's better nature. In the seventeenth and eighteenth centuries, for example, the bear was the largest and fiercest creature of the North American and western European forests. Along with wolves, they posed real danger, as Peter, of Prokofiev's *Peter and the Wolf*, is repeatedly warned. By the beginning of the twentieth century, with the danger of the wild in retreat, Teddy and his stuffed animal compatriots became, like children, the last innocents, signifying what one writer called "the goodness of the wild in human nature."[38]

Signifying Animals

Animal symbols have become synonymous with childhood as both adults and children have lost intimate daily contact with actual domestic and wild animals. As the transformation of bears from grizzlies to teddies illustrates, domination and elimination of wild creatures have domesticated and infantilized their images, which then migrate from adult to child culture. Animal fables and fairy tales, originally serious entertainment for grownups—Socrates spent his prison days putting Aesop's fables into verse form—are now part of the juvenile canon. As one writer put it: "Once we stopped knowing animals as a direct matter of survival—as partners in work, as quarry to hunt, as predators to evade—fables could be read as stories about cute animals that could be safely given to children."[39]

Surrounding children with lovable creatures may also signal a collective disquiet with the scientific, detached, institutionalized treatment of animals in an age when genetically engineered animals are patented and sheep are cloned.[40] There may be whiffs of a Romantic idealization of "pure" Nature lost to the inroads of "cold" urbanization and industrialization. Cuddly creatures may be a reassuring way to underscore a childhood innocence in which we no longer believe. These social undercurrents have rendered children's culture more animal-saturated than ever.

On the other hand, the appeal of animal symbols antedates today's media blitzes. The propensity to refract human experience through an animal prism is older than recorded history. The earliest deliberately produced human work of art in existence, a 30,000-year-old statuette carved from a mammoth's tusk, depicts a man with a lion's head. Dating from about the same time are more than 300 animal figures—lifelike bulls, bison, rhinos, lions, and horses—as well as human-animal fusions, such as the head and torso of a bison on human legs, that gallop across the walls of the Chauvet cave, in the Ardèche region of France.

A universal human urge turns to animal beings as a means of reflecting upon and understanding human emotions and social organization. Anthropologist Claude Lévi-Strauss saw the forms of human cultures as modeled on observations of wild animals, "nature as a language and guide to human life." For him, totemism, universal among hunter-gatherer groups, and pervasive in human societies for at least 60,000 years, was the emblematic human belief system. Clans or other groups identified with their totem animals—for Ojibwas, for example, they were catfish, cranes, loon, bears, and martens—and these different animal species represented by analogy different forms of human society. "Because man originally felt himself identical to all those like him (among which we must include animals) that he came to acquire the capacity to distinguish *himself* as he distinguishes *them*, i.e., to use the diversity of species as conceptual support for social differentiation."[41]

Creation stories across varied cultures tell of original human-animal bonds, often describing a fall from the unity of all beings. For example, the Aztec myth of origin describes the union of the jaguar and a humanlike creature, the "jaguarman," out of which both humans and animals emerged. According to Hopi beliefs, humans were first ants, then became other animals in the "second world," and humanlike but with long tails in the "third world." Mircea Eliade identified humans living in harmony and communion with animals as the core feature common to all depictions of paradise: "Animals are charged with a symbolism and a mythology of great importance for the religious life; so that to communicate with animals, to speak their language and become their friend and master is to appropriate a spiritual life much richer than the merely human life of ordinary mortals."[42] Only shamans have the ability to reenter this lost world, to appeal to animal spirits by talking to them in their own language.

In the myths of many cultures, gods take animal forms—Jupiter appears as a bull, Arachne becomes a spider, Buddha is born as an elephant, Vishnu is incarnated as a tortoise.[43] Belief in the shape-shifting of humans into animals and animals into humans, visible in Paleolithic drawings and sculptures and universal among early hunter-gatherers, took root in ancient Egypt, spread to Greece, and by the sixth century B.C.E. entered the teachings of Buddha and the fables of Aesop. By then the iconography of animals was so elaborate that animal symbols could represent the full panoply of human relationships. Poking fun at human frailties via talking animals decked out in human attire—the animal burlesque—is one of the oldest of literary conventions. In the ancient Greek mock epic *Batrachomyomachia,* the battles between the "frog people" and the "mice people" satirized the Trojan War. The animal-filled European fairy tales of the Brothers Grimm and Charles Perrault trace their roots to oral traditions that may date back to Ice Age hunter societies.[44] The oldest toys so far discovered—Bronze Age clay rattles with the heads of foxes, birds, and dogs, and wooden crocodiles and lions from 1000 B.C.E. Egypt—depict animals.[45]

Humans have always invested animals with moral urgency and emotional power. Medieval bestiaries praised turtle doves for their chastity but condemned wolves as vicious and pigs as lazy.[46] Animals carry the weight of every human failing and accomplishment. Because animal symbols project our deepest fears, wishes, and conflicts, "when we look at animals, we see ourselves," as writer Boria Sax says.[47] Modern metaphors continue to sketch humans in animal hues—"hogging the road," "wolfing down food," "chickening out"—even though living hogs, wolves, and chickens are long gone from daily life. The bulls and bears of the stock market, the MGM lion, the Republican elephant and Democratic donkey, the Chicago Bulls, Detroit Tigers, and other animal mascots of dozens of sports teams—all are examples of an animal shorthand that permeates contemporary popular culture, just as a different animal shorthand described religious life in the Middle Ages. As one writer observed: "most animal symbols are traditional, belonging to the mythology of everyone, eternally present in the collective unconscious memory and in the dream world where everything is a symbol."[48]

What accounts for the persistence and centrality of animal metaphors? Because animals were the most salient aspect of the environment of human evolution, the human mind may be prewired to vibrate to *animal* as an innate category of thought and emotion.[49] Steven Mithen, in *The Prehistory of the Mind,* describes the evolution of the human brain in terms of three equally important domains of thought, which he calls "social" (thinking about other humans), "natural history" (thinking about animals), and "technological" (thinking about things). On the basis of the fossil record, he argues that the hallmark of the modern human brain, as contrasted to the brains of earlier hominids, is cognitive fluidity, or integration of thought across these three domains. The fusion of social and natural-history thinking allows humans to think about animals as if they were people, as well as put themselves imaginatively into animal minds and bodies. The integration of natural-history thinking with technological thinking lets humans treat animals as objects. (People can be easily objectified when social and technological thinking merge.)[50]

In this view, culture is following more than leading children's fascination with all things animal. If, as Mithen argues, thinking about animals and flexibly considering them as people or as things is a core feature of human intelligence, we would expect children to draw spontaneously on animal imagery and characters as their sense of self emerges and crystallizes.[51] Children's writer Rosemary Wells summed up this view: "Animals live in a world that children seem to climb right into."[52] Seventeenth-century philosopher John Locke felt the same way. He advocated the illustrated *Aesop's Fables* and *Reynaud the Fox* to convey lessons in virtue because of their "natural" appeal to young minds.

Whether we emphasize cultural conditioning or human predilection for thinking in animal symbols, the question remains: What are these animals of children's dreams, stories, and make-believe saying to them? What do they say to us about what animals mean to children? Why are animal symbols most potent in childhood?

The Good Me, the Bad Me

Historically, the dominant response to these questions has come from psychoanalytic theory. In this account, young children, under the sway of unruly instincts and under pressure to control their messy impulses, express their "wild," "bad" parts through animal characters. For Freud, animal and child formed a natural fraternity and sorority of the untamed. This interpretation was a spinoff of the still pervasive cultural metaphor entwining young children, animals, and so-called "primitive peoples" in the skeins of instinct. Because the child was a sort of primitive, outside refined (that is, bourgeois Viennese) society, children's responses to animals seemed to Freud to parallel the totemistic worship of animal ancestors by so-called primitive tribes:

> The relation of the child to animals has much in common with that of primitive man. The child does not yet show any trace of the pride which afterwards moves the adult civilized man to set a sharp dividing line between his own nature and that of all other animals. The child unhesitatingly attributes full equality to animals; he probably feels himself more closely related to the animal than to the undoubtedly mysterious adult, in the freedom with which he acknowledges his needs.[53]

Animals appear in children's and adults' dreams and fears as code for what Ernest Jones, the psychoanalyst biographer of Freud, called "crude and unabridged wishes."[54] A small child's storms of anger against a kid brother or sister turn into a bear who roars, bites, and devours. Wild animals personify the child's own frightening rages. Three-year-old Bart's story—"Once there was a lion. He ate everybody up. He ate himself up."—was, to Evelyn Pitcher and Ernest Prelinger, an example of how "wild, fierce, and ferocious animals . . . may serve as a convenient representative of the child's consciously not acceptable wishes to harm and to destroy, of his anger and his resentments."[55] "Monstrous" feelings that a child finds too terrifying to acknowledge take life, in Maurice Sendak's classic children's book, *Where the Wild Things Are,* as monsters conjured up by an angry little boy, Max, banished to his room.

In the psychoanalytic explanation, animals make convenient targets for the real objects of a child's anger, fear, and desire. Like the totemic figures studied by anthropologists, animals are the repository of feelings that, if directed toward authority figures like mother or father, would be unacceptable. Karl Menninger recalled how in childhood he lavished "definitely romantic and somewhat consciously erotic" attention on his pet horse. Through psychoanalysis, Menninger came to recognize that in such attachments "the animal represents a sister, mother, father, or other relative."[56]

In Freud's famous (and only) analysis of a young child, four-and-a-half-year-old "little Hans" became fearful that a horse in the street would bite him. (These were the days of horse-drawn wagons and carriages.) Soon his phobia made him afraid even to go out into the street. He became convinced that a horse would come into his room at night. At the same time, horses fascinated Hans. As he explained to his father, who was sending in regular reports to Herr Professor Freud, "I have to look at horses, and then I'm frightened."[57] Soon Hans's fear spread to other large animals; at the zoo he now refused to see the giraffes or elephants. He recounted night terrors involving "big giraffes" and "crumpled ones."

For Freud, little Hans's phobia stemmed from a potent Oedipal brew of angry wishes to destroy his father, fear of his father's retaliatory power and his mother's abandonment, and Hans's guilt and anxiety over the anger he felt toward the father he loved. The big, long-necked giraffe signified his father's penis, the crumpled one his mother's genital organs. When Hans confided he was particularly afraid of horses with "something black on their mouths," Freud linked the image to Hans's father and his black moustache. Large, powerful, towering horses and long-necked giraffes could hold all these frightening and ambivalent feelings, preserving the warmth and closeness of Hans's bond with his father. As Freud imparted these interpretations to the child, little Hans slowly shed his fears. With a note of self-satisfaction, Freud concluded: "the only results of the analysis were that Hans recovered, that he ceased to be afraid of horses, and that he got on to rather familiar terms with his father."[58]

The bundle of instincts with which young children wrestle may at times frighten them, but for psychoanalytic theory the untamed id also signifies freedom. Bruno Bettelheim's analysis of children's fairy tales, *The Uses of Enchantment,* describes dogs in these stories as representing "instinctual freedom—freedom to bite, to excrete in an uncontrolled way, and to indulge sexual needs without restraint." To Bettelheim, horse stories fascinated girls because horses stood for "the sexually animalistic within herself."[59] Freud noted that "animals owe a good deal of their importance in myths and fairy tales to the openness with which they display their genitals and their sexual functions to the inquisitive little human child."[60] Little Hans initially became preoccupied with horses, Freud surmised, because their large penises, on public display, fascinated him.

As in "Beauty and the Beast," the inner beast of unbridled sexual urges must be tamed, but first it must be accepted and loved. As Beauty loves the Beast, she accepts his "wild parts" and, by doing so, allows them to be integrated into a now humanized person. Adherents to a Jungian perspective describe animal motifs in art as symbols of "man's primitive and instinctual nature" and argue that "acceptance of the animal soul is the condition for wholeness and a fully lived life."[61]

For Freud, Jung, and the other psychoanalysts following in their wake, animals were flexible symbol systems taking myriad shapes to express a wide range of instinctual feelings and ideas. Animals could be the raging self or the feared and loved parent. They could be sexual urges or the terror of them. A few animals seemed to be universal, biologically based symbols; for example, snakes always represented phalluses. Even children's delight in animal companions, real and imaginary, and their intense attachment to pets supposedly derived from an infantile primitivism, a childish "tenacious, fantastic bond," as a 1917 essay in the *Psychoanalytic Review* put it, that adult rational thought must ultimately sever.[62]

Because of the plasticity of animals in signifying the urges and conflicts that the child could not directly acknowledge, creatures popped up everywhere in children's dreams, fantasies, and fears. Imagery from animal-laden fairy tales resonated with a scarcely buried substrate of primitive urges. For example, the young man dubbed "the Wolfman" recalled a recurring nightmare, when he was five years old, of six or seven white wolves threatening to eat him. To Freud, the dream merged "Little Red Riding Hood" and "The Wolf and the Seven Little Goats" into an "anxiety-animal" known to the child only from stories and picture books.[63] The devouring wolves stood for the Wolfman's aggressive impulses, terrifying superego, and fear of being castrated by his father.[64]

While not discarding the insights of a psychoanalytic interpretation of animal symbolism, we can reach for a broader, more compelling account. The animal kingdom of the imagination does more than screen unacceptable or conflicted childhood passions. Animals also are a first vocabulary for many other aspects of oneself. When young children make up stories, their animal descriptions often blur with descriptions of themselves. To dream researcher David Foulkes, "the animal character is the first form in which children's own interests are invested."[65] Animal dreams, stories, fantasies, and play can be viewed as central to young children's "self-work." Rather than standing in for an already fully realized, self-aware self, animal characters are the raw material out of which children construct a sense of self.

Ignored in the equation of animal instinct with wild child is the way animal stories and symbols guide children into deeper understanding of what it means to have a *human* self. Young children use animal characters much as Lévi-Strauss saw hunter-gatherer groups using their animal

totems—as visible manifestations of invisible human feelings and relationships. As Paul Shepard notes, "animals have a critical role in the
shaping of personal identity and social consciousness. Among the first
inhabitants of the mind's eye, they are basic to the development of
speech and thought. Later, they play a key role in the passage to adulthood. Because of their participation in each stage of consciousness, they
are indispensable to our becoming human in the fullest sense." To fully
appreciate being human, he suggests, we must trace the threads linking
us to other animals.[66]

Children enlist both real and make-believe animal characters in a
wide range of developmental challenges—achieving mastery and a
sense of competence, balancing independence with dependence on parents and peers, exploring and integrating different facets of their emerging selves. Animal characters play out issues of power and powerlessness, responsibility, and freedom. C. S. Lewis, the distinguished author
of *The Lion, The Witch, and the Wardrobe* and other children's books,
was not quite sure himself why he gravitated to animal characters. Perhaps, he mused, his own creations, as well as characters like Mr. Toad in
Kenneth Grahame's *Wind in the Willows,* appeal to children because
they combine a child's freedom from adult "domestic cares" with
grownup license to "go where they like, do what they please, and ar-
range their own lives."[67]

With animal characters, children explore the boundary between human and animal. As children sing "Old MacDonald" and "Eensy
Weensy Spider," play fox-and-goose chase games, or get lost in *The Jungle Books,* they are carving out a common ground with other beings. In
animal play and animal stories, children imaginatively cross the gulf between the human and animal worlds, as Mowgli, the wolf boy of
Kipling's *Jungle Books,* does when he learns the ways of the animals'
world. Through animal symbols, children are laying down the roots of a
childhood ecology. They are considering what it might feel like to be in
an animal's body, as Stuart Little inhabits the body of a mouse.[68]
Children rely on animals, real and fanciful, to situate themselves in a
multicreature world.

Harnessing Animal Powers

A slight, shy eight-year-old boy I know hurries home after school each day to go back to the age when dinosaurs roamed the Earth. A walking encyclopedia of dinosaur lore, he never tires of playing out battles between Brontosaurus and Tyrannosaurus Rex, using his six-inch-high replicas. Unlike the power of adults or other bigger, more assertive peers, dinosaur power is, literally, under his thumb. As he moves his dinosaur kingdom around the table, like chess pieces on a large board, he is the supreme deity of his miniature kingdom of terrifying beasts. Is his fascination with dinosaurs, and the remarkable knowledge he's accumulated as a result, just a redirection of unacceptable sexual and aggressive urges? While these may be elements in his play, his life among the dinosaurs primarily serves other functions. In that life is an interplay of power and powerlessness—the small child as master of larger, rampaging forces, the dinosaur creatures miniaturized. No matter that the dinosaur expert's handwriting is nearly illegible, and that the teacher keeps telling him to sit still.

Scary creatures—Godzilla, King Kong, the dinosaurs of *Jurassic Park* and *The Land before Time*—mix a frisson of fear into children's exhilaration at the sight of even grownups getting stomped. At the same time, dinosaur and monster tales read as parables of the small and dependent ultimately outwitting, taming, or destroying overwhelming beasts. Another variation on animal stories as power plays is the "reluctant dragon." Like the Kenneth Grahame story of the same name (1899), reluctant dragons—Barney is the latest incarnation of the breed—reveal soft centers that render them as harmless as floppy dogs.[69]

Animal Guides

In some children's stories, the special gifts of animals shepherd the child on a perilous adventure. This theme of animal guides, deeply resonant in Native American tales and the legends of many other cultures, gets a modern reworking in "dangerous survivor" stories.[70] For example, in *The Grey King*, a 1976 Newbery Award book based on Welsh legends, a boy searches for a golden harp, guided by a magical white dog with silver eyes who can see the wind.[71] The thirteen-year-old Inuit heroine of *Julie of the Wolves* survives in the Artic wilderness because a pack of wolves adopts her, showing her how to track game and protecting her from bear attack. In *The Music of Dolphins*, dolphins raise Mila from the age of four until her "rescue" as a teenager off an unpopulated Florida island.[72] Karana, the Indian heroine of *Island of the Blue Dolphins*, survives Robinson Crusoe style on a deserted island by taming wild dogs, birds, and even otters as companions.[73]

Such adventures echo the "wild child," the ancient theme of children suckled by wolves, as were Romulus and Remus, the traditional founders of Rome, or raised in the forest by bears, as was Orson, in the fourteenth-century English tale, "Valentine and Orson," of twin brothers separated at birth.[74] Like the "wild boy" of Aveyron, the wild child grows up in the animal world, never knowing human society. In modern animal guide stories, the child—often a young girl—owes more than her survival to her animal saviors. She enters the world of the wolves (or dolphins) not as a human observer but as one of them. The child parts the curtain that separates animal societies from human experience. Because the child truly understands the animals, from inside their world, she can become their intermediary with often hostile, uncomprehending adult humans. There comes a moment when the child, so long protected by her animal guides, in turn saves them from human predation, as Julie saves one of her wolf "family" from sporthunters gunning down wolves from a plane.

The animal guide stories tell of a protective Mother Nature, literally mothering the lost child. Here, wild animals signify a purity of acceptance and care, in contrast to the confusing mixed signals of human hypocrisy and deceit. The animal guide erases the barrier between the young human and the surrounding animal world.

Saving the Animals

In the movie *Fly Away Home,* a young girl comes from Australia after her mother's sudden death to live in New England with the father she hardly knows. Depressed, she finds solace in handraising some wild Canadian goslings whose abandoned eggs she found when hunters had killed their parents. As the goslings mature, their survival depends upon learning to fly and then to migrate, skills their parents would have taught them. Now it is up to the girl, with her father's help, to teach the goslings in their parents' place. Father and daughter build a plane and paint it to resemble a giant goose. She learns to fly it, and, one step ahead of unfeeling hunters and real estate developers, she guides the birds on their journey south. Her depression lifts, a bond forms between father and daughter, and the girl grows daily more competent and assertive. At the end, piloting the "goose" plane, she stands down a cigar-chomping, pot-bellied developer about to bulldoze a crucial wetland. In saving the geese, she has saved herself, metamorphosing from withdrawn sadsack to a pint-sized Amelia Earhart adventurer.

Fly Away Home taps a recurring theme in animal stories—children as allies and often saviors of vulnerable animals against an unfeeling, cruel adult world. The child and animal form a bond, share a common language. The goslings, imprinted to the young girl, follow her around as she clucks and hoots to them in fluent Canada goose. Both child and animal are outsiders in the adult world, marginal to its rules but subject to their arbitrariness. For both of them, freedom is tenuous and threatened. To save the animal from the clutches of adult authority, the child must marshal every ounce of juvenile strength and skill. The rescue of the animal becomes a rite of passage, a test of maturity. Sometimes a lone, kindly adult mentor, like the father in *Fly Away Home,* imparts to the child the skills needed to do battle on behalf of the animal.

In the process of saving the animal, the child grows stronger. Often the endangered animal is, like the Canada geese, as big as the child, or much larger, like the whale of *Free Willy* movies or the horse of *The*

Black Stallion, but its size and strength are not enough to save it. Its massive force must be harnessed to the child's resourcefulness and courage. The animal may be big and seemingly powerful, but it needs the small child's help. At some point in the story, however, the animal's strength comes to the rescue when the child is most vulnerable. The Black Stallion saves young Alec Ramsey when the steamer *Drake* is shipwrecked, only to be later saved by the boy. "Saving the animals" stories affirm the child's sense of mastery through a special, mysterious bond to a large and usually wild animal.

These stories depict children as the true stewards of embattled nature. In *Friends in Deed Save the Manatee,* they, not the indifferent, heedless adults, rescue endangered species. In the sixteen-volume Pony Pals series, preteen girls come to the aid of horses animals in danger.[75] As in C. S. Lewis' Chronicles of Narnia and Rudyard Kipling's *Jungle Books,* children mediate between the realms of animals and adults.

Scamps and Rascals

A variant on the motif of power and powerlessness depicts animal characters as diminutive but crafty creatures, who get out of scrapes by using their wiles and small size to outsmart those with superior brawn. This is the animal as little, spunky kid. Here animal characters act out a child's "underdog" status in the family pecking order.[76] From folk wisdom and ancient fables through contemporary cartoons, we see animals as mischievous rascals. As one scholar remarked, "small animals like cats give us an opportunity to see our small, cute, and guileless pet (and potential alter ego) improbably succeed in getting his or her way in a world of larger animals, including human adults."[77] Peter Rabbit disregards his mother's warnings and wanders into Farmer McGregor's cabbage patch, barely escaping with his life. Curious George can't resist scrambling up to dangerous heights to retrieve a banana. Toad, in the popular Frog and Toad series by Arnold Lobel, is an impulsive show-off. Chester

Cricket, the eponymous hero of *Cricket in Times Square*, creates a miniature world with his cat and rat pals. His sly adventures skirt the real-
life consequences of children's misdeeds. These animals, almost always
male, play out the mixed messages of masculine socialization. Peter
Rabbit is the errant boy, simultaneously admired for his naughty spirit
of adventure and (with a wink) punished for transgressing the big people's rules.

Characters like Sterling North's beloved pet raccoon Rascal, in the
1964 adult best-seller of the same name, evoke a boyhood of camping,
fishing, and trapping in a manly society unfettered by female demands.
(Twelve-year-old Sterling, living alone with his father after his mother
has died and older siblings have moved away, is free to build a canoe in
the living room. When his proper older sister visits, she is horrified by
the mess and insists that Rascal be penned up.) When Rascal grows to
adult size and evinces an interest in mating, Sterling sadly releases his
pet and thereby relinquishes his own freewheeling boyhood.[78]

The Animal Me

Sixteen-year-old Tricia props herself up in the hospital bed, swings her
legs over the side, and rolls the computer table into reach. Quickly she
logs on and enters the chatroom as her favorite cyber-identity, a silver
pony. Whenever she's on line at the Starbright World, a computer network for hospitalized children, this is the being she assumes.[79]
Cyberspace is just the latest arena in which children take on animal
identities.

In many children's stories, as well as in much adult fiction featuring
children and animals, there is an easy identification of child with animal.
In the recent book and movie *The Horse Whisperer*, Grace, a young
teenage girl, and her beloved horse, Pilgrim, are severely injured in a
horrible accident, in which Grace's best friend is killed. As the Horse
Whisperer, Tom Booker, rehabilitates Pilgrim, Grace too is made well.
Girl and horse move in parallel through an arduous struggle to regain
wholeness.

Such equating of child with animal is quite different from that of psychoanalytic interpretations. Here, they are not joined as instinctual beings, but as comrades sharing remarkably similar emotions despite the species divide. This parallelism of child with animal emphasizes the capacity of children to connect directly with animals, to enter their emotional life, even when the animal is culturally despised. In *A Little Princess*, by Frances Hodgson Burnett, a little girl, Sara, meets a rat in the attic: "'I dare say it is rather hard to be a rat,' she mused. 'Nobody likes you. People jump and run away and scream out. 'Oh, a horrid rat!' I shouldn't like people to scream and jump and say, 'Oh, a horrid Sara!'"[80]

Animal characters are particularly well suited to playing out themes of identity. Animal metaphors, refracting facets of human personality and behavior, put us in touch with the animal (in a broader, rather than, narrower, instinctual sense) within us. Shakespeare penned more than four thousand metaphors and similes involving animals.[81] Mermaids, centaurs, and other human-animal hybrids, and magical transformations—human into animal and back again—recur in many folk and fairytales. Ananse, the Spider Man of African legends, spins a web up to the sky. In the Native American folktale "The Serpent of the Sea," a girl must marry a serpent, who then turns into a handsome man.[82] The Frog Prince assumes both roles in the course of his story, the Twelve Brothers are changed into ravens before resuming human form, and the Enchanted Stag begins life as a human boy but falls under the spell of a wicked stepmother.

In the DonkeySkin tales, of which Charles Perrault's 1694 version is the best known, the beautiful princess escapes detection by hiding under the mangy pelt of a donkey, so that she is known only as "DonkeySkin." The donkey skin represents a saving disguise from the incestuous advances of the princess' father. At the same time, the skin that cloaks the princess' radiance is the cultural repository of bestial hairiness—associated with the devil in seventeenth-century symbolism—filth, and ugliness. The princess uses the donkey skin for survival, but it is she who had demanded that her father kill the enchanted beast. Animal-human shape-changing stories, like the DonkeySkin tales, mirror the multiple ways in which a particular culture and historical time use animals as sources of both positive and negative identity.[83]

The transformation theme sports a modern update in the best-selling Animorph series of books, in which five junior high school students—Jake, Rachel, Cassie, Tobias, and Marco—battle evil aliens through their ability to turn themselves into animals and, once in their animal beings, to communicate with one another telepathically. Each Animorph episode shows one of the youngsters morphing into an animal—cat, bear, dolphin, hawk.[84] For the Animorphs, like the Frog Prince or Enchanted Stag of the old fables, the matter-of-fact commuting and communicating across species boundaries illustrates what Paul Shepard calls "the glue of real kinship" between the human child and the animal world.[85]

Why do children, but not adolescents or adults, live quite comfortably and consciously in the world of animal symbols, a world their adult caretakers embroider for them with animal stories, toys, and every imaginable product? Why is the rich texture of animal imagery and meaning driven underground as children move into maturity? One conjecture is that young children graft animals into their inner worlds and themselves into the imagined worlds of animals because of a fundamental cognitive and emotional immaturity. Unable to sustain the intricacies of human friendships, a first-grader takes Winnie the Pooh for temporary best pal. Struggling to contain waves of rage at being denied her wishes, a preschooler defangs her inner beasts with friendly monsters.

This view of animals as childish things to be put away ignores the positive, growth-promoting features of the animals of the imagination and of real life. If we embrace a different premise, based on the legacy of our coevolution with animal species, that life begins with an openness toward animals as creatures in equal standing with us, then animals become the essential first vocabulary for understanding ourselves and other humans. As children develop into adolescence and adulthood, this vocabulary, encoded in metaphors and folktales, retains its symbolic power.

7

Victims and Objects

In the early morning of Saturday, March 8, 1997, a volunteer arrived for her shift at the Noah's Ark Foundation, a "no-kill" animal shelter that rescues stray cats and dogs, in the rural community of Fairfield, Iowa.[1] As she swung the door open, a war scene of blood and body parts greeted her. Sixteen cats were dead, apparently bludgeoned, and at least six more lay injured, with broken legs, smashed jaws, and multiple fractures. The surviving animals were shell-shocked, cowering in corners. Others had disappeared entirely.

A week later, following tips from local residents and helped by a reward that quickly grew to $5,000, the police arrested Justin Tobin, eighteen; Chad Lamansky, eighteen; and Daniel Myers, seventeen; and charged them with third-degree burglary, illegal entry, and destruction of property and animals. Justin and Chad were seniors, Daniel a junior, at the local Fairfield High School, where Chad played on the football team. None of the three had ever been in trouble with the law before. When Justin plea-bargained in exchange for testifying against the other two, the events of the "cat massacre" quickly emerged.

That Friday night, after a few beers at the Hy-Vee, a popular Fairfield High hangout, the three young men drove to Justin's house to pick up baseball bats. With Justin driving, they went to the Noah's Ark shelter. The converted white clapboard house seemed deserted. There was no sign of human presence, but it was home to more than fifty stray cats. Laura Sykes, who, with her former husband, David, had founded the shelter a decade earlier, was in Idaho on her first vacation in fifteen years. As Justin waited by the door—he described himself as "doorman and driver"—Chad and Daniel began the killing. After about five minutes, at Justin's insistence, they left, but may have returned later that night with another individual.

The news of the Fairfield cat killings stunned the small community. The local St. Gabriel and All Angels church held a special "healing service for all those traumatized by the tragedy," as the local newspaper put it.[2] Veterinary clinics donated their services to treat the surviving injured cats. Outraged letters poured into area newspapers calling the accused youngsters "two vile bubba breeds" and "sadistic monsters" with "evil and sickness in their minds." Many of those writing echoed an Iowa City pastor who saw "a symptom of something terribly, deeply wrong inside" the accused youngsters. Some warned that "notorious criminal monsters . . . began their infamous activities by doing what these kids did."[3] But others agreed with their defense attorney, who labeled the killings simply "a stupid teenage mistake." According to one local resident, Dixie Haynes, whose son Donny was an acquaintance of Chad Lamansky: "It's a thing that boys have. You used to see them out hunting, targeting cats with .22s."[4]

As more details leaked out about the accused, especially Chad, the "thing that boys have" took on darker tones. On Chad's truck a bumper sticker read: "If you're missing your cat, look at my tires." A few days before the cat killings, according to witnesses at the Hy-Vee, Chad had waved around the pelt of a freshly skinned black and white cat. As a "practical joke" on his kid brother, Chad had killed and skinned one of his mother's cats that closely resembled his brother's own pet. High school acquaintances remembered that Chad had earlier got in trouble by bringing a hunting rifle in his car onto school grounds.

The Fairfield case attracted wide media attention. By the end of September 1997, crews from *The Today Show, 48 Hours,* and Fox network had filmed at the shelter and around town. *People* magazine gave prominent coverage to the November trial and December sentencing of Chad and Daniel. At the trial, both young men admitted breaking and entering into the shelter and intentionally killing the cats, but gave no motive. Because the jury found that the total value of all the killed and injured cats was less than $500, the felony conviction automatically dropped to aggravated misdemeanor. Although their conviction carried a maximum sentence of five years in prison, Judge Wilson sentenced them to twenty-three days in jail, one day for each cat killed or injured, $2,500 each in fines, and three years' probation. No psychological counseling or humane education was required. While Laura and David Sykes bemoaned the verdict as "a slap on the wrist," other local residents pointed to spending Christmas in jail as proof of the severity of the punishment. One of the jurors, nineteen-year-old Jeremie McCoy, when asked if he had ever killed a cat, replied, "I think everybody has in his childhood."

The cat killings in Fairfield momentarily focused attention on a generally underplayed facet of children's relationships with animals. The idea of childhood cruelty toward animals challenges deeply rooted notions of young innocence and goodness contrasted to adult exploitation. In 1942 a writer gushing over the just-released movie *Bambi* perfectly captured this cultural assumption: "The message of Bambi is sweeping the country; it is appealing above all to the men and women of tomorrow who are now our children. To a child, in his simplicity, the life of an innocent, harmless, and beautiful animal is just as precious as that of a human being, so many of whom do not appear altogether innocent and harmless and beautiful."[5]

But anyone who has been bullied in the schoolyard or teased unmercifully by an older brother or sister—just about all of us, that is—know how cruel children can be at times. Honest reflection on our own childhoods brings back moments of astonishing meanness. Hitting, pushing, taunting, grabbing, kicking, teasing—all surface at one time or another in every child, along with kindness, helping, empathy, and nurturing. Childhood is, in part, a struggle to dampen and channel those aggressive, destructive urges with which all humans contend. Animals, so entwined in children's intimate lives, are on hand for the ups and downs of that struggle. Precisely because children connect so readily to animals as symbols of every emotional hue, pets and other small animals are vulnerable to a child's rages and resentments.

The same qualities that call forth nurturing—small size, child- likeness, and dependency—make pets and small wild animals like squirrels, chipmunks, and rabbits vulnerable to abuse. Pets live under a (usually) benevolent, affectionate dictatorship, but they remain wholly subject to human power. They are the first living creatures over whom children can wield absolute control. Every relationship with great disparities in power carries the potential for abuse. When those in power are inexperienced, with uncertain dominion over their own rages, and carrying their own history of utter dependency—in other words, children—the probability of cruelty, casual mistreatment, and neglect increases. The honorary family-member status of pets adds to their vulnerability, as they get drawn into the swirl of family dynamics. When violence takes root in a family, its tendrils are likely to ensnare the family's animals as well.

Given the shaky, "one-down" position of pets and other small animals, perhaps we should be surprised that more children do *not* commit acts of intentional cruelty and killing of animals. Most animal mistreatment at childish hands stems from isolated incidents motivated by curiosity or ignorance rather than from a recurring pattern of premeditated, serious injury.[6] The terms *animal abuse* and *animal cruelty* are overly broad; they cover a wide range of mistreatment differing in motive and circumstance, from passive neglect, depriving a pet of adequate food, water, or shelter, to excessively harsh discipline, such as whipping a dog into obedience, to abandonment of unwanted pets, to beating, stoning, and torturing in order to maim and kill. Many, perhaps even most, young children at some time stomp on bugs, pull wings off insects, throw stones at birds, or handle small creatures so roughly as to injure or kill them. Usually these early destructive experiments do not escalate into a pattern of deliberate cruelty.[7]

Nonetheless, we should be wary of dismissing any animal mistreatment as mischief that youngsters naturally outgrow along with last year's high-tops. Because scholarship hasn't yet uncovered the triggering mechanisms that make some children go on to ever-more-abusive acts, a zero-tolerance stance is prudent. When we countenance needless animal suffering, even of "lower" beings like insects and rodents, we send a message that shrinks rather than expands the boundaries of empathy. Children may bring an open, wholehearted interest to their encounters with animal life, but this interest is not automatically focused on enhancing animal well-being. As the biophilia hypothesis suggests, culture, family, and individual experiences converge to channel children's intrinsic interest in animals into benign or destructive pathways. Even if only a small minority of children go on to commit intentional, serious injury of animals, thousands of animals and children are being harmed.

The First Kill

A recent spate of highly publicized schoolyard killings has prompted a closer look for early-warning signs of violence in children. Cruelty to animals—often elaborate torture killings—surfaces repeatedly as part of a constellation of ominous signs. A month before the Fairfield trial, on October 1, 1997, Luke Woodham, a sophomore at Pearl High School, in a suburb of Jackson, Mississippi, stabbed his mother to death and later opened fire on classmates with a hunting rifle, killing two girls and injuring seven other students. Investigators found Woodham's account of his gruesome torture and killing of his pet dog, Sparkle, which Woodham described as "his first kill." He and another teenager had beaten the dog with a club, wrapped it in garbage bags doused with lighter fluid, set the dog ablaze, and finally thrown the animal into a pond. He wrote: "I'll never forget the sound of her breaking under my might. I hit her so hard I knocked the fur off her neck . . . It was true beauty."[8] On May 21, 1998, Kip Kinkel, a fifteen-year-old, slight for his age, shot his parents to death before emptying three guns at his classmates in the Thurston High School cafeteria in Springfield, Oregon, leaving one dead and twenty-six injured. Described by classmates as an angry, "mean" child, Kip often bragged to them about how he tortured animals.[9]

Systematic research tends to confirm the pattern suggested by these sensational cases. Frank Ascione has reviewed most existing studies and case reports of children who are cruel to animals.[10] He concludes that serious, intentional harm to animals is one of the earliest appearing signs—usually before age seven—of conduct disorder, a complex of behavioral and psychological problems including high impulsivity, violence, and disregard for others' feelings. Repeated, intentional cruelty to animals almost never appears as an isolated aberration in an otherwise well-adjusted child. Characteristically it is part of a constellation of symptoms, including fighting, tantrums, truancy, vandalism, and firesetting.[11]

Conduct disorder itself puts children at risk for delinquency and crime. In 1992 Ascione assessed ninety-six teenage boys who were either incarcerated or undergoing evaluation by the Utah Department of Corrections. Fifteen percent of the imprisoned youth and 21 percent of those being evaluated reported torturing or hurting animals on purpose within the last twelve months.[12] Another study reviewed the case histories of twenty-one homicidally aggressive eight-to-twelve-year-olds hospitalized for psychiatric treatment. Mention of animal abuse appeared in 14 percent of the records (as compared to 3 percent of same-age youngsters hospitalized for nonviolent disorders).[13] On the bright side, these figures suggest that the vast majority of even seriously disturbed children probably do not abuse animals. Still, as Ascione points out, if only 5 percent of children with conduct disorder abuse animals—and this is probably a serious underestimate—this translates into thousands of children (over 100,000 children are diagnosed with conduct disorder each year) and thousands of mistreated and killed animals.[14]

Cruelty to animals, often spectacularly inventive and filled with sadistic pleasure, is much more common in the childhood histories of rapists, murderers, and other violent criminals than in the backgrounds of nonviolent criminals or noncriminals. Jeffrey Dahmer; Albert DeSalvo, the "Boston Strangler"; David Berkowitz, the "Son of Sam"; and Carroll

Edward Cole, a serial killer accused of thirty-five deaths, all recounted animal torture as their first violent act.[15] Stephen Kellert and Alan Felthous asked counselors at federal penitentiaries in Danbury, Connecticut, and Leavenworth, Kansas, to rate the habitual aggression while in prison of 102 inmates under their supervision. Each convict also gave a detailed account of his childhood experiences with animals. Almost 70 percent of the most aggressive criminals acknowledged at least one childhood episode of cruelty to an animal; a quarter of them admitted to five or more acts of cruelty, indicating a persistent pattern. By contrast, 6 percent of the nonaggressive criminals reported five or more acts of cruelty. The litany of childhood animal mistreatment was worthy of professional torturers in totalitarian regimes; exploding a cat in a microwave, putting rat poison in fishbowls, tying cats' tails together, snapping the necks of animals, feeding dogs gunpowder. When Felthous compared violent psychiatric inpatients with nonaggressive ones, the results were similar: 23 percent of the violent inpatients (versus 10 percent of nonaggressive ones) said that as children they had killed dogs or cats for no apparent reason. Eighteen percent of aggressive inpatients as children had tortured animals, in contrast to 5 percent of the nonaggressive inpatients.[16]

These studies and case histories tell a consistent story: as boys, criminally violent adult males are much more likely than other men to have abused animals.[17] The more violent and antisocial the adult, the more severe the childhood mistreatment of animals. Nonviolent psychiatric patients and nonaggressive prison inmates do not differ from a group of "average" men, drawn from the general population, in their reported childhood histories of animal abuse.[18] This is one of the most disturbing implications of these retrospective studies. If their findings hold up when tested more rigorously and widely, the sobering conclusion is that between 3 and 10 percent of adult men without violent histories may, as boys, have purposely abused animals.[19]

The research data are not conclusive; it's not clear how often children intentionally abuse animals and which children are most at risk. One problem is that no one has gathered prevalence rates for cruelty to animals in the general population of children or even of adults. U.S. census-based studies are nonexistent.[20] Because of this, there is no baseline by which to evaluate the incidence of animal cruelty in specific groups of children or adults. Linking childhood abuse of animals to later violence against humans by tapping the recollections of adults is a suspect strategy. Memory tends to be selective and self-serving, even when a person is not doing time in a federal prison. Violent prisoners or psychiatric patients may have particularly distorted recollections of their childhoods. Half of the inmates that Felthous and Kellert approached refused to tell their stories, leaving us to wonder whether tales of animal torture might be part of the braggadocio of especially violent men. Working backward—from adult violence to childhood cruelty to animals—misses the many, perhaps majority of, children who display some mistreatment of animals but do not go on to threaten humans or other animals.

Getting valid evidence of abuse directly from children is tricky because animal mistreatment tends to be hidden. In a few cases, children brag about their misdeeds or, like Chad Lamansky in Fairfield, show off the gruesome evidence; but typically, parents, relatives, and neighbors are unaware of it. There are only a few small-scale studies that directly ask youngsters, rather than their parents, about current mistreatment of animals.[21] Children themselves may not be forthright about animal abuse when questioned about it; violent children may exaggerate to appear "tough," while other children may not want to admit what they realize are shameful actions. In general, great interviewing skill is required to probe suggestible youngsters about sensitive issues.

Even with these qualifications, reliable evidence of animal abuse at the hands of children fills the files of humane societies. In the Milwaukee area alone, the Wisconsin Humane Society documented the following cases in a single year, 1993. Several youths doused a pit bull puppy, Hank, with gasoline, threw him into a trash bin, and burned him alive. A thirteen-year-old boy threw a kitten on a lit barbecue grill. Patrons at a fast-food restaurant witnessed a group of eight-to-eleven-year-old boys in the parking lot playing hackysack by using a five-week-old kitten, which died from their kicking and tossing. Several boys poked out the eye of a shepherd mix dog. In 1998, in Pennsylvania, two boys, eight and nine years old, taped a dog's mouth, bound its legs together, cut off its ears, and left it for dead in the woods. In Kansas, four youths, ranging from seventeen to twenty, set fire to a dog and then videotaped it burning to death.[22]

Until recently, except for humane societies and anti-animal-cruelty groups, animal abuse was often either ignored or downplayed when it came to light. Case workers and law enforcement officers would fail to record episodes of cruelty in their notes. Randall Lockwood, the education director of the Humane Society of the United States, points out that most cases of animal abuse involving juveniles are never reported.[23] Witnesses to children's cruelty often are silent, perhaps because they are unclear what laws were being broken or feel it's a matter best resolved within the family. A shocking example of this occurred in the notorious case of Jeffrey Dahmer, who killed and mutilated seventeen young men. As a boy he collected road kill, dismembered small wild animals, and impaled their skulls on crosses in a perverse "animal cemetery" that he constructed in his backyard. His neighbors photographed the skulls and kept the pictures for years but never reported the incidents to police or social service agencies.[24]

In 1987 the American Psychiatric Association added the phrase "physically cruel to animals" to the description of conduct disorder in its *Diagnostic and Statistical Manual,* the standard guide that psychologists, psychiatrists, and social workers use to diagnose children. The inclusion of cruelty to animals in this diagnostic "bible" has helped sensitize therapists to animal mistreatment as a symptom of conduct disorder.

Law enforcement officials increasingly are red-flagging animal abuse when they build profiles of habitually violent offenders. FBI Special Agent Alan Brantley, who focuses on animal abuse cases, underscored what he sees as the link between childhood cruelty to animals and subsequent violent crime: "Something we believe is prominently displayed in the histories of people who are habitually violent is animal abuse . . . You have to look at the quality of the act and at the frequency and severity." Brantley has noticed that symbolic animal abuse, such as cutting up a stuffed animal, appears very early in the childhoods of some multiple murderers.[25]

"A Righteous Man Regardeth the Life of His Beast"

The idea of animal abuse as an early-warning sign of murderous tendencies toward humans has a long history. In the thirteenth century Thomas Aquinas (1225–1274), drawing on biblical passages such as Proverbs 12:10 (quoted above), cautioned that "Holy Scripture seems to forbid us to be cruel to brute animals . . . through being cruel to animals one becomes cruel to human beings." The sixteenth-century French essayist Michel de Montaigne (1533–1592) pointed out that "Natures that are bloodthirsty toward animals give proof of a natural propensity toward cruelty."[26] From the seventeenth through nineteenth centuries, sermons from the pulpits of western Europe and America decried the brutalizing effect of animal mistreatment among the lower classes—foxhunting and other diversions of the aristocracy were excluded. Every seedling of cruelty to animals must be rooted out when children are still young, urged the British philosopher John Locke (1632–1704) in *Some Thoughts concerning Education:* "I have frequently observed in children that, when they have got possession of any poor creature, they are apt to use it ill; they often torment and treat very roughly young birds, butterflies, and such other poor animals, which fall into their hands, and that with a seeming kind of pleasure."[27]

Immanuel Kant (1724–1804), the German philosopher, considered kindness to animals "man's duty to himself." When Kant lectured on the subject, he displayed a series of four engravings by the British artist William Hogarth, titled *Four Stages of Cruelty* (1751). In the first, Tom Nero—the name of this Everyman evokes the dissipated Roman emperor—and other lads disport themselves in various animal torments. They are depicted hanging cats upside down and driving a rod into the anus of a captive dog. The second engraving shows Tom as a young man, beating a carriage horse to death. In the third, Tom has turned his murderous impulses on his wife, stabbing her with a knife. Tom's comeuppance is revealed in the last engraving, as, after being hanged for murder, he lies disemboweled on an anatomical dissecting table. Underneath the table, a dog nibbles at his discarded vital organs.

Earlier, Hogarth had created similar sets of moralizing narratives, such as the six engravings showing *The Harlot's Progress,* and the eight-engraving set *The Rake's Progress.* Both mercilessly displayed the downfall that awaits those who succumb to vice. Throughout the nineteenth century, social reformers continued to link the treatment of animals by the laboring classes to social ills, among them slavery, child labor, and the inhumane treatment of prisoners and inmates in insane asylums.

Some of the earliest stories written especially for children admonished against inflicting misery on small creatures. In the eighteenth and nineteenth centuries, promoting kindness to animals joined with antislavery sentiments and benevolence to the poor in a noblesse-oblige crusade to soften the hearts of the young. In the first English-language book of fiction for children, *Goody Two Shoes* (1765), Margery Meanwell underscores her heroine's goodness by examples of her solicitude for animals. The popular British children's book *Sandford and Merton* (1783–1789), penned by an English antislavery activist Thomas Day, recounted the story of Harry Sandford, who went without supper so that he could feed hungry birds in winter.[28] Sarah Trimmer's ponderously titled *Fabulous Histories Designed for the Instruction of Children Respecting Their Treatment of Animals* (1786) put moral exhortations into the beaks of Mr. and Mrs. Robin, a talking bird family nesting in the garden of the human Benson family: "As every living creature can feel, we should have a constant regard to these feelings and strive to give happiness rather than inflict misery."[29]

These and other children's books and Sunday School lessons of the period exhorted kindness to animals as the true mark of a gentleman (and presumably, a gentlewoman). School readers, given to didactic moralizing on a range of subjects, included cautionary tales of comeuppance for youngsters who pulled wings off flies, tormented cats, flogged horses, snared birds, or indulged in other animal-directed nastiness. In the closing decades of the nineteenth century, the American Humane Education Society sponsored "Bands of Mercy" clubs. Children who joined took a pledge to be kind to animals and earned badges and certificates attesting to their humaneness.[30] George Angell, who founded the Massachusetts Society for the Prevention of Cruelty to Animals in 1868, distributed thousands of copies of his *Ten Lessons on Kindness to Animals* (1884) to schools throughout the United States. The goals of all these efforts were twofold: to counteract children's apparently widespread cruelty toward animals and to use treatment of animals to extend a more kindly orientation toward needy humans. As Margaret Marshall Saunders wrote in *Beautiful Joe* (1894), a paean to its eponymous dog hero: "Children who are taught to love and protect dumb creatures will be kind to their fellow men when they grow up."[31]

The most famous anticruelty tract pitched to both children and adults remains Anna Sewell's *Black Beauty*, originally published in 1877, and still widely read and loved. In this autobiography of a beautiful and noble horse, Black Beauty rails against boys pulling the wings off flies, throwing stones at horses to make them gallop faster, and whipping ponies. Through the eyes of the suffering beast, we feel the pain of harsh breaking-in techniques, overwork, and, most of all, the mutilations then in fashion to produce a spirited, prancing look—the "bearing rein," which yanked the horse's head tautly high, the breaking and resetting of tailbones at a more jaunty angle, the use of bits painful enough to fracture the horse's jaw.[32] *Black Beauty* proved to be an effective weapon in the crusade against the mistreatment of horses. Copies reached thousands of grooms, stablemen, and drivers; the book is credited for helping to abolish the bearing rein.[33]

The view that animal maltreatment is an early symptom of human depravity is part of a long tradition of animals as visible symbols standing in for human virtues and vices in morality tales. Justifying the crusade against animal cruelty only in terms of human betterment also unintentionally served to reinforce the subordination of animal well-being to human needs. Cruelty to animals was abhorrent, not because of animal suffering or animal rights, but solely for its corrupting effects on human relationships. The first animal protection laws, appearing in the nineteenth century, were designed to ameliorate human society, not to protect animals.[34]

During the twentieth century, as the claims of women, children, and animals for rights gained legitimacy, animal welfare increasingly became sufficient justification for calls to reduce unnecessary animal suffering. At the same time, easy generalization from cruelty practiced on animals to cruelty practiced on humans did not withstand scientific scrutiny. No single childhood predictor could explain the phenomenon. It remains unclear what events occurring in childhood are most relevant to producing human-human violence later in adulthood.

Today children's books dwell less than their predecessors on discouraging overt cruelty to animals. This trend may reflect real declines over time in the pervasiveness of the more egregious abuses. Paralleling social trends, humane treatment is justified not because it edifies children's characters, but because it prevents needless animal suffering. Neglect and casual mistreatment fueled by ignorance or impatience draw the attention of today's writers of juvenile fiction. Children discover that the cute puppy chews their toys, the cat scratches if persistently annoyed, and the gerbil cage requires daily cleaning.[35] "How-to" books on the proper care of pets and nature books detailing the habits of different species aim to help youngsters appreciate the world according to the animal. The hope is that once the animal's needs are understood, children will behave more sensitively toward them, with encouragement and monitoring from adults.

Explaining Cruelty toward Animals

Historically, the explanation for cruelty to animals was sought in original sin, in unwholesome companions, or in parents' and teachers' failure to inculcate virtues. Contemporary research is only now beginning to shed light on *why* some children knowingly mistreat animals. Violent youngsters like Kip Kinkel and Luke Woodham often seem at a loss to explain why they tortured and killed animals. If they give any reason, it's usually "for fun." (This is the only motive that Lamansky and Myers gave for the Fairfield cat killings.) "For fun," "for kicks" were also common explanations given by aggressive criminals to Kellert and Felthous for their childhood abuse of animals.

Freud speculated that cruelty to animals or playmates could fuse with "erogenous impulses" in early childhood, and, once established, the link would be difficult to break.[36] Sadistic pleasure in causing pain may be one motive, but its origin is still obscure. *Why* do some children derive pleasure from injuring animals? There is a tangled web of causes, almost all of which children are unaware of or can't articulate.[37] Many influences interact, including a child's biological temperament, family relationships, neighborhood climate, and cultural context.

Risk may begin with a "difficult" temperament. Children whose constitutional makeup combines poor impulse control, high activity, and low tolerance for change—a mix far more common in boys than in girls—are more likely to hurt other children and adults, break the law, and, not surprisingly, show symptoms of conduct disorder. It is possible that even from infancy some children may have a temperamental vulnerability to harm animals.

We know much more about another skein of the web—family violence. When children are growing up witness to batterings of their mothers or siblings or are themselves victims of abuse, animal abuse routinely becomes part of the deadly mix. Laurie Rovin, clinical director of Crossroads Group Home, a residential treatment center in Greenville, South Carolina, for girls who have been severely traumatized by sexual abuse, told me that animal abuse incidents often come to light in the histories of girls being treated there. One ten-year-old girl came to Crossroads deeply disturbed; among other symptoms, she would stick peanut butter up her vagina. When the staff caught her pulling on the tails of the resident dogs, a chocolate Lab and a collie, and of the many cats who wandered around Crossroads' farmlike setting, she soon confided that her father had made her watch as he hung and strangled a cat.[38] This girl's trauma is by no means unusual in cases of sexual and physical abuse. Abusers—usually a father, stepfather, or boyfriend—often threaten or actually injure or kill family pets to send a chilling message about what is in store for the child who tells about abuse or the battered woman who attempts to escape.

Frank Ascione has been doing pioneering work at shelters for battered women in Utah, gathering evidence of how thoroughly animal abuse permeates domestic violence. Most of the women seeking shelter described to him how their partners repeatedly threatened family pets and routinely carried out their threats with deadly consequences. Animals were kicked, hit, drowned, strangled, poisoned, thrown from moving cars, intentionally run over, even nailed to the woman's bedroom door. Most of the children had witnessed the cruelty. Many had tried vainly to protect the animals by hiding them or even trying to block assaults, despite endangering their own safety. They described how upset they were by the pet abuse—undoubtedly compounded by the violence they witnessed against their mothers—and how they wished that pets would be better treated. Yet some of the children themselves severely hurt or killed their pets. Not surprisingly, these children of violence showed alarming levels of behavior problems; nearly 40 percent fell within the clinically significant range of conduct disorder, indicating immediate need for treatment.[39]

Women's shelters and domestic violence centers around the country have begun to track the interconnections among wife battering, child abuse, and animal abuse. Their reports confirm Ascione's findings in Utah. For example, three-quarters of all women seeking refuge in twelve Wisconsin shelters during 1994–95 reported that the men battering them had abused or threatened to hurt a pet or livestock animal (some of the shelters were in farm areas). Almost always the women and their children witnessed the abuse; in large part, it was for their "benefit." More than half of the children who had been forced to watch as a cat or dog was beaten, thrown out of a car, strangled, or tortured had repeated a similar act upon an animal, their mothers said.[40]

The connection between animal abuse and domestic violence surfaces again when investigators crosscheck humane society records of animal abuse against reports of child abuse made to child protective services. In New Jersey, for example, 88 percent of pet-owning parents who had physically abused their children and were being supervised by the state Division of Youth and Family Services admitted to animal abuse. Caseworkers monitoring these families were eyewitnesses to many cruel acts, including hitting, kicking, and throwing objects at the pet.[41] In Massachusetts, 70 percent of all those convicted of animal abuse over a twenty-year period had committed at least one serious crime against people. These animal abusers also were three times more likely than a comparison group to have drug offenses, disorderly conduct, or property crimes on their records.[42]

The association of animal and child abuse is not new. The history of animal protection in the United States has been intertwined with the history of child protection. The movement to counteract cruelty to animals came first. Largely through the crusading efforts of Henry Bergh, a prominent New Yorker, in 1866 New York State passed "An Act Better to Prevent Cruelty to Animals," the first law punishing "unjustifiable" pain to animals. At the same time Bergh spearheaded the first humane society, the American Society for the Prevention of Cruelty to Animals, or ASPCA. By 1874 Bergh's watchdog group was in full swing, monitoring Barnum's circus elephants, bringing suit against trolleymen for beating horses, and castigating livestock producers for causing their cattle to suffer unnecessarily. Then "little Mary Ellen," as she became known, was found. She was emaciated, far too small for her ten years, clothed in rags, and covered with the scabs of a lifetime of abuse. The social worker who discovered her, Etta Angell Wheeler, appealed to Bergh for help.

Bergh's attorney, Elbridge Gerry, got a writ of habeas corpus to remove the child from the home and bring the case to court. Gerry and Bergh soon launched the first organized movement for the defense of children, the Society for the Prevention of Cruelty to Children, building on their track record in fighting animal abuse.[43] Today the American Humane Association and other anti-animal-cruelty groups still maintain joint mandates—advocating for the welfare of both animals and children, the two most helpless and dependent groups in the social fabric. In the policy arena, their work underscores how frequently violence against animals and against children coexists in households.

Violent adults infect children by multiple routes. When parents settle conflicts by force, children tend to learn that might is the only way to change someone's, including an animal's, behavior. In violent families, parents model aggression. Their children see them taking pleasure in hurting others. John Locke's words in 1693 still ring as relevant: "People teach children to strike, and laugh when they hurt, or see harm come to others."[44] In this way children become desensitized to physical coercion and begin to adopt it as their everyday mode of communication. Around the country, directors of programs for children with animal abuse histories describe these children's families in depressingly similar ways. The parents endorse a "good whippin'" for child and dog alike as the surest remedy for disobedience. Children from such families often have distorted ideas about animals, assuming that cats don't have feelings or that dogs need to be choked or hit to obey commands.

Another route from family violence to children's cruelty to animals runs through the familiar psychological mechanism of displacement. Children who are victims of adult violence or who witness someone they love—usually their mother—being beaten or psychologically tormented, become enraged. Their anger is shunted from the feared abuser to "safer" outlets at the bottom of the pecking order, the pet or a small wild animal such as a bird, squirrel, or rabbit. Violent inmates or psychiatric patients recount childhoods that sound numbingly the same—a father who oils his abuse with drugs and alcohol, a child in whom rage builds until it lashes out in animal cruelty to "get even." As teenagers, these youngsters might "retaliate" with massive force against an animal for some imagined slight—such as killing a neighbor's dog for barking too much.[45]

Displacement may coexist with distorted self-identity. Children subjected to a steady diet of physical, sexual, and emotional abuse readily come to see themselves as evil and unworthy. Treated like monsters, they begin to feel and act monstrously. Inflicting cruelty on animals (together with bullying other children and vandalizing property) becomes "fun."

Violence is not confined behind the front doors of family homes. Children growing up in violent families are likely to be at double risk of getting extra doses of mayhem from neighborhoods steeped in violent traditions that encompass animals as well as people. Dogfighting, cockfights, torture of cats, and other forms of animal cruelty have taken hold in the underbelly of some communities. One fifth-grade boy attending an inner-city Milwaukee school wrote to the Wisconsin Humane Society pleading for them to "do something to stop all the dogfighting. People get drunk and want to fight and go get their dogs to fight them. When the dog doesn't want to fight, they burn their mouths and jaws to make them fight."[46] In Toledo, Ohio, both the Humane Society and the police department view dogfighting as a big problem that is getting bigger. Officer Doug Allen, who heads the gang task force for the Toledo police department, described to me how gangs kidnap other dogs and use them to bait their pit bulls for training. Then they kill that dog, and if the pit bull doesn't do very well, they may kill it too. Younger children watching the dogfights may get mauled by the dogs.[47] In those inner-city and rural areas most ravaged by poverty and crime, the family dog is likely to be a pit bull or Doberman "toughened" for maximum meanness. A student at Washington High School, in downtown Milwaukee, described a local "recipe" for turning a dog into an attack machine—don't feed him for three or four days and then put hotsauce in his food.[48] Humane society educators are not shocked when, in some inner-city classrooms, every hand shoots up in answer to the question: "How many of you children have seen someone mistreat a cat?" As one humane educator told me, "We are always hearing about kids putting firecrackers up the butts of cats."[49]

In poor neighborhoods stressed by crime, drugs, and family violence, "pet turnover," a frightening euphemism for the violence and neglect visited on animals, is especially high. Robert Bierer, the lone counselor at the 780-pupil Emerson Elementary School in Albuquerque, New Mexico, works with a group of impoverished Hispanic-American and Native-American children. Just outside the city limits roam packs of stray wild dogs, he told me, products of the routine abandonment of pets these children see. When he asks his pupils about their own pets, he often hears that the dog "ran away" or "somebody stole him." When pets have such a short shelf life, he wonders, what is the impact on these children's feelings of an animal's worthiness, and perhaps their own?[50]

A recurring theme in reports of animal abuse around the country is the potentially lethal mix of cats, or other small animals, and groups of preadolescent or adolescent boys itching for trouble.[51] As in the Fairfield cat-killing case, the scenario typically includes boredom, macho posturing—watch me do something *really* bad—alcohol or drugs, and at least one boy fueled by anger. Tormenting and killing cats, for some groups of boys, is a way to impress, to be "cool." Unconfirmed reports of animal abuse in gang initiation rituals have cropped up. John Caruso, of the Anti-Cruelty Society in Chicago, told me of his suspicion that this kind of organized cruelty is going on, although it remains hidden.

Cutting the "Tangled Web"

As a result of the overlap among wife battering, child abuse, other forms of violence against people, and animal abuse, coalitions of humane officers, social workers, and law enforcement are forming around the country. In 1996 the San Francisco Council on Child Abuse and the Department of Animal Care and Control worked together to pass legislation mandating state humane officers, among others, to report child abuse. The two organizations set up crosstraining—for humane officers, on how to recognize signs of child abuse; for social workers, on how to spot "the battered pet syndrome" as well as other forms of animal abuse and neglect. In Toledo, Ohio, the Animal Advocates for Children program gives animal welfare agents training in crisis intervention and in detecting child abuse and neglect, as well as elder abuse.

In Colorado Springs, DVERT, the Domestic Violence Enhanced Response Team, brings together the local police, humane society, child protective services, district attorney, center for prevention of domestic violence, and social service agency, among others—fifteen groups in all—to identify the county's most lethal perpetrators. The agencies do crosstraining, share records, and coordinate their investigations. Donna Straub, assistant director of the Pike's Peak Humane Society and a member of the DVERT team, explained to me how this approach is uncovering hidden abuse: "The hammer case—that's what we call it—is a perfect example." Three children, ages ten, eight, and six, had written on the back of their father's business card "Call my Dad; the dog is in the garage" and thrown it onto a neighbor's lawn. (The parents were divorced, and the father was living in California.) The neighbor alerted the humane society, and when animal control officers arrived, they found a dog beaten almost to death and in the garage, a hammer with blood and dog hairs on it. The children's mother soon confessed to the beating. When veterinarians examined the dog, they found numerous fractures in various stages of healing, indicating a long history of vicious abuse. "Our people thought something was not right about the kids," Donna recalled, "even though we couldn't see anything. Sure enough, it turned out the children were being abused, too. Because of DVERT, we could immediately bring in Child Protection."[52] DVERT has become a national model for a coordinated rapid response to all forms of abuse, animal as well as human.

Nationwide, there are calls to legally require veterinarians to report suspected child abuse or neglect and social workers to report suspected animal abuse. (Currently only a few states even require veterinarians to report suspected animal cruelty.)[53] State groups are organizing to toughen penalties for animal cruelty; currently twenty-one states made some form of animal cruelty a felony, while forty-three states classified organized dogfighting as a felony. Other proposals include federal legislation, modeled after the 1974 Child Abuse Prevention and Treatment Act, to establish national standards for defining and prosecuting animal abuse, and a national registry to track the incidence of animal abuse.[54] The American Humane Association and other organizations are lobbying for more federally funded research on the link between violence against animals and humans. In 1997 the Humane Society of the United States launched the "First Strike" campaign, a coordinated effort to increase public awareness of the connection between cruelty to animals and violence against humans.[55]

Humane education is a relatively recent front opened in the battle for the hearts and minds of children. Formal programs to foster children's compassion and respect toward animals and, through a process of generalization, toward other humans date back only about one hundred years. G. Stanley Hall, in his classic 1904 text, *Adolescence,* expressed the rationale behind such programs in this way: "If pedagogy is ever to become adequate to the needs of the soul, the time will come when animals will play a far larger educational role than has yet been conceived, that they will be curriculized, will acquire a new and higher humanistic or cultural value in the future compared with their utility in the past."[56]

Current examples of curricula include "Pets and Me," from the University of Pennsylvania; the People and Animals program, developed by the National Association for Humane and Environmental Education (NAHEE); the Operation Outreach–USA program of the American Humane Education Society; and Project Wild, developed by the Western Regional Environmental Council. Each curriculum has a slightly different focus. The "Pets and Me" curriculum, for preschool through grade five, centers on promoting responsible pet ownership and "personalizing" animal welfare and environmental conservation issues through the pet connection. Project Wild, on the other hand, focuses on wildlife appreciation through nature study. Both Operation Outreach–USA and the People and Animals programs have the broad goal of fostering respect for all living things.[57]

Do these classroom humane education curricula work? There are few evaluations, and their results are inconclusive. After a yearlong exposure to the People and Animals curriculum, first- and fourth-graders in Utah reported more humane attitudes—for example, answering no to questions like "Should you spank a cat to teach it to mind you?" and "Do you think it's fun to break up a spider's web?"—than did other children from the same schools who had not received the program. A year after the fourth-graders had completed the program, they continued to express more humane attitudes than the control group. Second- and fifth-graders at the same schools showed no change in humane attitudes as a result of the curriculum. Regardless of grade level, however, children who received the humane curriculum expressed more empathy toward other children, at least on a questionnaire.

It's not clear how much or what kind of humane education is most beneficial in shaping attitudes toward the treatment of animals; in this study, teachers devoted only forty hours, on average, over the entire school year, the equivalent of barely a week of children's television viewing.[58] Another question is why the intervention "took" with fourth-graders and not with younger or older children. Humane education certainly needs testing with a wider diversity of children as well; in this study, they were overwhelmingly white and Mormon. Finally, documenting changes in attitudes immediately after an educational "treatment" is a far cry from showing long-term changes in behavior.

Formal programs may be less important than a general classroom climate extending respect and care across species. However fine-tuned humane education becomes, it's likely to take only a small fraction of classroom time and reach a limited number of students, given the many competing demands on instruction. Another persistent issue is generalization to human relationships. Why should we expect exhortations to treat animals kindly, or at least without unnecessary cruelty, to "rub off" on children's behavior toward their classmates, particularly when humane education does not address interpersonal violence directly? Would humane education focused on animal welfare necessarily promote tolerance of vulnerable humans, such as persons with disabilities or minorities?

A more fundamental birthing ground for humane attitudes lies within the family. Families are the primary context in which children watch birds at a feeder, go camping, hunt and fish, protect, or endanger animals. Children's first outings to the zoo, aquarium, or nature park are usually family ones. The first lessons in responsible pet ownership or messages of neglect take place at home. Even at first grade, humane education works not on a "blank slate," but on an already developing ethic of animal treatment. As one humane educator told me: "You sometimes hear things [on kindergarten visits] like 'Dad kicks the dog on purpose, to make him mean.' Some children seem aware that this is not right; they'll say, 'You shouldn't do that,' but more often the child thinks, 'This is the way it's done; they're just animals.'"[59]

When children feel safe and protected at home, they can practice role-taking skills under parental guidance. Research documents that children are more empathic toward other children when parents routinely direct their attention to others' feelings, using the disciplinary strategy called *induction,* with questions like "How do you think that makes her feel?" Such children may also be more likely to extend protection to others, including animals. Supporting this idea, a study of eight-to-thirteen-year-olds in California found that children who felt that their parents were emotionally available and responsive also endorsed more humane attitudes toward animals. Those children who reported fathers and older siblings as punitive were less humane.[60]

Kindness and Abuse

We must be careful not to reach for family, community, or school programs as the sole explanation for childhood cruelty (or kindness) to animals. Not all abused children pass on the cycle of abuse to animals. In fact many children bombarded by violence seek solace in their pets, are careful and solicitous of their well-being, and, as Ascione found, often try to protect them from an abuser. For these children, losing pets is one of the more painful losses in their far-from-idyllic childhoods. One boy, the product of an abusive childhood, ended up at age fifteen in a Minnesota training school for delinquent youth. There he talked about his dog Duke: "He was eleven years old, and my mother had my little brother, and Duke started being grouchy and nipping at people. So my brother-in-law shot him. It really hurt bad, like one of my brothers died, it was really hard to accept."[61] While some children's grief fuels runaway anger that engulfs animals, others are so shaken by the animal abuse they've been forced to observe that, in one battered mother's words, they turn into "animal lovers, very protective and caring."[62]

Both kindness and cruelty to animals coexist in many children, whether they have experienced family violence or not. Children can compartmentalize their feelings, apportioning protection to some creatures, indifference or even hate to others. "Let's see what happens" curiosity, poor impulse control, and mistaken ideas about animals can be a combustible mixture. Susan Isaacs observed both tenderness and cruelty, often in the same children, among the two-to-eight-year-olds at her school in Cambridge:

When the children were changing the water of the goldfish, Frank had a sudden impulse of cruelty, and said to the others, "Shall we stamp on it?" . . . Before she [the teacher] could stop them, they had thrown the fish out into the sand and stamped on it. They stood round and looked at it, rather excited, and obviously wishing they hadn't done it, and Frank said, "Now let's put it into water, and then it'll come alive again."[63]

Barbara Boat, a psychologist who treats abused and abusing children at the University of Cincinnati Medical School, reported a case involving two boys who set a kitten on fire. (They were caught only because the kitten ran under a car, exploding the vehicle.) One of the boys described the solace he derived from his two beloved dogs. Why, then, had he killed the kitten? "Well," he explained with a shrug, "we thought it was a stray." Both destructive and nurturing urges are intimately connected within our psyches. Both turn on easily when we're in charge of anything small, helpless, and demanding—as any doting parent who has come close to shaking a baby knows.

In general, we know little about what prompts children to be actively kind to animals and concerned about their welfare, particularly beyond their own pets, as distinct from refraining from acts of mistreatment. While family violence may predispose some children to mistreatment of animals, there is no evidence that absence of violence promotes kindness. When it comes to animals, as well as other people, the predictors of antisocial and prosocial behaviors may be different.

Cultural Contradictions

The cultural niche that animals occupy makes them especially vulnerable. Societal messages about animal treatment swirl around children in confusing, often conflicting crosscurrents. Pets are pampered like favorite children, while chickens, pigs, and other domestic animals are raised in extreme confinement in huge computer-operated factory farms. Pet owners bestow family membership on their companion animals, yet every year at least 5 percent of the entire pet population—between five and six million dogs and cats—are given up to shelters and euthanized.[64] Many thousands more—no one knows exactly how many—are abandoned, winding up as roadkill or wandering as strays. In one survey, 45 percent of those who relinquished their dogs to a shelter (with the high probability that the dog would be killed) "strongly agreed" that the dog was a family member; most of these owners carried or displayed a picture of it.[65] Households with children were more likely than childless couples or singles to give up their dogs or cats to shelters, ensuring that many children learned the lesson that inconvenient animals are disposable. Americans may lavish love on their pets, but for far too many, they are disposable family members, love *objects* rather than objects of love.

Attitudes toward some species resonate with a particularly ambiguous subtext. Consider cats, which have been both worshipped as gods and reviled as witches' familiars. Today, television ads show them rhinestone collared, lolling about as lord or queen of the manor, the ultimate picky eaters, in a role reversal of master and pet. At the same time, feral stray cats foraging in alley garbage cans inspire revulsion as disease-carrying pests. When I've asked humane educators around the country why so many cases of animal mistreatment seem to involve groups of boys and cats, their answers tap into a cultural reservoir of contradictory images. As Peggy Smith, school psychologist at Washington High School in Milwaukee, put it: "It's the reputation cats have. They sit back and hiss at you, they're more aloof. People see them as less worthwhile. You see more running loose on the streets." Cats may be especially vulnerable to mischief-seeking boys not just because they're small and available for victimization. In popular culture, feline often stands for "female." Cats may bear the projective burden of adolescent male sexual unease. The sexual connection in boys' torments of cats—the most common version describes boys putting firecrackers in the anuses of cats—seems obvious, but researchers, humane educators, and therapists have paid little attention to it.

Like treatment of pets, cultural attitudes about killing animals are rife with unacknowledged contradictions, what one writer called "moral schizophrenia."[66] For Susan Isaacs, "There is probably no moral field in which the child sees so many puzzling inconsistencies."[67] Is it wrong to kill animals? Clearly not, learns the child biting into a Big Mac; but pets like dogs and cats are out of bounds as food. (Elsewhere cows are revered, and dogs are eaten.) The exterminator should come to rid the house of insect pests, but pulling the wings off flies to watch them die would be cruel. Fishing and hunting are fun family outings for many, but using stray cats for target practice is barbaric. Cows, pigs, sheep, and horses past their prime are "processed" by the thousands every day in killing sheds, but slaughterhouse workers should not enjoy the process of killing or want to prolong the animals' suffering; that would be inhumane.

Every culture has a complicated set of confusing strictures, a calculus of killing, conveyed to each new generation. The institutionalized killing of animals for human needs is fundamental to every culture of our carnivorous species. At the same time, every human culture protects pet species, whose members are rarely eaten, and invests animals with spiritual power. As anthropologist Margaret Mead put it: "Delicately, precisely, carefully, within each subculture, in the country, in the city, on the farm, by the sea, the lines are drawn. Pests to be killed, food to be eaten, pets to be loved, are discriminated for the growing child." These fine distinctions understandably mystify many youngsters. When a child, especially one prone to aggression and impulsive acting out, violates one of the "taboos" regulating a culture's treatment of animals and is not caught, or is too violently punished, Mead suggested, "the temptation to try it again, try something bigger, kill a cat instead of a bird, wring a dog's neck instead of a canary's, can take possession of the child."[68] Children's cruelty to animals illuminates the fault lines in a culture's mix of utilitarian use, companionship, harshness, and benevolence in its treatment of animals.

Human history is replete with animal abuse masquerading as forms of entertainment, not as the unavoidable by-product of human needs for food, clothing, and labor. From the blood-spattered carnivals in the Roman Coliseum, where more than 10,000 animals might be slaughtered in a single day, to centuries-old popular European and then American entertainments of bearbaiting, chasing greased pigs, "throwing at cocks," "coon in a log," and "gander pulling," we can trace an unbroken line of animal torture and killing as family fun enjoyed by seemingly well-adjusted, upstanding citizens of the community. In "throwing at cocks," the game was to kill a rooster (sometimes a cat), tied down so that only its head was visible, by hurling sticks and clubs at it. In "coon in a log," a pastime on the American frontier, dogs were set upon a raccoon who was chained to a log or barrel, as onlookers cheered until the dogs tore the coon to pieces. "Gander pulling" involved greasing a live goose with lard and stringing it up head down, swinging from a pole. As riders galloped by, each tried to grab the neck of the goose and pull its head off. The trials would continue, amid the wailing and flailing of the suffering animal, until the goose was decapitated.[69]

An unblinking historical examination of Western practices since animal domestication makes human cruelty to animals seem the norm, and calls for kindness small glimmers of a better nature.[70] In this light, children's mistreatment of animals resists distillation to individual pathology, a violent symptom in a violent child. We can't explain it away as a few "bad seed" children produced in the cauldron of abusive families. Instead, we must recognize a cruel streak running through all human cultures. Contemporary attitudes may recoil at the barbaric "amusements" that persisted in the United States until the beginning of the twentieth century, but remnants of these practices still lurk in dark corners of our society. Even "mainstream" popular culture derives slapstick humor from animal suffering. In the film comedy *A Fish Called Wanda*, hilarity builds—or so the writers assume—from repeated attempts to kill some pesky lapdogs. Ads for the wildly successful movie *There's Something about Mary* touted its wacky fun by featuring a completely bandaged small dog (whose injuries resulted when the film's hero hurled it through a window). A 1999 music video aired on MTV, "What's My Name?" by the rapper DMX, pans from two pit bulls set to destroy each other to the rapper as he sings of killing and death, surrounded by a smiling audience. As a recent column in the *New York Times* noted, "pretending to hurt animals has become an intentional laugh-getter in movies, television, and advertising."[71] Fear of animals, fascination with their suffering and death, and urges to kill them "for fun" have a history as old as the human species. When children are cruel to animals, they show us a part of ourselves that we'd rather not confront.

Today we remain confused about exactly where animals lie on our moral compass. Does hunting whip up a boy's bloodlust, or does it teach him to appreciate where meat really comes from? Is all meat eating animal cruelty, or do vegans ignore our carnivorous human nature? Are zoos inherently prisons that objectify animals, or are they our best hope for rescuing and rehabilitating endangered species? Are rodeos "cruelty packaged as Americana" or an innocent expression of cultural heritage falling victim to the correctness police?[72] Is animal experimentation essential in order to save human lives, but cruel if conducted to find a better wrinkle cream?

Animal-rights groups square off against medical scientists and agricultural producers in noisy, often acrimonious public debates. Behind the headlines lies a fundamental reexamination of age-old questions: Do animals have rights? What are they? How do we apportion them? Do animals share the same feelings as humans? What forms of treatment of animals are cruel?[73] Our own lack of clarity about the answers to these questions muddies the messages that we send children.

There is an area of common ground on which all can agree, however. Intentionally harming animals purely for the pleasure of causing their suffering, and not for any human need, fits everyone's definition of cruelty. Even as we call for more systematic documentation of children's animal abuse and more rigorous research, we should not lose sight of what we already know. To make human society less violent and reduce unnecessary animal suffering, we must shelter both children and animals under the umbrella of our concern and empathy.

8

Deepening the Animal Connection

We need a biocentric perspective on children's development. Grounded in the biophilia hypothesis, such a perspective assumes that from infancy, children are predisposed to attend to life, to its nonhuman as well as human forms. The "animal pull" of our human natures makes animals intrinsically interesting; just looking at animals is its own reward. Human brains are wired to vibrate to animals as dense packets of information. Added to this are three interrelated products of human evolution that together make animals particularly interesting to children. First, children, like the young of other species, are less fearful, more curious, and more ready to approach other species. Second, human infants, like other primate young, are strongly attracted to other young. For example, babies who are wary of adult strangers will leave their mother's side to approach an unfamiliar infant.[1] It's not small size that draws them, since twelve-month-olds respond to an adult midget in the same wary manner. Third, as we noted earlier, the neoteny of most pets and domesticated animals makes them appear "childlike." As a result, young children respond to animals as if they were interesting peers.

Shaping this innate animal pull are experiences of many kinds—cultural values, social norms, parents' behaviors, neighborhood resources, and media images. Children's involvement with animals, their attitudes toward animal treatment, and their emotional ties to pets unite biological predisposition and environmental influence, "nature" and "nurture" working in concert. The animal pull can strengthen into a respectful kinship, imparting a sense of place in the natural world, a grounded membership in the community of living beings. Or the animal pull can weaken and eventually atrophy into indifference. Curiosity can twist into cruelty. Interest can flip over to fear and disgust. Even biophobia, aversion to animal and plant life, can spring from the soil of biophilia.[2]

Looking at children through a biocentric lens, as this book has done, reveals how thickly animal threads run through children's everyday lives. There are the pets, of course, and the farm animals. There is the wild animal life wriggling, chirping, squeaking, and scurrying underfoot, at arm's reach, and overhead. In children's imaginations, more creatures take up residence. Monsters roar in dreams, humanoid animals tell story-book tales, and furry and feathered "pals" wisecrack on their own Web sites.

In an anthropocentric take on development, this childhood animal world buzzes, squeals, and purrs only as background music to the central dramas of human relationships. At most, childish fascination with animals is a scaffolding that falls away as the edifice of maturity rises. In a biocentric view, by contrast, the animal connection is the foundation of the building that children construct of their lives.

Charting a Biocentric Course

What might a biocentric vision of childhood look like? We might ask how infants and young children come to understand different modes of being, how they conceptualize being human versus nonhuman but animal, and what distinctions among animals they make. We might investigate animal imagery in children's dreams, play, imagination, and art, testing whether animal motifs fuel creativity, order chaotic emotions, or rehearse and thus tame preoccupations. We might explore how communicative competence develops across, not just within, species, as children speak, gesture, hold, and make nonverbal sounds to animals. We might take children at their word, and appreciate the child-pet bond as the repository of love no less intense than that between humans. We might see in the child-pet relationship a full-body, full sensory tuning-in to the subjective experience of a very different being.[3] We might try to pinpoint the process by which children shift from engaging animals as coequal other beings to straddling the barrier of a radical species divide. We might pursue the implications of children's acceptance of animals as partners for the development of both empathy and cruelty in the face of difference. We might trace the childhood roots of adult debates over the moral standing of animals posed by human assault on other species and their habitats.

Opening up the study of children's development, currently framed solely in terms of other people, to include nonhuman animals illuminates neglected corners of childhood. Social cognition, "ideas about self and others," would expand to "ideas about self and other beings." Theory of mind would be reframed from "understanding people as mental beings"[4] to "understanding the mental life of other beings." Emotional intelligence encompasses insight into the inner lives of other creatures. Attachment, defined by one best-selling textbook as "the strong affectional tie that humans feel for special people in their lives," recognizes the affection, love, and sometimes selfless devotion that children invest in their pets.[5] John Bowlby's concept of attachment security broadens to acknowledge the potential of responsive animal presence to affirm a child's psychological security. If neoteny predisposes children to treat their pets and other domestic animals "as if" they were other children, theory and research on peer relationships—the development of social competence, the growth of friendships, for example—need to encompass the animal "peer." Children's feelings with and for animals become part of the study of the development of empathy and sympathy. Moral reasoning wrestles with the rights and obligations raised for children by their membership in Earth's multispecies ecology as well as in the human species.

Such issues, if reframed biocentrically, may lead to new insights about children's thoughts, feelings, and ties to other humans. To what extent do thinking about, feeling for, empathizing with, and loving members of other species influence, reflect, or compensate those parallel processes directed toward other humans? In an anthropocentric view of development, a child's imaginative and real life with animals counts only to the extent that it pays off in better understanding children in their human context. From a biocentric perspective, however, even if the animal world of children proved to be wholly unconnected to human interchange, its importance would not be diminished. The imperative to grasp its significance, to understand children's animal connections on their own terms, not simply because of their implications for human relationships, remains.

In all likelihood, we will discover that children's life with animals and life with humans are interwoven in complex ways. Making that assumption at the outset may prevent an overly narrow focus on the human-animal bond to the exclusion of other developmental influences. Animal connections are only one of multiple factors acting on development. For example, we should be wary of distilling out a child's attachment to his or her pet dog, cat, or gerbil from other relationships and thinking of this child-pet bond in isolation. Does the child have good friends, or is he or she a loner? Is the child a welcome addition to neighborhood playgroups or always the last picked? Does the child have a secure attachment to mother and father? What's the tone of sibling relations? How do the parents treat the family pets? What is the family climate?

The meaning of pets for children remains embedded within their family systems. Just as sibling relationships cannot be understood apart from a child's ties to mother and to father, so too child-pet relationships are colored by all other family ties. Exactly how may be exceedingly complex and not easily predicted. Children create their own relationships with pets, influenced but not wholly determined by other family ties. Children bring their own biologically based individuality, their own temperaments, to every relationship, including that with pets. The animal's individual temperament and personality color the relationship as well.

The concept of environmental specificity is helpful here.[6] This refers to the view that aspects of children's environments interact in complicated ways with children's preexisting characteristics. If we use the lens of environmental specificity to study how pets and other animals influence development, we would not ask: Do pets or other animals affect children? Instead, we would pose the far more focused and tempered question: *Which* aspects of the child-pet relationship affect *which* children in *which* ways at *what* times?

For instance, having a dog, cat, gerbil, or bird does not automatically mean that a child's need to nurture will now be fulfilled, or his or her responsibility, empathy, or sense of acceptance enhanced. Pets *may* often have these effects, but clearly not always, not for all children, and not in all circumstances. Such variability might be expected, if the meaning of a child's bond with his or her pet depends on the child's individual characteristics, all other family ties, other relationships such as with friends and classmates, and the animal's own characteristics.

A Biocentric Education

A biocentric framework for understanding development has yet to be filled in. Meanwhile, given what we already know, a few voices plead for a more holistic approach to education, childrearing, and intervention. Gary Paul Nabhan singles out three strategies that parents and educators should adopt to stave off what he calls "the extinction of experience": intimate involvement with plants and animals, exposure to a wide variety of wild animals in their natural habitats, and teaching by community "elders" who pass on their knowledge of flora and fauna.[7] In middle childhood, David Hutchison argues, children search for meaning and purpose in the natural world. They construct a "working theory," a "functional cosmology" of the world. For Hutchison this childhood ecology is pivotal, not only for the subsequent healthy development of the individual but for "the recovery of sustainable relations with the natural world."[8] David Orr, who coined the term *environmental literacy,* laments that "we are still educating the young as if there were no planetary emergency." Drawing inspiration from curricula pioneered in Montessori, Steiner, and Waldorf schools, he advocates biocentric educational reforms that build on children's sense of awe at nature, emphasize interconnections with other species, and forge a new convenant of respect toward animals. In such an ecologically sensitive curriculum, kindergarteners would play with twigs, stones, and seashells instead of plastic materials. In middle school, children would study local natural environments, testing the water quality of the local river, for example. Concrete playgrounds would become vegetable gardens or meadows designed to attract wildlife.[9]

Public schools with an environmental education theme—many of them magnet schools—are sprouting up around the country. (At the end of 1998 there were about 100.) At the Environmental Middle School in Portland, Oregon, for example, students roleplay Northwest animals living in and around a local river, such as the salmon or great horned owl, to imagine how a storm would affect them.[10] This kind of exercise forges ecological awareness by building on children's fascination with animals and readiness to cross species lines. Other school systems have set up less ambitious environmental and humane education curricula. In Memphis, Tennessee, for example, eleven elementary schools have adopted the Caretaker Classroom curriculum, which incorporates recycling, planting trees and flowers, "adopting" endangered animals, maintaining school grounds, and setting up bulletin boards for environmental issues.[11] The Common Roots program, in rural Vermont elementary schools, involves each grade level in active study of the local ecosystem. Kindergarten children help grow sunflowers, carrots, and pumpkins in an Earth-friendly "kinder garden," while fourth-graders evaluate the water quality of local streams and ponds.[12]

"Kindness" curricula—teaching respect for animals, humans, and the environment—are finding their way into many school systems, driven by the rising tide of school-based violence. Despite countervailing educational currents to strip away "frills" and focus on testable basics, there is a growing sense that schools cannot be havens of learning when children bring their rage and shame to class with their lunchboxes. *Kind News*, a "for kids" newspaper put out by the National Association for Humane and Environmental Education, the youth education division of the Humane Society of the United States, reaches thousands of KIND clubs in schools around the country with a steady drumbeat of proper pet-care tips and exhortations to kindness. In a recent issue, for example, Scott Servais, catcher for the Chicago Cubs, passed on his advice—"Good pet owners care for their pets as if they were people!"—in the celebrity column. Young readers wrote in their answers to the question "What does being a responsible pet owner mean?" (Meaghan: "It means feeding pets and treating them right.") Dr. Kind, veterinarian Candace Ashley, answered the question "How can you be a friend to pets?" with the admonition to take good care of them.

Educational materials like *Kind News* explicitly make the connection between kindness to animals and ecological sensibility. Protecting animals means protecting their habitats, and this fact leads children to address issues of endangered species, air and water pollution, energy conservation, and wild/pet animal distinctions. "Don't keep wild animals as pets—they have a role to play in nature," urges the *Kind News Guide to Protecting Animals and the Earth,* along with "Take short showers instead of baths." Environmental educators strive to help children see the interconnections among animals, environments, and themselves, and thereby foster a stewardship identity toward all living things. A new philosophy of education, dubbed "biophilic education," is emerging. Its principles emphasize examining a community's relationship to its physical, social, and cultural setting, learning through direct encounters with natural places, and developing an orientation of "bonding, caring, and sharing necessary for nurturing biophilic relationships," as one advocate put it.[13]

For children who have already abused animals or are starting to build violent histories, innovative programs like PAL (People–Animals–Love) in Milwaukee and the Shiloh Project in Fairfax, Virginia, are models for ways to deflect youngsters from a destructive path. Both programs pair hard-to-adopt shelter dogs who are in urgent need of obedience training and troubled children or teens who need to learn new, nonviolent ways of behaving. PAL brings fourth- through sixth-grade children nominated by their teachers as at risk for violence to the local humane shelter for three-week summer sessions. Most of these ten-to-thirteen-year-olds are failing in school and struggling at home. They include J, who lives with his mother and father, both of whom are crack addicts; and T, who with her mother doubles up with a houseful of relatives in a chaotic, dilapidated dwelling. In the PAL program, children work in teams of two with a shelter dog for three hours a day. At first the children practice reward-based obedience techniques under the guidance of a professional trainer. The goal is to get "their" dog to learn basic dog manners—to sit, heel, stay, come when called, and wait at the door—by "graduation" in a brief three weeks. (PAL staff evaluate each shelter dog and select only highly trainable dogs for the program.) The children work in a wildlife rehabilitation center, feed baby ducks, and keep a program journal to supplement the training sessions. The result, says executive director Jill DeGrave, is a better-behaved, more adoptable dog, and children who've learned to work as a team while acquiring nonviolent strategies to get the dog to obey. The children get a boost of self-confidence—look what this dog can do because of me!—and begin to see dogs as affectionate, responsive companions rather than as menacing guard dogs. "Most of these kids have pets," says DeGrave, "but they're often pit bulls . . . Many are afraid of [our] dogs when they first see them."[14]

Because of the high level of cat abuse in the community, PAL recently added a "cat socialization program." After the dog training session, children spend time playing with and observing shelter cats. Each child writes up a profile of one of the cats, describing how the feline behaves and what it likes to play with. The shelter then shares these descriptions with potential adopters, giving them a fuller picture of the cat's personality. The experience changes the children's perceptions of cats, DeGrave believes: "Before, these kids believed that cats can't be trained, that they don't have feelings."

At Shiloh, juvenile offenders at a boys' probation home spend a month practicing reward-based dog obedience training and hearing messages about humane treatment of animals. The teenagers are "pretty hard guys who have committed some serious crimes," says John Tuell, assistant director of the Boys' Probation Home. "There's a lot of animal abuse; we just don't have it documented . . . Many times they'll speak about it and their other crimes without the remorse we'd like to see."[15] Some of the boys had participated in pit-bull fighting, had injured stray cats, or while high had shared their drugs and alcohol with pets. By the end of the program, boys like sixteen-year-old T were marveling at what rewards and encouragement will produce: "It's amazing how I can teach Sparky something and he learns it the first time. It makes me sad sometimes. I need to hear it a thousand times in my head before I know I do something wrong." At the "graduation" ceremony, each boy shows off his dog's accomplishments and makes a presentation. Nancy Katz, founder of the Shiloh Project, is surprised at what most boys choose to do: "Here are these tough guys, and they get up there and read these sappy poems about how much they love their dogs." The key moment comes at the end, when each boy is asked to sign a written pledge never to abuse or neglect an animal. In the history of the program, all but two boys who have completed the training signed the pledge.

Will the Shiloh experience make a permanent change in teens like T? There is no documentation that it will, but the staff at the Boys' Probation Home see some immediate improvements. "We see them let down their defenses, relax a bit, and care for another being," said John Tuell. These boys have "horrendous relations" with other people, Rice Lilly, the director of the home, explained: "Animals are not nearly so complex as humans . . . The boys definitely get an attachment to these animals. They develop lasting concern about the animal they are working with. That's what we're aiming for—empathy."[16]

Broad-based education efforts like *Kind News* and focused programs like PAL and Shiloh are sparking interest around the country as local school systems, juvenile justice, and humane societies team up in search of ways to reduce animal abuse and, they hope, even violence toward humans. Participating children and program staff are uniformly enthusiastic that these initiatives are transforming children's attitudes and behavior. So far, however, there are no systematic, long-term evaluations of these efforts. Social scientists have been late to join with grassroots organizers, and as a result there are no "hard data" that would argue for expansion of these programs, or identify which aspects of the interventions are most effective for certain children. Programs like PAL and Shiloh have twin treatment goals of reducing both animal abuse and antisocial behavior, yet the interventions target only the first, in the hope that benefits there will spill over to the second. However, there is no clear evidence that animal-based interventions reduce human-directed violence. The likelihood of this happening is probably reduced further when programs fail to draw explicit comparisons between humane treatment of animals and nonviolence toward humans. Another problem is that despite widespread recognition of how embedded children's mistreatment of animals is in the context of family and community violence, all the programs target children alone, without their parents, and away from their homes.

A few innovative initiatives are reframing the idea of nurturance more broadly than the care of animals. Tending a garden, feeding wild birds, watering houseplants, environmental conservation activities, even mowing a lawn, share with animal care the potential to appreciate a living system and its needs.[17] Building such experiences into a child's life may be just as effective in encouraging a nurturing orientation as caring for a pet. Well-conceived programs centering on contacts with nature may prove as therapeutic as animal-assisted therapy for distressed children. In research studies, stressed adults report feeling better after viewing nature scenes. Adult hospital patients recover from surgery more quickly when their window overlooks a small stand of trees rather than a brown brick wall.[18] The hope is that children with emotional and physical disabilities may benefit from nature therapies—growing plants, walking in natural settings, even just observing scenes of nature—in ways that are similar to animal-assisted therapies.

Such healing through nature has the added advantage of not stressing or overworking the "therapists." Critics of animal-assisted therapies and activities maintain that many programs are insufficiently sensitive to the welfare of the animals or to children's safety around animals. Lynn Loar of the San Francisco Child Abuse Council cautions that children who have observed violence may threaten the safety of small animals. Gardening, she argues, teaches children to be gentle with living things and instills a sense of nurturance. "If a child lost control and threw or destroyed a plant, the damage would be smaller, and the burden to the child of having harmed a living thing reduced," she notes. "Once the children have demonstrated mastery of gentle caretaking with plants and flowers, they could then be promoted to playing with animals, ideally, large, gentle and sturdy animals at first."[19] Carol Rathmann, shelter manager at the Sonoma County Humane Society in Santa Rosa, California, enlisted volunteers to transform an acre of tall weeds and decrepit animal corrals into the Forget Me Not Farm, a spacious garden and animal-petting area where women from a battered women's shelter and a drug treatment center, together with abused and emotionally disturbed children, grow plants and vegetables, using the harvest to feed animals awaiting adoption. Forget Me Not Farm practices greater vigilance about animal welfare than most animal-based therapies. The farm underscores multiple pathways toward healing and reconnection. Its "horticulture therapy," mixed with supervised, limited animal contact, seeks to envelop frightened mothers and children within the safety of a living shelter, redolent with freshly tilled earth, growing plants, and animals.

Contemporary urban, suburban, and even rural children in North America, and increasingly throughout the globe, live in a world that in terms of animals has become ever more impoverished and denatured. Our youngsters encounter only a tiny fraction of the world's species. Opportunities for close, leisured examination of creatures in their natural habitats grow rarer. Animals more often appear cut off from their natural settings, in zoo dioramas and recreations, on television nature shows, or as humanoid characters at the bottom of a McDonald's Funmeal box. Whether called "the extinction of experience" or a "vicarious view of nature," children's claim on a place within the buzzing, blooming confusion of life forms is endangered.[20] Two naturalists, Gary Paul Nabhan and Stephen Trimble, warn in *The Geography of Childhood* of ever-shrinking "wild places" for children to "wander, be outside, watch ants . . . contemplate clouds and chickadees."[21] A geographer, Roger Hart, documenting children's favorite places in a small town, found that they were animal places as well—frog ponds, horse paddocks, brooks, fields, and hills: "All children have the urge to explore the landscape around them, to learn about it, give order to it, and invest it with meaning."[22] Young children have an intuitive grasp of the truth that we are human *and* animal.

The diverse animal life of our planet is essential for children to gain a sense of their own place in a multispecies world. As Earth is denuded of species and habitat diversity, we deny our children this sense of connection. A new generation, lacking any deeply felt conviction of a shared environment, comes of age only to further accelerate ecological degradation.

Biophilia—our intrinsic connectedness with animals and nature— cautions us that a denatured environment, stripped of a rich diversity of animal inhabitants, will be a toxic one for our children. All humans, pint-sized and full-grown alike, possess a human nature that is part of Nature. Children learn about themselves and their place in the world through engagement with the animal kingdom. We remove this essential learning at our peril.

What can children's life with animals teach us? Rather than viewing fascination with animals as a childish thing that maturation puts aside, we might see children's attunement to animals as nature's gift to our species. It is a reminder that each generation of humans needs an environment of living beings to thrive as surely as it needs oxygen and water. It is an alert, warning us to ensure that children not lose their sense of connection to other species as they grow into adulthood. Instead, childhood should become a time of deepening connection, a time when respectful interest builds on children's intuitive reaching toward animal life. Children are untutored and easily corrupted ecologists, but they set out on life's journey as ecologists nonetheless. In their intimacy with other species, in their ease at crossing species lines, lie the seeds of their future stewardship of the planet.

NOTES

Introduction

1. For an overview of the health benefits of animal contact for adults, see Alan M. Beck and Aaron H. Katcher, *Between Pets and People: The Importance of Animal Companionship*, rev. ed. (West Lafayette, Ind.: Purdue University Press, 1996); and Cindy C. Wilson and Dennis C. Turner, eds., *Companion Animals in Human Health* (Thousand Oaks, Calif.: Sage Publications, 1998).

2. I am using the term "biocentric" differently from Peter H. Kahn Jr. in *The Human Relationship with Nature: Development and Culture* (Cambridge, Mass.: MIT Press, 1999). Kahn (p. 87) labels as "biocentric" moral reasoning focused on issues of welfare, fairness, and respect for nature, as distinguished from "anthropocentric" or human-centered moral reasoning, based on the welfare of humans.

3. For greater clarity, throughout this book I follow the conventional practice of referring to nonhuman animals as "animals" and to human animals as "humans."

1. Animals and the Study of Children

1. John Bowlby, *Attachment and Loss* (London: Hogarth, 1969) and *Secure and Insecure Attachment* (New York: Basic Books, 1989). See also Gail F. Melson, "Studying Children's Attachment to Their Pets: A Conceptual and Methodological Review," *Anthrozoös* 4 (1991): 91–99.

2. Urie Bronfenbrenner, *The Ecology of Human Development* (Cambridge, Mass.: Harvard University Press, 1979), quotation p. 19.

3. For definitional issues related to personal (or social) networks, see J. C. Mitchell, "The Concept and Use of Social Networks," in J. C. Mitchell, ed., *Social Networks in Urban Situations* (Manchester: Manchester University Press, 1969), pp. 1–50. For examples of assessment strategies restricted to human networks, see James Garbarino, N. Burston,

S. Raber, R. Russell, and Ann Crouter, "The Social Maps of Children Approaching Adolescence: Studying the Ecology of Youth Development," *Journal of Youth and Adolescence* 7 (1978): 417–428; and Moncrieff Cochran and David Riley, "The Social Networks of Six-Year-Olds: Context, Content, and Consequence," in Moncrieff Cochran, Mary Larner, David Riley, Lars Gunnarsson, and Charles R. Henderson, Jr., eds., *Extending Families: The Social Networks of Parents and Their Children* (New York: Cambridge University Press, 1990), pp. 154–177.

4. Ernest S. Wolf, "Selfobject Experiences: Development, Psychopathology, Treatment," in Selma Kramer and Salman Akhtar, eds., *Mahler and Kohut: Perspectives on Development, Psychopathology, and Technique* (Northvale, N.J.: Jason Aronson, 1994), pp. 65–96.

5. On the developmental significance of play, see Catherine Garvey, *Play* (Cambridge, Mass.: Harvard University Press, 1977).

6. Sigmund Freud, *Totem and Taboo: Some Points of Agreement between the Mental Lives of Savages and Neurotics* (New York: W. W. Norton, 1950) and *The Interpretation of Dreams* (New York: Avon/Basic, 1965).

7. M.-L. von Franz, "The Process of Individuation," in Carl G. Jung and M.-L. von Franz, eds., *Man and His Symbols* (New York: Dell, 1972), pp. 158–229; quotation p. 207.

8. For a summary of blood-pressure studies on children and adults, see Alan M. Beck and Aaron H. Katcher, *Between Pets and People: The Importance of Animal Companionship*, rev. ed. (West Lafayette, Ind.: Purdue University Press, 1996).

9. See Susan Carey, *Conceptual Change in Childhood* (Cambridge, Mass.: MIT Press, 1985); and Henry M. Wellman and Susan A. Gelman, "Cognitive Development: Foundational Theories of Core Domains," *Annual Review of Psychology* 43 (1992): 337–375.

10. Sherry Turkle, "The Digital Future: From Rorschach to Relational Artifact," *Radcliffe Quarterly* 85 (2000): 29.

11. Claude Lévi-Strauss, *Totemism*, trans. Rodney Needham ((Boston: Beacon Press, 1963), p. 89.

12. William A. Corsaro, *Friendship and Peer Culture in the Early Years.* (Norwood, N.J.: Ablex Publishing, 1985).

13. Beck and Katcher, *Between Pets and People*, p. 89.

14. Aaron H. Katcher, "The Future of Educational Research on the Animal-Human Bond and Animal-Assisted Therapy," in Aubrey H. Fine, ed., *Handbook on Animal-Assisted Therapy* (New York: Academic Press, 2000), pp. 468–469.

15. Arnold Arluke, a sociologist at Northeastern University, is currently addressing this question.

16. I am indebted to an anonymous reviewer for this point. See Arnold Arluke and Boria Sax, "Understanding Nazi Animal Protection and the Holocaust," *Anthrozoös* 5 (1992): 6–31. However, the extent to which Nazi behavior toward animals was congruent with their strict antivivisectionist laws is debatable. See Ulrich Fritzsche, "Nazis and Animal Protection," *Anthrozoös* 5 (1992): 218.

17. Peter H. Kahn, *The Human Relationship with Nature: Development and Culture* (Cambridge, Mass.: MIT Press, 1999).

18. This does not imply that one set of changes has caused the other.

19. See Edward O. Wilson, *Biophilia* (Cambridge, Mass.: Harvard University Press, 1984); Stephen R. Kellert and Edward O. Wilson, eds., *The Biophilia Hypothesis* (Washington, D.C.: Island Press, 1993); and Stephen R. Kellert, *Kinship to Mastery: Biophilia in Human Evolution and Development* (Washington, D.C.: Island Press, 1997).

20. Freud, *Totem and Taboo*, p. 7.

21. Gene Myers, *Children and Animals: Social Development and Our Connection to Other Species* (Boulder, Colo.: Westview Press, 1998); p. 165.

22. Gillian Avery, *Nineteenth-Century Children: Heroes and Heroines in English Children's Stories, 1780–1900* (London: Hodder and Stoughton, 1965), p. 39.

2. Reaching across the Divide

1. According to recent mitochondrial DNA analyses, wolves and dogs diverged genetically about 135,000 years ago, far earlier than the earliest fossil evidence, dating to about 12,000 years ago, would suggest; Stephen Budiansky, "The Truth about Dogs," *Atlantic Monthly,* July 1999, pp. 39–54.

2. Human petkeeping is thought to have originated in a process of mutual adaptation in which wolves played an active, perhaps primary part, rather than in deliberate acts of taming by humans. See Stephen Budiansky, *The Covenant of the Wild: Why Animals Chose Domestication* (New York: Morrow, 1992); R. Fiennes and A. Fiennes, *The Natural History of Dogs* (New York: Natural History Press, 1970); C. Reed, "Animal Domestication in the Prehistoric Near East," *Science* 130 (1959): 1629–39; and Mark Derr, *Dog's Best Friend: Annals of the Dog-Human Relationship* (New York: Henry Holt, 1997).

3. Tim Ingold, a social anthropologist at the University of Manchester, describes the "rites" employed by modern hunter-gatherers to ensure that their prey will not be "offended" by unnecessary killing and will instead offer themselves for human consumption in the future. Animal prey are viewed in a relationship of free will with human hunters whose respect is repaid when the animal allows itself to be killed. "From Trust to Domination: An Alternative History of Human-Animal Relations," in Aubrey Manning and James Serpell, eds., *Animals and Human Society: Changing Perspectives* (New York: Routledge, 1994), quotation p. 15.

4. Elizabeth Marshall Thomas describes the traditional relationship between !Kung bushmen of the Kalahari desert in southwestern Africa and lions who share their environment as one of mutual understanding and adaptation. See "The Old Way," *New Yorker,* October 15, 1990, pp. 78–110. See also Thomas, *The Tribe of Tiger: Cats and Their Culture* (New York: Simon and Schuster, 1994). In *The Prehistory of the Mind* (New York: Thames and Hudson, 1996), Steven Mithen describes the deep respect that modern hunter-gatherers extend to their prey, whom they view as fellow kinsmen. Such respect in no way diminishes, and in fact may help justify, the hunter-gatherer's readiness to eat these same animals.

5. Juliet Clutton-Brock, *Domesticated Animals from Early Times* (London: British Museum, 1981), p. 14.

6. Juliet Clutton-Brock, "The Unnatural World: Behavioral Aspects of Humans and Animals in the Process of Domestication," in Manning and Serpell, *Animals and Human Society,* pp. 23–35. Clutton-Brock points out that whereas any mammal can be tamed if

reared from an early age by humans, the adult animal will remain tame only if it is from a highly social species.

7. A sensitive depiction of twentieth-century hunter-gatherer life, now disappeared, appears in Elizabeth Marshall Thomas, *The Harmless People* (New York: Alfred A. Knopf, 1959). For an account of the origins of animal domestication, see Clutton-Brock, *Domesticated Animals from Early Times.*

8. James Serpell, *In the Company of Animals: A Study of Human-Animal Relationships* (London: Cambridge University Press, 1996), p. 4.

9. James Serpell provides cross-cultural evidence for the extreme reluctance of humans to eat their own pets, even though in periods of food shortage humans may eat other members of those species kept as pets. See "Pet-keeping and Animal Domestication: A Reappraisal," in Juliet Clutton-Brock, ed., *The Walking Larder: Patterns of Domestication, Pastoralism, and Predation* (London: Unwin Hyman, 1989), pp. 10–21.

10. Konrad Lorenz, *Studies in Animal and Human Behavior,* vol. 2 (London: Methuen, 1971).

11. Stephen Jay Gould, "A Biological Homage to Mickey Mouse," in *The Panda's Thumb* (New York: W. W. Norton, 1982), p. 101.

12. S. M. J. Davis and F. R. Valla, "Evidence for Domestication of the Dog 12,000 Years Ago in the Natufian Culture of Israel," *Nature* 276 (1978): 608.

13. Mithen, "Epilogue," in *Prehistory of the Mind.*

14. W. Halliday, "Animal Pets in Ancient Greece," *Discovery* 3 (1922): 151–154.

15. Juliet Clutton-Brock, "Introduction," in *The Walking Larder,* pp. 1–3.

16. As reported by Calvin W. Schwabe, "Animals in the Ancient World," in Manning and Serpell, *Animals and Society,* pp. 36–58.

17. Quoted in Clutton-Brock, *Domesticated Animals from Early Times,* p. 15. Evidence for petkeeping across cultures is presented by Serpell, "Petkeeping and Animal Domestication: A Reappraisal," in Clutton-Brock, *The Walking Larder.* Domestication is most easily achieved with species that breed readily in captivity and have social structures allied to those of humans.

18. Harriet Ritvo, *The Animal Estate: The English and Other Creatures of the Victorian Age* (Cambridge, Mass.: Harvard University Press, 1987).

19. Albert the Great, *Man and the Beasts. De Animalibus,* trans. James J. Scanlon (Binghamton, N.Y.: SUNY at Binghamton, 1987), p. 78.

20. *Oxford English Dictionary* (New York, Clarendon Press, 1989), 11: 625.

21. James Serpell attributes the social respectability of petkeeping to the growth of cities and corresponding decline of rural populations who needed a value system rationalizing their killing of animals for food, clothing, and other products. See "Animal Companions and Human Well-Being: An Historical Exploration of the Value of Human-Animal Relationships," in Aubrey H. Fine, ed., *Handbook on Animal-Assisted Therapy* (New York: Academic Press, 2000), pp. 3–19.

22. Kathleen Kete, *The Beast in the Boudoir* (New Haven: Yale University Press, 1994), p. 7.

23. Katherine Grier, personal communication.

24. Ruth M. Baldwin, *One Hundred Nineteenth-Century Rhyming Alphabets in English* (Carbondale: Southern Illinois University Press, 1972), p. 83. Christopher Manes estimates that one-third of all nineteenth-century English-language alphabet books used animals as examples. See *Other Creations: Rediscovering the Spirituality of Animals* (New York: Doubleday, 1997).

25. Stephen R. Kellert, "American Attitudes toward and Knowledge of Animals," *International Journal of the Study of Animal Problems* 1 (1980): 87–119.

26. Gary Paul Nabhan has documented that even rural children living next to national parks and protected wilderness areas are now gaining their knowledge about other organisms second-hand. In interviews with eight-to-fourteen-year-olds, 61 percent of the Anglo-American, 77 percent of the Hispanic-American, and 60 percent of the Yaqui (Native American) children felt they had seen more animals on television and in the movies than in the wild. See Gary Paul Nabhan and Stephen Trimble, *The Geography of Childhood: Why Children Need Wild Places* (Boston: Beacon Press, 1994), p. 88.

27. Paul Shepard, *The Others: How Animals Made Us Human* (Washington, D.C.: Island Press, 1995).

28. David Elkind, *The Hurried Child: Growing Up Too Fast Too Soon* (Reading, Mass.: Addison-Wesley, 1981).

29. Christopher Lasch, *Haven in a Heartless World* (New York: Basic Books, 1979).

30. David Elkind, *Ties That Stress* (Cambridge, Mass.: Harvard University Press, 1994).

31. Similar figures from the American Veterinary Medical Association (hereafter AVMA) are reported in Alan M. Beck and N. M. Meyers, "Health Enhancement and Companion Animal Ownership," *Annual Review of Public Health* 17 (1996): 247–257.

32. Andrew N. Rowan, "Pet Ownership and Use of Superstores on the Rise," *Anthrozoös* 8 (1995): 111; Beck and Meyers, "Health Enhancement"; "Americans Spend Twenty Billion Dollars per Year on Pets and Investors Are Cashing In," *Anthrozoös* 9 (1996): 116; AVMA, *Veterinary Economic Statistics, August 1997* (Schaumburg, Ill.: Center for Information Management, 1997).

33. Serpell, *In the Company of Animals*, pp. 13–14.

34. AVMA, *The Veterinary Service Market for Companion Animals* (Schaumburg, Ill.: Center for Information Management, 1992); Serpell, *In the Company of Animals*.

35. AVMA, *Veterinary Economic Statistics, August 1997.*

36. "Americans Spend Twenty Billion Dollars per Year on Pets."

37. Kathleen Szasz, *Petishism: Pets and Their People in the Western World* (New York: Holt, Rinehart and Winston, 1969). See also Richard Klein, "The Power of Pets," *New Republic,* July 10, 1995, pp. 18–23.

38. Beck and Meyers, "Health Enhancement"; AVMA, *Veterinary Economic Statistics, August 1997.*

39. AVMA, *The Veterinary Service Market for Companion Animals.*

40. *Reader's Digest Eurodata: A Consumer Survey of 17 European Countries* (Pleasantville, N.Y.: Reader's Digest Association, 1991), pp. 267–268.

41. Alberta Albert and Kris Bulcroft, "Pets and Urban Life," *Anthrozoös* 1 (1986): 9–23.

42. Gail F. Melson, "Availability and Involvement with Pets by Children: Determinants and Correlates," *Anthrozoös* 2 (1988): 45–52; Gail F. Melson, Rona Schwarz, and Alan Beck, "The Importance of Companion Animals in Children's Lives: Implications for Veterinary Practice," *Journal of the American Veterinary Medical Association* 211 (1997): 1512–18.

43. Brian Fogle, *Pets and Their People* (New York: Viking, 1983), p. 72.

44. See Jeffrey J. Sacks, Randall Lockwood, Janet Hornreich, and Richard W. Sattin, "Fatal Dog Attacks, 1989–1994," *Pediatrics* 97 (1996): 891–895; Alan Beck and Barbara A. Jones, "Unreported Dog Bites in Children," *Public Health Reports* 100 (1985): 315–321; Thomas V. Brogan, Susan L. Bratton, M. Denise Dowd, and Mary A. Hegenbarth, "Severe Dog Bites in Children," *Pediatrics* 96 (1995): 947–950.

45. Jean C. Filiatre, Jean L. Millot, and Hubert Montagner, "New Findings on Communication: The Young Child and His Pet Dog," in Institute for Interdisciplinary Research on the Human-Pet Relationship, *The Human-Pet Relationship* (Vienna, 1985), pp. 50–57. Particularly gentle, even-tempered dogs were probably selected for the study. Clearly, not all dogs would respond similarly.

46. Judith M. Siegel, "Pet Ownership and the Importance of Pets among Adolescents," *Anthrozoös* 8 (1995): 217–223.

47. Siegel, "Pet Ownership." Ethnic and racial differences in pet ownership and in the meaning of pets once they are part of a household are poorly understood and, to date, the subject of almost no research; Dr. Caroline Schaffer, personal communication.

48. Michael Robin, Robert ten Bensel, Joseph S. Quigley, and Robert K. Anderson, "Childhood Pets and the Psychosocial Development of Adolescents," in Aaron H. Katcher and Alan M. Beck, eds., *New Perspectives on Our Lives with Companion Animals* (Philadelphia: University of Pennsylvania Press, 1983), pp. 436–448.

49. Ann Ottney Cain, "Pets as Family Members," in Martin B. Sussman, ed., *Pets and the Family* (New York: Haworth Press, 1985), pp. 5–10; Nienke Endenberg and Ben Baarda, "The Role of Pets in Enhancing Human Well-Being: Effects on Child Development," in Ian Robinson, ed., *The Waltham Book of Human-Animal Interaction: Benefits and Responsibilities of Pet Ownership* (Tarrytown, N.Y.: Elsevier Science, 1995), pp. 7–17.

50. James Serpell, "Childhood Pets and Their Influences on Adults' Attitudes," *Psychological Reports* 49 (1981): 651–654.

51. Elizabeth S. Paul and James Serpell, "Childhood Petkeeping and Humane Attitudes in Young Adulthood," *Animal Welfare* 2 (1993): 321–337.

52. Robert A. Palmatier, *Speaking of Animals: A Dictionary of Animal Metaphors* (Westport, Conn.: Greenwood Press, 1995), p. 207. See *Oxford English Dictionary,* 11: 625. The *OED* cites a 1508 Scottish proverb that conveys well the sense of "pet" as "indulged and spoiled child": "He has fault of a wife who marries mam's pet."

53. Leslie Fiedler, *Freaks: Myths and Images of the Secret Self* (New York: Simon and Schuster, 1978), p. 28.

54. See Gene Myers, *Children and Animals: Social Development and Our Connection to Other Species* (Boulder, Colo.: Westview Press, 1998), pp. 19–44.

55. Georges Bataille, *The Accursed Share: An Essay on General Economy,* trans. Robert Hurley, vols. 2 and 3 (New York: Zone Books, 1992) (originally published as *L'histoire de l'érotisme et la souserainêté,* vol. 8 of *Oeuvres complètes* [Paris: Gallimard, 1976]).

56. Grace Glueck, "Before the Flowers Fade: The Eden of Childhood," *New York Times,* December 5, 1997, p. B30.

57. For Montreal, see Anne Salomon, "Montreal Children in the Light of the Test of Animal Affinities," *Annales Medico-Psychologiques* 140 (1982): 207–224; for the San Francisco Bay area, see Aline H. Kidd and Robert M. Kidd, "Children's Attitudes toward Their Pets," *Psychological Reports* 57 (1985): 15–31; for Syracuse, see Ruth L. Wynn, "Children's Satisfaction with Self-Care as a Function of Dog Ownership and Neighborhood Safety," paper delivered at the annual meeting of the Delta Society, Vancouver, October 1987.

58. Albert and Bulcroft, "Pets and Urban Life."

59. Sociologists Kris Bulcroft and Alexa Albert conducted a telephone survey of a random sample of households in Providence, Rhode Island, in 1985. The results were presented in "Similarities and Differences between the Roles of Pets and Children in the American Family," paper delivered at the annual meeting of the Delta Society, Vancouver, October 1987.

60. Brenda K. Bryant, "The Relevance of Pets and Neighborhood Animals to the Social-Emotional Functioning and Development of School-Age Children," Final Report to the Delta Society, Renton, Wash., 1986. See also Bryant, "The Neighborhood Walk: Sources of Support in Middle Childhood," *Monographs of the Society for Research in Child Development* 50 (1985): 1–114.

61. James Serpell, "Does Contact with Animals Affect Humane Attitudes?" paper delivered to the Humane Education Symposium, Animal Care Expo '99, Orlando, Florida, February 24, 1999.

62. Gail F. Melson and Alan Fogel, "Parental Perceptions of Their Children's Involvement with Household Pets: A Test of a Specificity Model of Nurturance," *Anthrozoös* 9 (1996): 95–105. A similar pattern of results was found by Brenda Bryant in her study of seven- and ten-year-olds in California. See "The Neighborhood Walk."

63. Filiatre, Millot, and Montagner, "New Findings on Communication."

64. Judy Dunn and Carol Kendrick, *Siblings: Love, Envy, and Understanding* (Cambridge, Mass.: Harvard University Press, 1982).

65. Bryant, *Relevance of Pets and Neighborhood Animals,* p. 11.

66. Alexa Albert and Marion Anderson, "Dogs, Cats, and Morale Maintenance: Some Preliminary Data," *Anthrozoös* 10 (1997): 121–124.

67. Murray Bowen, *Family Therapy in Clinical Practice* (New York: Jason Aronson, 1978).

68. Ann Ottney Cain, "A Study of Pets in the Family System," in Katcher and Beck, *New Perspectives on Our Lives with Companion Animals,* pp. 72–81; Cain, "Pets as Family Members."

69. Leon J. Saul, "Psychosocial Medicine and Observation of Animals," *Psychosomatic Medicine* 24 (1962): 8–61.

70. E. K. Rynearson, "Humans and Pets and Attachment," *British Journal of Psychiatry* 133 (1978): 550–555. For an example of nervous breakdowns, see a case description of a sixteen-year-old girl's acute depression following the death of her dog in K. M. D. Keddie, "Pathological Mourning after the Death of a Domestic Pet," *British Journal of Psychiatry* 131 (1977): 21–25.

3. Love on Four Legs

1. For another scale measuring children's attachment to their pets, see Robert H. Poresky, Charles Hendrix, Jacob E. Mosier, and Marvin L. Samuelson, "Young Children's Companion Animal Bonding and Adults' Pet Attitudes: A Retrospective Study," *Psychological Reports* 62 (1988): 419–425.

2. Aaron H. Katcher and Alan M. Beck, "Dialogue with Animals," *Transactions and Studies of the College of Physicians of Philadelphia* 8 (1986): 105–112.

3. Charles Darwin, "A Biographical Sketch of a Young Child," *Kosmos* 1 (1877): 367–376.

4. Kathryn Hirsh-Pasek and Rebecca Treiman, "Doggerel: Motherese in a New Context," *Journal of Child Language* 9 (1982): 229–237; Aline H. Kidd and Robert M. Kidd, "Children's Attitudes toward Their Pets," *Psychological Reports* 57 (1985): 15–36.

5. Hirsh-Patek and Treiman, "Doggerel."

6. Aaron H. Katcher, Erika Friedman, Alan M. Beck, and James J. Lynch, "Talking, Looking, and Blood Pressure: Physiological Consequences of Interaction with the Living Environment," in Aaron H. Katcher and Alan M. Beck, eds., *New Perspectives on Our Lives with Companion Animals* (Philadelphia: University of Pennsylvania Press, 1983), pp. 351–359.

7. There is no observational evidence to date contrasting children's speech to babies with children's speech to pets. For comparison of adult speech to babies and to pets, see Aaron Katcher and Alan Beck, "Health and Caring for Living Things," *Anthrozoös* 1 (1987): 175–183.

8. Gene Myers, *Children and Animals: Social Development and Our Connections to Other Species* (Boulder, Colo.: Westview Press, 1998), p. 119.

9. Ibid., chap. 1.

10. Brenda K. Bryant, "Relevance of Pets and Neighborhood Animals to the Social-Emotional Functioning and Development of School-Age Children," Final Report to the Delta Society, Renton, Wash., 1986.

11. Juliet Clutton-Brock, *Domesticated Animals from Early Times* (London: Heinemann, 1989), p. 36.

12. Daniel Goleman, *Emotional Intelligence* (New York: Bantam Books, 1995).

13. Ibid., p. 97.

14. See Stephen Nowicki and Marshall Duke, *Helping the Child Who Doesn't Fit In* (Atlanta: Peachtree Publishing, 1992); and Byron Rourke, *Nonverbal Learning Disabilities* (New York: Guilford Press, 1989). See also G. Guttman, M. Predovic, and M. Zemanek, "The Influence of Pet Ownership on Non-Verbal Communication and Social Competence in Children," in *The Human-Pet Relationship: Proceedings* (Vienna: Institute for Interdisciplinary Research on the Human-Pet Relationship, 1985).

15. For evidence that five- and six-year-olds who are more attached to their pets report greater empathy toward other children, see Gail F. Melson, Susan Peet, and Cheri Sparks, "Children's Attachment to Their Pets: Links to Socioemotional Development," *Children's Environments Quarterly* 8 (1992): 55–65. In another study comparing three-to-five-year-olds who had dogs or cats with same-age children without pets, the pet-owning children were more skilled at predicting the feelings of other people in a series of

hypothetical situations. See Cindee Bailey, "Exposure of Preschool Children to Companion Animals: Impact on Role-Taking Skills" (Ph.D. diss., Oregon State University, 1987). Brenda Bryant found that seven- and ten-year-olds who reported often having "intimate talks" with their pets expressed greater empathy toward peers. See Bryant, "Relevance of Pets and Neighborhood Animals," p. 1.

16. Myers, *Children and Animals*, p. 111.

17. An animal may serve as part of what Erik Erikson called "the small world of manageable toys that the child can retreat to" or what Donald Winnicott termed "transitional objects." See Erikson, "Toys and Reasons," in *Childhood and Society* (New York: W. W. Norton, 1963); and Winnicott, *The Maturational Process and the Facilitating Environment* (New York: Internatrional Universities Press, 1965).

18. Recent elaborations of attachment theory explore intergenerational links in quality of attachment. Secure attachment in infancy and early childhood, a product of responsive parenting, predicts later adult effectiveness as a caregiver of one's own young children. See Mary Main, N. Kaplan, and Jude Cassidy, "Security in Infancy, Childhood, and Adulthood: A Move to the Level of Representation," in Inge Bretherton and Everett Waters, eds., "Growing Points of Attachment Theory and Research," *Monographs of the Society for Research in Child Development* 50 (1985).

19. Beatrice B. Whiting and John W. M. Whiting, *Children of Six Cultures: A Psychocultural Analysis* (Cambridge, Mass.: Harvard University Press, 1975). An extension and elaboration of the Whitings' classic work is Beatrice B. Whiting and Carolyn P. Edwards, *Children of Different Worlds: The Formation of Social Behavior* (Cambridge, Mass.: Harvard University Press, 1988). See also Thomas Weisner, "Sibling Interdependence and Child Caretaking: A Cross-cultural View," in Michael Lamb and Brian Sutton-Smith, eds., *Sibling Relations: Their Nature and Significance across the Life-span* (Hillsdale, N..J.: Erlbaum, 1982); and Thomas Weisner and Robert Gallimore, "My Brother's Keeper: Child and Sibling Caretaking," *Current Anthropology* 18 (1977): 169–190.

20. For a fuller discussion of nurturing others as a developmental process beginning in childhood, see Alan Fogel and Gail F. Melson, eds., *Origins of Nurturance: Developmental, Biological, and Cultural Perspectives on Caregiving* (Hillsdale, N.J.: Erlbaum, 1986).

21. Robert Weiss, "The Provisions of Social Relationships," in Zick Rubin, ed., *Doing unto Others* (Englewood Cliffs, N.J.: Prentice-Hall, 1974), pp. 17–26.

22. For example, Rost and Hartmann found that 25 percent of the eight-to-ten-year-olds in their study indicated sole responsibility for the care of their pets, 25 percent said they rarely looked after their animals, and the rest shared caregiving with other family members. Children with small animals—gerbils, hamsters, rabbits, birds, and fish—took on more caregiving than did youngsters with dogs or cats. But 92 percent of these children considered caring for their pets a "very important" or "important" part of their relationship with the animal. See Detlef H. Rost and Anette Hartmann, "Children and Their Pets," *Anthrozoös* 7 (1994): 242–254. In a telephone survey of Providence, Rhode Island, households, mothers claimed responsibility for most pet care. See Alexa Albert and Kris Bulcroft, "Pets and Urban Life," *Anthrozoös* 1 (1987): 19–26.

23. Thomas F. Juster, Martha S. Hill, Frank P. Stafford, and Jacquelynne Eccles, *Time Use Longitudinal Panel Study, 1975–1981* (Ann Arbor: Survey Research Center, Institute for Social Research, University of Michigan, 1981). I am indebted to the Henry A. Murray Research Center, Radcliffe College, for making these data available to me and for providing research support.

24. See a review of ethnographic data from fifty cultures from the Human Relations Area Files by Barbara Rogoff et al., "Age of Assignment of Roles and Responsibilities to Children: A Cross-Cultural Survey," *Human Development* 18 (1975): 353–369. For discussion of sex differences in nurturance, see Alan Fogel, Gail F. Melson, and Jayanthi Mistry, "Conceptualizing the Determinants of Nurturance: A Reassessment of Sex Differences," in Fogel and Melson, *Origins of Nurturance.*

25. R. G. Slaby and K. S. Frey, "Development of Gender Constancy and Selective Attention to Same-sex Models," *Child Development* 46 (1975): 849–856.

26. Marsha Weinraub, L. P. Clemens, A. Sockloff, T. Ethridge, E. Gracely, and B. Myers, "The Development of Sex Role Stereotypes in the Third Year: Relations to Gender Labelling, Sex-typed Toy Preference and Family Characteristics," *Child Development* 55 (1984): 1493–1503.

27. For detailed discussion of gender differences, see Phyllis W. Berman, "Young Children's Responses to Babies: Do They Foreshadow Differences between Maternal and Paternal Styles?" and Alan Fogel, Gail F. Melson, and Jayanthi Mistry, "Conceptualizing the Determinants of Nurturance: A Reassessment of Sex Differences," both in Fogel and Melson, *Origins of Nurturance.*

28. Gail F. Melson, Alan Fogel, and Sueko Toda, "Children's Ideas about Infants and Their Care," *Child Development* 57 (1986): 1519–27. See also Gail F. Melson and Alan Fogel, "Children's Ideas about Animal Young and Their Care: A Reassessment of Gender Differences in the Development of Nurturance," *Anthrozoös* 2 (1989): 265–273.

29. Gail F. Melson and Alan Fogel, "Parental Perceptions of Their Children's Involvement with Household Pets," *Anthrozoös* 9 (1996): 95–106.

30. In 1975 Boris Levinson noted that "showing affection for a pet is not considered . . . unmanly in our society, the child can openly and freely kiss and fondle the pet without anyone thinking something is wrong"; "Pets and Environment," in Robert S. Anderson, ed., *Pet Animals and Society* (London: Bailliere Tindall), pp. 8–18.

31. Elizabeth S. Paul and James Serpell, "Childhood Petkeeping and Humane Attitudes in Young Adulthood," *Animal Welfare* 2 (1993): 321–337. Historically, many prominent European advocates for humane treatment of animals were pet-lovers, who explicitly linked their concern for animal welfare to the "lessons" their pets had taught them. For example, Michel de Montaigne (1533–1592) felt that his pet dog and cat had convinced him of the needs of other creatures. For a discussion of the links between petkeeping and humane attitudes toward animals, see James Serpell and Elizabeth Paul, "Pets and the Development of Positive Attitudes to Animals," in Aubrey Manning and James Serpell, eds., *Animals and Human Society: Changing Perspectives* (New York: Routledge, 1994), pp. 1–22.

32. Quoted in Steven A. Holmes, "Children Study Longer and Play Less, a Report Says," *New York Times,* November 11, 1998, p. A18.

33. See David Elkind, *The Hurried Child: Growing Up Too Fast Too Soon* (Reading, Mass.: Addison-Wesley, 1981).

34. Rost and Hartmann, "Children and Their Pets."

35. Anita M. Covert, Alice P. Whirren, Joanne Keith, and Christine Nelson, "Pets, Early Adolescents, and Families," *Marriage and Family Review* 8 (1985): 95–108. By contrast, when Brenda Bryant interviewed ten-year-olds in California, only 13 percent spontane-

ously volunteered their pets in answer to the question: "To whom do you turn when you are feeling sad?" See Brenda K. Bryant, "The Neighborhood Walk: Sources of Support in Middle Childhood," *Monographs of the Society for Research in Child Development* 50 (1985): 1–114. Differences in question wording and mode of administration (face-to-face interview versus questionnaire) may account for some of this variation.

36. Gail F. Melson and Rona Schwarz, "Pets as Social Supports for Families with Young Children," paper delivered at the annual meeting of the Delta Society, New York, October 1994.

37. See S. Cohen and G. McKay, "Social Support, Stress, and the Buffering Hypothesis: A Theoretical Analysis," in A. Baum, J. E. Singer, and S. E. Taylor, eds., *Handbook of Psychology and Health* (Hillsdale, N.J.: Erlbaum, 1984), 4: 253–267.

38. Glyn M. Collis and June McNicholas, "A Theoretical Basis for Health Benefits of Pet Ownership: Attachment versus Psychological Support," in Cindy C. Wilson and Dennis C. Turner, eds., *Companion Animals in Human Health* (Thousand Oaks, Calif.: Sage, 1998), p. 118.

39. Wyndol Furman, "The Development of Children's Social Networks," in Deborah Belle, ed., *Children's Social Networks and Social Supports* (New York: Wiley, 1989), pp. 151–172.

40. "Children's Representations of Pets in Their Social Network," manuscript.

41. Ruth L. Wynn, "Children's Satisfaction with Self-Care as a Function of Dog Ownership and Neighborhood Safety," paper delivered at the annual meeting of the Delta Society, Vancouver, October 1987.

42. Michael Robin, Robin ten Bensel, Joseph Quigley, and Robert K. Anderson, "Abused Children and Their Pets," in Robert K. Anderson, Benjamin Hart, and Lynette Hart, eds., *The Pet Connection* (Minneapolis: Center for the Study of Human-Animal Relationships and Environment, 1984).

43. Nancy M. Bodmer, "Impact of Pet Ownership on the Well-Being of Adolescents with Few Familial Resources," in Wilson and Turner, *Companion Animals in Human Health,* pp. 237–247.

44. Interview with veterinarian Myrna Milani, October 9, 1998. A Minnesota study of 507 adolescents found that more than half had lost a pet, while Mary Stewart, a veterinarian in Scotland, reported that 77 percent of the primary-school-age children and 80 percent of the secondary-school-age children she interviewed—a total of 137 children—had experienced the death of a pet. See Michael Robin, Robert ten Bensel, Joseph S. Quigley, and Robert K. Anderson, "Childhood Pets and the Psychosocial Development of Adolescents," in Katcher and Beck, *New Perspectives on Our Lives with Companion Animals,* pp. 436–443; and Mary Stewart, "Loss of a Pet—Loss of a Person: A Comparative Study of Bereavement," ibid., pp. 390–404.

45. A small percentage of America's children—fewer than 3 percent—live on farms that contain farm animals and there routinely see animals being born, suffering illness and injury, and dying.

46. Brenda K. Bryant has developed a Pet Costs questionnaire that taps sources of distress that children may feel because of their pet. Distress over pet health, safety, needs, and death figure prominently. See "The Richness of the Child-Pet Relationship: A Consideration of Both Benefits and Costs of Pets to Children," *Anthrozoös* 3 (1990): 253–261.

47. Virginia Morrow, "My Animals and Other Family: Children's Perspectives on Their Relationships with Companion Animals," *Anthrozoös* 11 (1998): 218–229; quotation p. 222.

48. Interview with Robert Bierer, July 1, 1998.

49. To provide additional background for this discussion of pet loss and its significance, Dr. Sandra Diskin, a family therapist, conducted an informal survey of how parents respond to children when their pets die.

50. Christopher Manes, *Other Creations: Rediscovering the Spirituality of Animals* (New York: Doubleday, 1997), p. 4.

51. For an extended discussion of pet loss and children, see Laurel Lagoni, Carolyn Butler, and Suzanne Hetts, *The Human-Animal Bond and Grief* (New York: W. B. Saunders, 1994).

52. Iris Nowell, *The Dog Crisis* (New York: St. Martin's Press, 1978), p. 22, claims that parental ineptitude in the face of pet death is so pervasive as to render it useless or even damaging as a learning experience.

53. Adults who live alone, are intensely attached to their pet, and lose the pet suddenly, report bereavement reactions that strikingly parallel those after the loss of human loved ones. See John Archer and Gillian Winchester, "Bereavement Following Death of a Pet," *British Journal of Psychology* 85 (1994): 259–271.

54. John Fleming, "Livestock Projects Teach Values," *4-H Doings,* March 1986, p. 4.

55. For example, interviews in 1978 with a random sample of 150 4-H animal science members, ages sixteen to eighteen, from thirty Wisconsin counties found that 73 percent felt that they learned "quite a bit" or "a lot" about "understanding and respecting animals"; "4-Hers Learn from Animal Projects," report from the 4-H and Youth Development Program Area and Division of Program and Staff Development, University of Wisconsin Extension, October 1978.

56. J. H. Davis and A. M. Juhasz, "The Preadolescent/Pet Bond and Psychosocial Development," in Martin B. Sussman, ed., *Pets and the Family* (New York: Haworth Press, 1985), pp. 90–91.

4. Learning from Animals

1. Gene Myers, *Children and Animals: Social Development and Our Connection to Other Species* (Boulder, Colo.: Westview Press, 1998), pp. 15–16.

2. Paul Shepard, *The Others: How Animals Made Us Human* (Washington, D.C.: Island Press, 1995); and Yi-Fu Tuan, *Dominance and Affection: The Making of Pets* (New Haven: Yale University Press, 1984). See also Paul Shepard, *Traces of an Omnivore* (Washington, D.C.: Island Press, 1996), pp. 51–74.

3. John Berger, *About Looking* (New York: Vintage Books, 1991), p. 16.

4. On the ethical dilemmas raised by use of live animals in high school biology classes, see Heather McGiffin and Nancie Brownley, eds., *Animals in Education: The Use of Animals in High School Biology Classes and Science Fairs* (Washington, D.C.: Institute for the Study of Animal Problems, 1980).

5. Stephen R. Kellert, *Kinship to Mastery: Biophilia in Human Evolution and Development* (Washington, D.C.: Island Press, 1997), p. 98.

6. The most useful and comprehensive treatment of this question may be found in Myers, *Children and Animals;* and in Hubert Montagner, *L'enfant, l'animal, et l'école* (Paris: Bayard, 1995).

7. A small-scale survey of elementary school teachers in Indiana found that about half had, or would have liked to have, animals in their classroom; unpublished data from A. G. Rud and Alan Beck. In a survey of thirty-seven northern California elementary school teachers in thirty schools, 59 percent reported having living animals in the classroom, most commonly small "pocket pets," like hamsters, guinea pigs, and gerbils, or small reptiles, such as iguanas, snakes, and lizards, and fish; R. Lee Zasloff, Lynette A. Hart, and Harold deArmond, "Animals in Elementary School Education in California," *Journal of Applied Animal Welfare Science* 2 (1999): 347–357. Cheryl McCrindle, a veterinarian at the University of Pretoria, South Africa, surveyed preschool classrooms in and around Pretoria and concluded that although the majority of classrooms contained animals, and preschool teachers felt they contributed to the children's development, many teachers lacked knowledge about animal management and behavior and were concerned about the hazards of zoonotic diseases; Cheryl M. E. McCrindle, personal communication.

8. Susan King and Pat MacIsaac, "What Did You Do with Sophie, Teacher?" *Young Children,* January 1989, pp. 37–38. See also Marjan Margadant-van Arcken, "There's a Real Dog in the Classroom: The Relationships between Young Children and Animals," *Children's Environments Quarterly* 1 (1984): 12–16; and J. Vollmer, "The Passing of Muffin: A Classroom Pet Dies," *Instructor* 89 (1979): 99–100.

9. For an overview of the potential benefits of involvement with pets for young children's development in these areas, see Gladys F. Blue, "The Value of Pets in Children's Lives," *Childhood Education* 63 (1986): 84–90. For overworked teachers, living classroom animals can impose additional burdens. Teachers who do not have living animals cite as problems the need for continuing care over weekends, vacations, and summer, sanitation problems, and concern over liability as a result of animal bites or allergies; Zasloff, Hart, and deArmond, "Animals in Elementary School." There are no written guidelines for animal care in public elementary and secondary schools. The U.S. Animal Welfare Act specifically excludes animals in precollege education. Concern over the welfare of animals in school settings has prompted the ASPCA to urge alternatives to living animals in the classroom (e.g., visits, animal specimens, such as feathers or bones, and media presentations of animals).

10. On self-regulation, see Ross A. Thompson, "On Emotion and Self-Regulation," in Ross A. Thompson, ed., *Nebraska Symposium on Motivation,* vol. 36 (Lincoln: University of Nebraska Press, 1990), pp. 383–483.

11. Montagner, *L'enfant, l'animal et l'école,* p. 16.

12. For examples of preschoolers spontaneously expressing moral concern for the well-being of animals see Myers, *Children and Animals,* pp. 147–154.

13. Madeleine Antonelli, Alan M. Beck, Elizabeth Bennett, Elizabeth Bradley, Carole C. Freeman, Sally Fricke, Barbara Grippi, Dolly Ketterer, and Harris J. Sokoloff, *Pets and Me: A Thematic Learning Experience Built on the Relationship between People and Animals. Pre-K through Grade 5* (Philadelphia: University of Pennsylvania Graduate School of Education, 1991). Teacher training packages geared to the early grades have been developed in several European countries as well. An example is "Children and Animal Life"

available from l'Afirac (French Association of Information and Research on Companion Animals), 7 rue du Pasteur Wagner, 75011 Paris.

14. Myers, *Children and Animals*.

15. John Richard Schrock, "Animals in the Classroom," *Carolina Tips* 54 (1991): 15.

16. The socially embedded nature of children's thinking is central to Lev S. Vygotsky's theory of cognitive development. See *Mind and Society* (Cambridge, Mass.: Harvard University Press, 1978). An extensive literature documents variability in children's thinking, based on task demands, on children's expertise or prior knowledge, and on the match between them. See, for example, Howard Gardner and Barbara Rogoff, "Children's Deliberateness of Planning according to Task Circumstances," *Developmental Psychology* 26 (1990): 480–487; and M. T. H. Chi, "Knowledge Development and Memory Performance," in J. P. Das and N. O'Conner, eds., *Intelligence and Learning* (New York: Plenum Press, 1981).

17. Robert S. Siegler, *Children's Thinking* (Upper Saddle River, N.J.: Prentice-Hall, 1998), pp. 114–115.

18. Eleanor J. Gibson, "Exploratory Behavior in the Development of Perceiving, Acting, and the Acquiring of Knowledge," *Annual Review of Psychology* 39 (1988): 1–41.

19. Elizabeth S. Spelke, Ann Phillips, and Amanda L. Woodward, "Infants' Knowledge of Object Motion and Human Action," in Dan Sperber, David Premack, and Ann James Premack, eds., *Causal Cognition: A Multidisciplinary Debate* (Oxford: Clarendon Press, 1995), pp. 44–78.

20. Aline H. Kidd and Robert M. Kidd, "Reactions of Infants and Toddlers to Live and Toy Animals," *Psychological Reports* 61 (1987): 455–464.

21. Marcelle Ricard and Louise Allard, "The Reaction of 9-to-10-Month-Old Infants to an Unfamiliar Animal," *Journal of Genetic Psychology* 154 (1992): 14.

22. J. A. Nielsen and L. A. Delude demonstrated that varied species of live animals, including dogs, birds, and spiders, hold preschoolers' interest and act as catalysts for social interaction, while toy animals do not. Mammals induce physical contact, while birds and even tarantulas evoke verbal interaction. See "Behavior of Young Children in the Presence of Different Kinds of Animals," *Anthrozoös* 3 (1989): 119–129.

23. Katherine Nelson, "Structure and Strategy in Learning to Talk," *Monographs of the Society for Research in Child Development* 38, no. 149 (1973).

24. M. C. Caselli, E. Bates, P. Casadio, J. Fenson, L. Fenson, L. Sanderl, and J. Weir, "Cross-Linguistic Lexical Development," *Cognitive Development* 10 (1995): 159–199. See also Siegler, *Children's Thinking*, p. 151.

25. Myers, *Children and Animals*, chap. 1.

26. Nielsen and Delude, "Behavior of Young Children in the Presence of Different Kinds of Animals." In general, adults and children respond more positively to soft, fuzzy animals than to hard, reptilelike ones. See S. J. Hunt, Lynette A. Hart, and R. Gomulkiewicz, "The Role of Small Animals in Social Interactions between Strangers," *Journal of Social Psychology* 132 (1992): 245–256.

27. Jean Piaget, *The Child's Conception of the World* (Totowa, N.J.: Littlefield, Adams, 1969), pp. 218–223.

28. See Kim G. Dolgin and Douglas A. Behrend, "Children's Knowledge about Animates and Inanimates," *Child Development* 55 (1984): 1646–50.

29. Susan Carey, *Conceptual Change in Childhood* (Cambridge, Mass.: MIT Press, 1985). I am indebted to Fiona K. Innes' insightful discussion of the development of children's concept of animal in "Children's Conceptualization of Animals," specialization paper submitted for the doctoral program in developmental studies, Purdue University, December 1997.

30. For example, see John D. Coley, "Emerging Differentiation of Folkbiology and Folkpsychology: Attributions of Biological and Psychological Properties to Living Things," *Child Development* 66 (1995): 1856–74; Kayoko Inagaki and Giyoo Hatano, "Young Children's Recognition of Commonalties between Animals and Plants," *Child Development* 67 (1996): 2823–40.

31. Giyoo Hatano and Kayoko Inagaki, "Desituating Cognition through the Construction of Conceptual Knowledge," in G. Salomon, ed., *Distributed Cognitions* (New York: Cambridge University Press, 1993), pp. 115–133. Because the children were not randomly assigned to goldfish raising or control, preexisting differences between the two groups cannot be ruled out. Parents may provide pets to cognitively more mature children.

32. Ibid., p. 126.

33. Montagner, *L'enfant, l'animal, et l'école,* p. 18.

34. David Paterson, "Beastly Images of Childhood," *New Scientist* 24 (1990): 53–55.

35. Interview with Jean McGroarty, Education Director, Tippecanoe County Humane Society, March 12, 1998.

36. Kellert, *Kinship to Mastery.*

37. Ibid.

38. Andrew N. Meltzoff, "Understanding the Intentions of Others: Re-Enactment of Intended Acts by 18-Month-Old Children," *Developmental Psychology* 31 (1995): 838–850.

39. Henry Wellman, *Children's Theory of Mind* (Cambridge, Mass.: MIT Press, 1990). See also Siegler, *Children's Thinking,* pp. 238–244.

40. Siegler, *Children's Thinking,* p. 238.

41. A simulation model holds that we use understanding of the workings of our own mind to simulate how another's mind works. Under this model, human understanding of animal minds will be fraught with many errors, arising out of inappropriate generalization of human desires, motives, and beliefs. See Paul L. Harris, "The Work of the Imagination," in A. Whiten, ed., *Natural Theories of Mind: Evolution, Development, and Simulation of Everyday Mindreading* (Oxford: Blackwell, 1991), pp. 283–304.

42. Similarly, preschoolers believe an adult would want to read a children's book rather than an adult book. See J. Astington and Alison Gopnik, "Developing Understanding of Desire and Intention," in Whiten, *Natural Theories of Mind,* pp. 39–50.

43. Peter H. Kahn Jr. argues persuasively for a view of biophilia as a flexible predisposition with the potential to develop both positive and negative attitudes and values toward animals and nature. See "Developmental Psychology and the Biophilia Hypothesis: Children's Affiliation with Nature," *Developmental Review* 17 (1997): 1–61.

44. Stephen Kellert, *The Value of Life* (Washington, D.C.: Island Press, 1996). James Serpell points out that in Kellert's surveys, second-graders tend to endorse apparently contradictory—from an adult perspective—stances, expressing equally high levels of ecologically sensitive and "dominionistic" or "utilitarian" views. Their cognitive immaturity may make them unaware of the logical inconsistencies in their positions, while their strong endorsement of animal-related attitudes "all over the map" supports biophilia's contention of intrinsic interest in animals. James Serpell, "Does Contact with Animals Affect Humane Attitudes?" paper delivered to the Humane Education Symposium, Animal Care Expo '99, Orlando, Florida, February 24, 1999.

45. Elliott Turiel, *The Development of Social Knowledge: Morality and Convention* (New York: Cambridge University Press, 1983).

46. Brenda K. Bryant, "An Index of Empathy for Children and Adolescents," *Child Development* 53 (1982): 413–425.

47. H. Hartshorne, M. A. May, and J. B. Maller, *Studies in the Nature of Character: Studies in Service and Self-Control,* vol. 2 (New York: Macmillan, 1929).

48. J. M. Sprafkin, R. M. Liebert, and R. W. Poulos, "Effects of a Prosocial Televised Example on Children's Helping," *Journal of Experimental Child Psychology* 20 (1975): 119–126. See also Marion R. Yarrow, P. N. Scott, and Carolyn Zahn-Waxler, "Learning Concern for Others," *Developmental Psychology* 8 (1973): 240–260.

49. Robert Coles, *The Moral Intelligence of Children* (New York: Random House, 1997), quotation p. 84.

50. Kahn, "Developmental Psychology and the Biophilia Hypothesis," p. 47. See also Peter H. Kahn Jr., *The Human Relationship with Nature: Development and Culture* (Cambridge, Mass.: MIT Press, 1999).

5. The Healing Lick

1. For a detailed description of the Green Chimneys therapeutic model, see Gerald P. Mallon, Samuel B. Ross Jr., and Lisa Ross, "Designing and Implementing AAT Programs in Health and Mental Health Organizations," in Aubrey H. Fine, ed., *Handbook on Animal-Assisted Therapy* (New York: Academic Press, 2000), pp. 115–127.

2. Gerald P. Mallon, "Some of Our Best Therapists Are Dogs," *Child and Youth Care Forum* 23 (1994): 94.

3. Ibid., p. 95.

4. Gerald P. Mallon, "Cow as Co-therapist: Utilization of Farm Animals as Therapeutic Aids with Children in Residential Treatment," *Child and Adolescent Social Work Journal* 11 (1994): 455–474; quotation p. 467.

5. Donald W. Winnicott, *The Maturational Process and the Facilitating Environment* (New York: International Universities Press, 1965).

6. The effectiveness of any comprehensive animal-assisted therapy (AAT) program depends on far more than exposure of children to animals. Green Chimneys staff caution that AAT programs must consider the following issues: (1) training and motivation of staff to infuse animal contact; (2) child safety, including allergies, infection control,

and prevention of zoonotic diseases; (3) animal welfare, including careful selection of animals; (4) variability in children's liking for and motivation to be with animals; and (5) cost effectiveness of interventions involving animals as compared with other available interventions. See Mallon, Ross, and Ross, "Designing and Implementing AAT Programs."

7. For the history of beliefs about animal healing of human sickness, see James Serpell, "Animal Companions and Human Well-Being: An Historical Exploration of the Value of Human-Animal Relationships," in Fine, Handbook on Animal-Assisted Therapy, pp. 3–17.

8. James Serpell, In the Company of Animals: A Study of Human-Animal Relationships: (New York: Cambridge University Press, 1986), p. 91. Calvin Schwabe contends that dogs and snakes were first associated with death (wild dogs were scavengers, eating dead bodies). Gradually the belief evolved that dogs and snakes could ward off death and, by implication, cure sickness. See "Animals in the Ancient World," in Aubrey Manning and James Serpell, eds., Animals and Human Society: Changing Perspectives (New York: Routledge, 1994), pp. 36–58.

9. Quoted in Juliet Clutton-Brock, Domesticated Animals from Early Times (London: Heinemann, 1981), p. 44.

10. Serpell, In The Company of Animals, p. 92.

11. Serpell, "Animal Companions and Human Well-Being," p. 10.

12. Albert the Great, Man and the Beasts. De Animalibus, trans. James J. Scanlon (Binghamton, N.Y.: SUNY at Binghamton, 1987), p. 31.

13. Mark Derr, Man's Best Friend: Annals of the Dog-Human Relationship (New York: Henry Holt, 1997), p. 305.

14. Florence Nightingale, Notes on Nursing: What It Is, and What It Is Not (New York: D. Appleton, 1914), p. 103.

15. Alan Beck, "The Use of Animals to Benefit Humans," in Fine, Handbook on Animal-Assisted Therapy, p. 21.

16. Boris Levinson, Pet-Oriented Child Psychotherapy, rev. ed., ed. Gerald P. Mallon (Springfield, Ill.: Charles C. Thomas, 1997), p. 38.

17. Ibid., pp. 40–41.

18. Mary R. Burch, "Animal-Assisted Therapy and Crack Babies: A New Frontier," Pet Partners Newsletter, 1991. See also Mary R. Burch, Leo K. Bustad, Susan L. Duncan, Maureen Frederickson, and Jean Tebay, "The Role of Pets in Therapeutic Programmes," in Ian Robinson, ed., The Waltham Book of Human-Animal Interaction: Benefits and Responsibilities of Pet Ownership (Tarrytown, N.Y.: Elsevier Science, 1995), pp. 55–69.

19. Ange Condoret, "Speech and Companion Animals: Experience with Normal and Disturbed Nursery School Children," in Aaron H. Katcher and Alan M. Beck, eds., New Perspectives on our Lives with Companion Animals (Philadelphia: University of Pennsylvania Press, 1983), pp. 467–471.

20. Jane Copeland Fitzgerald and Jean M. Tebay, "Hippotherapy and Therapeutic Riding," in Cindy C. Wilson and Dennis C. Turner, eds., Companion Animals in Human Health (Thousand Oaks, Calif.: Sage, 1998), pp. 41–58.

21. For more on therapeutic riding programs, see B. Engel, ed., *Therapeutic Riding Programs: Instruction and Rehabilitation* (Durango, Colo.: B. Engel Therapeutic Services, 1992).

22. D. Bertotti, "Effect of Therapeutic Horseback Riding on Children with Cerebral Palsy," *Physical Therapy* 68 (1988): 1505–12.

23. Natalie Bieber, "The Integration of a Therapeutic Equestrian Program in the Academic Environment of Children with Physical and Multiple Disabilities," in Katcher and Beck, *New Perspectives,* pp. 448–459.

24. David Nathanson, "Using Atlantic Bottlenose Dolphins to Increase Cognition of Mentally Retarded Children," in P. Lovibond and P. Wilson, eds., *Clinical and Abnormal Psychology* (Amsterdam, N.Y.: Elsevier Science, 1989), pp. 233–242; David Nathanson and Sherri de Faria, "Cognitive Improvement of Children in Water with and without Dolphins," *Anthrozoös* 6 (1993): 17–29; David Nathanson, "Long Term Effectiveness of Dolphin-Assisted Therapy for Children with Severe Disabilities," *Anthrozoös* 11 (1998): 22–32.

25. Lori Marino and Scott O. Lilienfeld, "Dolphin-Assisted Therapy: Flawed Data, Flawed Conclusions," *Anthrozoös* 11 (1998): 194–200.

26. Interview with Maureen Fredrickson, December 1, 1998. Some dolphin-assisted therapy programs do not allow children in the water with the dolphins. Marianne Klingel of the Clearwater Marine Aquarium uses the opportunity to feed, signal, or rub the dolphin's flipper (from poolside) as reinforcers.

27. Levinson, *Pet-Oriented Child Psychotherapy,* p. 3.

28. Ibid., p. 62; Selma Fraiberg, "The Analysis of an Eight-Year-Old Girl with Epilepsy," in E. D. Gerleerd, ed., *The Child Analyst at Work* (New York: International Universities Press, 1967), p. 235.

29. Aaron H. Katcher and Gregory G. Wilkins, "Dialogue with Animals: Its Nature and Culture," in E. O. Wilson and Stephen Kellert, eds., *The Biophilia Hypothesis* (Washington, D.C.: Island Press, 1993), pp. 179–180.

30. Alan M. Beck and Aaron H. Katcher, *Between Pets and People: The Importance of Animal Companionship* (West Lafayette, Ind.: Purdue University Press, 1996), p. 130.

31. Katcher reports that in over six years of Companionable Zoo programs at three treatment centers, staff have never needed to use restraints on any children in the zoo environment. For detailed description of the program and its evaluation, see Aaron H. Katcher and Gregory G. Wilkins, "The Centaur's Lessons: Therapeutic Education through Care of Animals and Nature Study," in Fine, *Handbook on Animal-Assisted Therapy,* pp. 153–177.

32. Ibid., pp. 173–174. High- and low-performing groups of boys were created by median splits on the Achenbach Teacher Report Total Problem Score and Externalizing Score. Other studies of AAT with adults find similar degree-of-program-involvement effects. For example, the presence of an aviary at an adult day health-care program had no overall effects, but elderly men who sought out the birds reported less depression and more interaction with family and staff than men who ignored the birds. See Ralph Holcomb, Connie Jendro, Barbara Weber, and Ursula Nahan, "Use of an Aviary to Relieve Depression in Elderly Males," *Anthrozoös* 10 (1997): 32–36.

33. Aaron H. Katcher and Alan M. Beck, "Dialogue with Animals," *Transactions and Studies of the College of Physicians of Philadelphia* 8 (1986): 105–112; Aaron H. Katcher, "The

Companionable Zoo Program at the Devereux Foundation," paper delivered at the Sixth International Conference on Human-Animal Interactions, Montreal, July 1992.

34. Erik Erikson, *Childhood and Society* (New York: W. W. Norton, 1963).

35. Gary Mallon, Samuel B. Ross, and Lisa Ross emphasize the importance of matching a child's temperament to a specific animal. For example, a quiet, fearful child should be paired with a reserved, gentle dog rather than a highly active one. See "Designing and Implementing AAT Programs."

36. Jennifer Limond, John Bradshaw, and Magnus Cormack, "Behavior of Children with Learning Disabilities Interacting with a Therapy Dog," *Anthrozoös* 10 (1997): 84–89.

37. Brenda Bryant, M. Djakovic, and Curt Acredolo in collaboration with Samuel Ross, Myra Ross, and Martin Vigdor, "The Ecological Imperative: The Daily Life of One Distressed Child," *Children's Environments* 11 (1994): 36–47.

38. See B. G. Esposito and W. J. Peach, "Changing Attitudes of Preschool Children toward Handicapped Persons," *Exceptional Children* 49 (1983): 361–363; and H. M. Inderbitzen and D. L. Best, "Children's Attitudes toward Physically Handicapped Peers," *Journal of Applied Developmental Psychology* 7 (1986): 417–428.

39. Bonnie Mader, Lynette A. Hart, and Bonnie Bergin, "Social Acknowledgments for Children with Disabilities: Effects of Service Dogs," *Child Development* 60 (1989): 1529–34.

40. Similar effects of friendly dog presence have been found with unsighted adults (Alyse Zee, "Guide Dogs and Their Owners: Assistance and Friendship," in Katcher and Beck, *New Perspectives on Our Lives with Companion Animals,* pp. 472–483) and with wheelchair-bound adults (J. Eddy, Lynette A. Hart, and R. P. Boltz, "The Effects of Service Dogs on Social Acknowledgments of People in Wheelchairs," *Journal of Social Psychology* 122 [1988]: 39–45; and Lynette A. Hart, Ben L. Hart, and Bonnie Bergin, "Socializing Effects of Service Dogs for People with Disabilities," *Anthrozoös* 1 [1987]: 41–44).

41. Fiona Innes, "The Influence of an Animal on Normally Developing Children's Ideas about Helping Children with Disabilities" (Ph.D. diss., Purdue University, 1999).

42. Social lubrication effects have been demonstrated only with a few species of animals, and mostly with adults. There may be species differences. Hunt and her colleagues found that strangers were more likely to initiate conversation when an adult was with a rabbit rather than with a turtle. See S. J. Hunt, L. A. Hart, and R. Gomulkiewicz, "The Role of Small Animals in Social Interaction between Strangers," *Journal of Social Psychology* 133 (1992): 245–256.

43. Randall Lockwood, "The Influence of Animals on Social Perception," in Katcher and Beck, *New Perspectives on Our Lives with Companion Animals,* pp. 64–71. Undergraduates rated photographs of unfamiliar adults shown next to golden retriever dogs as happier and more relaxed than the same adults depicted with flowers (red and white carnations in a tall white vase) or alone. In a second study, undergraduates indicated that they would feel more comfortable taking the place of a woman or man photographed walking with a golden retriever as compared to walking alone in a nature setting, a neighborhood scene, or an urban landscape.

44. Kelly A. Rossbach and John P. Wilson, "Does a Dog's Presence Make a Person Appear More Likeable? Two Studies," *Anthrozoös* 5 (1992): 40–51. See also R. Claire Budge, John Spicer, Boyd R. Jones, and Ross St. George, "The Influence of Companion Animals on Owner Perception: Gender and Species Effects," *Anthrozoös* 9 (1996): 10–18.

45. Innes, "Influence of an Animal."

46. Erika Friedmann, Aaron Katcher, Susan Thomas, James Lynch, and Peter Messent, "Social Interaction and Blood Pressure: Influence of Animal Companions," *Journal of Nervous and Mental Disease* 171 (1983): 461–465.

47. Healthy children who undergo a simulated physical medical examination in the presence of a friendly dog versus without an animal present have lower blood pressure and heart rate; S. L. Nagergost, M. M. Baun, M. Megel, and J. M. Leibowitz, "The Effects of the Presence of a Companion Animal on Physiologic Arousal and Behavioral Distress in Children during a Physical Examination," *Journal of Pediatric Nursing* 12 (1997): 323–330.

48. Adults with more positive attitudes toward dogs experience significantly lower blood pressure when reading aloud in the presence of an unfamiliar dog than do adults with a more negative attitude. However, among those with relatively negative attitudes, there is no increase in physiologic arousal; Erika Friedmann, "The Animal-Human Bond: Health and Wellness," in Fine, *Handbook on Animal-Assisted Therapy.* Friedmann identifies several other untested variables that may affect any relaxation response due to animal presence: relationship to animal, species, extent of interaction with animal, and type of stressor induced.

49. Peter Wolff, "The Causes, Controls, and Organization of Behavior in the Neonate," *Psychological Issues* 5 (1966): 7–11.

50. Katcher and Wilkins, "The Biophilia Hypothesis."

51. Aaron H. Katcher and Gregory G. Wilkins, "Animal-Assisted Therapy in the Treatment of Disruptive Behavior Disorders in Children," in Ante Lundberg, ed., *The Environment and Mental Health: A Guide for Clinicians* (Mahwah, N.J.: Lawrence Erlbaum, 1998), pp. 193–204. As Katcher and Wilkins point out, because many therapeutic interventions expose children to animals in the context of other natural elements, such as plants and trees, the effect of the animals alone cannot be determined.

6. Animal Selves

1. Evelyn Goodenough Pitcher and Ernst Prelinger, *Children Tell Stories: An Analysis of Fantasy* (New York: International Universities Press, 1963). Colin's story is on p. 44, Dulcy's on p. 59.

2. Ibid., p. 13.

3. Ibid., p. 126.

4. Roger G. Barker and Herbert F. Wright, *One Boy's Day: A Specimen Record of Behavior* (New York: Harper and Brothers, 1951), p. 349.

5. Susan Isaacs, *Intellectual Growth in Young Children* (London: Routledge and Paul, 1948), pp. 201–202.

6. Josephine C. Foster and John E. Anderson, "Unpleasant Dreams in Childhood," *Child Development* 7 (1936): 77–84. The results are based on seven-day records kept by 519 Minnesota parents of children aged one to twelve.

7. Louise Bates Ames, "Sleep and Dreams in Childhood," pp. 14–15.

8. David Foulkes, *Children's Dreaming and the Development of Consciousness* (Cambridge, Mass.: Harvard University Press, 1999), p. 62.

9. Arthur T. Jersild and Frances B. Holmes, *Children's Fears* (New York: Bureau of Publications, Teachers College, Columbia University, 1935).

10. Arthur T. Jersild and Frances B. Holmes, "A Study of Children's Fears," *Journal of Experimental Education* 2 (1933): 109–118.

11. Karl C. Pratt, "A Study of the 'Fears' of Rural Children," *Journal of Genetic Psychology* 67 (1945): 179–194. Sixty-nine percent of all fears mentioned involved animals.

12. Alan D. Bowd, "Fears and Understanding of Animals in Middle Childhood," *Journal of Genetic Psychology* 145 (1983): 143–144.

13. Nine-to-thirteen-year-old children identify spiders as their most intense fear; Peter Muris, Harald Merckelbach, and Ron Collaris, "Common Childhood Fears and Their Origins," *Behavior Research and Therapy* 35 (1997): 929–937. In a survey in Melbourne, Australia, of 439 eleven-to-eighteen-year-olds, fear of animals was one of the top three fears mentioned in response to an open-ended question, and fear of spiders was selected as the number one fear from a list of 78 fears. See Belinda Lane and Eleonora Gullone, "Common Fears: A Comparison of Adolescents' Self-Generated and Fear Schedule Survey Generated Fears," *Journal of Genetic Psychology* 160 (1999): 194–204. Both rural and urban fourth-, fifth-, and sixth-graders in the southeastern United States mention snakes and sharks among their ten most common fears; Phyllis N. White and Debbie J. Smith, "Content and Intensity of Fears in Middle Childhood among Rural and Urban Boys and Girls," *Journal of Genetic Psychology* 150 (1989): 51–58. M. Ferrari describes a developmental progression similar to that found by Jersild and Holmes. Preschoolers fear common animals and insects; children from five to six fear wild animals, ghosts, and monsters; and children over seven begin reporting more school- and relationship-based fears. See "Fears and Phobias in Childhood: Some Clinical and Developmental Considerations," *Child Psychiatry and Human Development* 17 (1986): 75–87.

14. Gene Myers, *Children and Animals: Social Development and Our Connections to Other Species* (Boulder, Colo.: Westview, 1998), p. 79. John Bowlby argued that animals often exhibit the cues that naturally arouse fear in young children—rapid approach, sudden movement, and unexpected noise; *Attachment and Loss,* vol. 2: *Separation* (New York: Basic Books, 1975).

15. Louise Bates Ames, Janet Learned, Ruth W. Metraux, and Richard N. Walker, *Child Rorschach Responses: Developmental Trends from Two to Ten Years* (New York: Paul B. Hoeber, 1952), pp. 273–274. See also L. Phillips and J. G. Smith, *Rorschach Interpretation: Advanced Technique* (New York: Grune & Stratton, 1953).

16. Leopold Bellak and Sonya S. Bellak, *Children's Apperception Test Manual,* 4th ed. (New York: C. P. S., 1961); quoted in Mary R. Haworth, *The CAT: Facts about Fantasy* (New York: Grune & Stratton, 1966), p. 1.

17. See, for example, Robert E. Bills, "Animal Pictures for Obtaining Children's Projections," *Journal of Clinical Psychology* 6 (1950): 291–293.

18. Arthur A. Schwartz and Israel H. Rosenberg, "Observations on the Significance of Animal Drawings," *American Journal of Orthopsychiatry* 25 (1955): 729–746.

19. Gerald Blum and H. F. Hunt, "The Validity of the Blacky Pictures," *Psychological Bulletin* 49 (1952): 239.

20. Marvin Spiegelman, Carl Terwilliger, and Franklin Fearing, "The Content of Comics: Goals and Means to Goals of Comic Strip Characters," *Journal of Social Psychology* 37 (1953): 115–125.

21. The Reader Rabbit series is designed to help children recognize letters, identify words, and develop other early reading skills. The Jump Start series, from *Jump Start Baby* to *Jump Start Second Grade,* as of 1998, focuses on the cognitive skills needed for each level. *Bailey's Book House* centers on learning the alphabet, creating stories, and developing writing and reading skills. Other CD-ROMs with animal themes include *The Big Bug Alphabet Book,* featuring cartoon bugs; *Zurk's Learning Safari;* and 3D *Dinosaur Adventure.*

22. For historical trends in animal characters in children's fiction, see Gillian Avery, *Nineteenth-Century Children: Heroes and Heroines in English Children's Stories, 1780–1900* (London: Hodder and Stoughton, 1965); and W. H. Magee, "The Animal Story: A Challenge in Technique," in S. Egoff, G. T. Stubbs, and L. F. Ashley, eds., *Only Connect: Readings on Children's Literature* (New York: Oxford University Press, 1969), pp. 221–232.

23. Compiled by Publishers Weekly; reported in *Information Please Almanac,* ed. Borgna Brunner (Boston: Houghton Mifflin, 1998), p. 738.

24. Kathryn Norcross Black, "Animals in Picture Books for Children," manuscript.

25. Cheryl M. E. McCrindle and Johannes S. J. Odendaal, "Animals in Books Used for Preschool Children," *Anthrozoös* 7 (1994): 135–146.

26. Mary H. Lystad, *From Dr. Mather to Dr. Seuss: 200 Years of American Books for Children* (Boston: G. K. Hall, 1980). For each year, 1776–1976, five books were randomly selected from the Rare Books Division of the Library of Congress. Other "counts" of animal content in children's storybooks find a similar preponderance of animals. See, for example, I. L. Child, E. H. Potter, and Estelle M. Levine, "Children's Textbooks and Personality Development: An Exploration in the Social Psychology of Education," *Psychological Monographs* 60 (1946): 1–7, 43–53.

27. Based on my analysis of U.S. school reader selections compiled by David McClelland. Four books used in public schools from each decade from 1800 to 1970 were selected, with every third page of each reader sampled for a ten-line story segment.

28. Martin J. Croghan and Penelope P. Croghan, *Role Models and Readers: A Sociological Analysis* (Washington, D.C.: University Press of America, 1980).

29. Nancy A. Boyd and George Mandler, "Children's Responses to Human and Animal Stories and Pictures," *Journal of Consulting Psychology* 19 (1955): 367–371.

30. Will James, *Smoky the Cowhorse* (New York: Charles Scribner, 1926), p. v.

31. Emily Neville, *It's Like This, Cat* (New York: Harper and Row, 1963), p. 8.

32. Marguerite Henry, *King of the Wind* (New York: Rand McNally, 1948); William H. Armstrong, *Sounder* (New York: Harper and Row, 1969); Jean Craighead George, *Julie of the Wolves* (New York: Harper and Row, 1972); Neville, *It's Like This, Cat.*

33. Karen Cushman, *The Midwife's Apprentice* (New York: Clarion Books, 1995).

34. Lynd Ward, *The Biggest Bear* (Boston: Houghton Mifflin, 1952); Evaline Ness, *Sam, Bangs, and Moonshine* (New York: Holt, Rinehart and Winston, 1966); Paul Goble, *The Girl Who Loved Wild Horses* (Scarsdale, N.Y.: Bradbury Press, 1978); Arnold Lobel, *Fa-*

bles (New York: Harper and Row, 1980); Eve Bunting, *Smoky Night* (San Diego: Harcourt Brace, 1994).

35. Michele Landsberg, *Reading for the Love of It* (New York: Prentice-Hall, 1986), p. 24.

36. Matt Cartmill, *A View to a Death in the Morning* (Cambridge, Mass.: Harvard University Press, 1993), p. 187.

37. Gary Cross, in *Kids' Stuff: Toys and the Changing World of American Culture* (Cambridge, Mass.: Harvard University Press, 1997), views Teddy and his successors as offering "both security and strength, a reassuring combination for the very young" (p. 97).

38. Marina Warner, *From the Beast to the Blonde: On Fairy Tales and Their Tellers* (New York: Farrar, Straus and Giroux, 1994), p. 307. Cartmill, in *A View to a Death in the Morning* (p. 188), suggests that this animalization "embodies an unspoken belief—and a message to children—that animals are good and innocent, whereas human beings are darker and more dubious creatures."

39. Nicolas Howe, "Fabling Beasts: Traces in Memory," in Arien Mack, ed., *Humans and Other Animals* (Columbus: Ohio State University Press, 1995), p. 244.

40. The first patent for an animal was issued in the United States in 1988 for a mouse genetically engineered to develop cancer; Boria Sax, *The Frog King: On Legends, Fables, Fairy Tales, and Anecdotes of Animals* (New York: Pace University Press, 1990), p. 159.

41. Claude Lévi-Strauss, *The Savage Mind* (Chicago: University of Chicago Press, 1966), quoted in Paul Shepard, *Traces of an Omnivore* (Washington, D.C.: Island Press, 1996), p. 53; Lévi-Strauss, *Totemism,* trans. Rodney Needham (Boston: Beacon Press, 1963), p. 101.

42. Mircea Eliade, *Myths, Dreams, and Mysteries* (New York: Harper and Row, 1960), p. 61. For animals in creation myths, see Yves Bennefoy, *American, African, and Old European Mythologies* (translated under the direction of Wendy Doniger) (Chicago: University of Chicago Press, 1993).

43. Many hunter cultures imagine divine beings as beasts of prey, for example, lions and leopards in Africa, jaguars in South America, crocodiles in Oceania. See Marcea Eliade, *Rites and Symbols of Initiation,* trans. Philip Mairet (New York: Harper, 1958), p. 23.

44. Sax, *The Frog King,* p. 32.

45. Christopher Manes suggests that these early toys probably also functioned as religious ritual objects; *Other Creations: Rediscovering the Spirituality of Animals* (New York: Doubleday, 1997), pp. 133–136.

46. See Sax, *The Frog King,* p. 20.

47. Ibid., p. 146.

48. Beryl Rowland, *Animals with Human Faces: A Guide to Animal Symbolism* (Knoxville: University of Tennessee Press, 1973), p. xvii.

49. Melissa Bowerman argues for innate semantic organization of language reflecting universal properties of human cognition and perception. See "Learning a Semantic System," in Paul Bloom, ed., *Language Acquisition: Core Readings* (Cambridge, Mass.: MIT press), p. 229.

50. Steven Mithen, *The Prehistory of the Mind* (New York: Thames and Hudson, 1996).

51. As Sax notes, "Our understanding of animals is so intimately bound up with our self-concept as human beings, we can hardly hope to separate the two completely"; *The Frog King*, p. 146.

52. Quoted in William Zinsser, ed., *Worlds of Childhood: The Art and Craft of Writing for Children* (Boston: Houghton Mifflin, 1990), p. 135.

53. Sigmund Freud, *Totem and Taboo,* trans. James Strachey (New York: W. W. Norton, 1980).

54. Ernest Jones, *On the Nightmare* (New York: Grove Press, 1951), p. 70.

55. Pitcher and Prelinger, *Children Tell Stories,* p. 173. Bart's story is quoted from p. 40.

56. Karl A. Menninger, "Totemic Aspects of Contemporary Attitudes toward Animals," in George B. Wilbur and Warner Muensterberger, eds., *Psychoanalysis and Culture* (New York: International Universities Press, 1951), pp. 43, 44.

57. Sigmund Freud, "Analysis of a Phobia in a Five-Year-Old Boy," (1909), in *Collected Papers of Sigmund Freud,* vol. 3, ed. Ernest Jones, trans. Alix and James Strachey (New York: Basic Books, 1959), p. 172.

58. Ibid., p. 285.

59. Bruno Bettelheim, *The Uses of Enchantment: The Meaning and Importance of Fairy Tales* (New York: Vintage Books, 1977), pp. 100 (about dogs) and 56 (about horses).

60. Freud, "Analysis of a Phobia in a Five-Year-Old Boy," pp. 152–153.

61. Aniela Jaffe, "Symbolism in the Visual Arts," in Carl G. Jung and M.-L. von Franz, eds., *Man and His Symbols* (New York: Dell, 1972), pp. 264, 266.

62. Smith Ely Jelliffe and Louise Brink, "The Role of Animals in the Unconscious, with Some Remarks on Theriomorphic Symbolism as Seen in Ovid," *Psychoanalytic Review* 2 (1917): 271.

63. Sigmund Freud, "The Occurrence in Dreams of Material from Fairy-Tales" (1916), in *Collected Papers,* 4: 236–243; quotation p. 242.

64. See Melanie Klein's discussion of the Wolfman in *The Psycho-Analysis of a Child* (New York: Humanities Press, 1969), p. 222.

65. David Foulkes, *Dreaming: A Cognitive-Psychological Analysis* (Hillsdale, N.J.: Erlbaum, 1985), p. 121. See Foulkes, *Children's Dreaming,* pp. 150–152, on consciousness and self-identity development.

66. Shepard, *Traces of an Omnivore,* p. 3.

67. C. S. Lewis, "On Stories," in M. Meek, A. Warlow, and G. Barton, eds., *The Cool Web: The Pattern of Children's Reading* (New York: Atheneum, 1978), pp. 84–85.

68. See Margaret Blount, *Animal Land: The Creatures of Children's Fiction* (New York: William Morrow, 1975). I am indebted to Blount's analysis of *The Jungle Books* and *Stuart Little* in chap. 12, "The Tables Turned at the Zoo: Mowgli and Stuart Little" (pp. 226–244).

69. Ibid. Blount ably reviews harmless monsters from E. Nesbitt's *Book of Dragons* (1900) to Maurice Sendak's *Where the Wild Things Are* (1967).

70. Sheila Egoff, *Thursday's Child: Trends and Patterns in Contemporary Children's Literature* (Chicago: American Library Association, 1981).

71. Susan Cooper, *The Grey King* (New York: Atheneum, 1975).

72. Karen Hesse, *The Music of Dolphins* (New York: Scholastic Books, 1996).

73. Scott O'Dell, *Island of the Blue Dolphins* (Boston: Houghton Mifflin, 1960).

74. See discussion of the wild child myth in Warner, *From the Beast to the Blonde,* p. 301. Valentine captures Orson in a hunt and redeems him through the "civilizing" powers of baptism and table manners.

75. Alison Friesinger, *Friends in Deed Save the Manatee* (New York: Random House, 1998). Jeanne Betancourt, Pony Pals series.

76. "It was expected," Leopold Bellak wrote, that children "would more readily relate to animals than to human figures . . . [because] the animals which children know are usually smaller than adult humans, or at any rate, are usually thought of as 'underdogs' like children, and even below children, in our pecking order"; Bellak and Bellak, *Children's Apperception Test Manual,* p. 66.

77. Russell W. Belk, "Metaphoric Relationships with Pets," *Society and Animals* 4 (1996): 125.

78. *Rascal* (New York: Dutton, 1964) was on adult best-seller lists for twenty-nine weeks, serialized twice by the BBC, broadcast on Voice of America, and translated into many languages. *Little Rascal* (New York: Dutton, 1965) adapted the bestseller for young readers.

79. Tricia's story appears in Catherine Greenman, "Network Helps Children Cope with Serious Illness," *New York Times,* May 28, 1998, p. D6.

80. As quoted in M. Meek, A. Warlow, and G. Barton, eds., *The Cool Web: The Pattern of Children's Reading* (New York: Atheneum, 1978), p. 25.

81. Mary Allen, *Animals in American Literature* (Champaign: University of Illinois Press, 1983), p. 4.

82. Chinese and Japanese folktales about marriages with owls, cranes, swans, and snakes are described in Mingshui Cai, "Folks, Friends, and Foes: Relations between Humans and Animals in Some Eastern and Western Folktales," *Children's Literature in Education* 24 (1993): 73–83. Transformation into an animal while retaining the mind and feelings of a human is vividly described in Ovid's *Metamorphosis.* Diana, goddess of the hunt, turns Acteon, prince of Thebes, into a stag with great horns and a spotted hide. His hounds fail to recognize the prince within, and as he groans, "Unhappy me!" they turn on him as prey.

83. See Warner, *From the Beast to the Blonde,* pp. 319–370, for discussion of the symbolic meanings of the DonkeySkin tales.

84. Alison Lurie notes, "Another great attraction of the Animorph books is that they provide thrilling, scientifically convincing descriptions of what it might be like to be an animal"; "Reading at Escape Velocity," *New York Times Book Review,* May 17, 1998, p. 51.

85. Shepard, *Traces of an Omnivore,* p. 4.

7. Victims and Objects

1. "No-kill" shelters will not euthanize healthy animals that are unclaimed for adoption.

2. "Cats Killed in Brutal Fairfield Attack," *Ottumwa Courier,* March 11, 1997, p. 1.

3. Letter to the editor from R. M. Zimmermann, *Bloomfield Democrat*, November 12, 1997.

4. "Cat Massacre at Iowa Shelter Splits a Town," *Los Angeles Times*, September 8, 1997, p. A14.

5. D. C. Peattie, "The Nature of Things," *Audubon Magazine* 44 (1942): 268; quoted in Matt Cartmill, *A View to a Death in the Morning* (Cambridge, Mass.: Harvard University Press, 1993), pp. 179–180.

6. There is very little research on children's understanding of animals' capacity for pain. One interview study of thirty-seven kindergarteners found that they believe that animals experience less pain than humans do; Alan D. Bowd, "Understanding of Animal Suffering by Young Children," *Humane Education Journal* 4 (1982): 5–7.

7. Arnold Arluke and Randall Lockwood point out how many fundamental questions about children's mistreatment of animals remain unanswered. In particular, we don't know why it occurs and why early mistreatment does or does not escalate. See "Understanding Cruelty to Animals," *Society and Animals* 5 (1997): 183–193. This is a special issue on animal cruelty.

8. "Grim Details Emerge in Teen-Age Slaying Case," *New York Times*, October 15, 1997, p. A10.

9. "The Tortured Path of a Troubled Youth," *New York Times*, May 22, 1998, p. 1.

10. Frank R. Ascione, "Children Who Are Cruel to Animals: A Review of Research and Implications for Developmental Psychopathology," *Anthrozoös* 6 (1993): 226–247.

11. According to parental reports. Precise estimates of children's cruelty to animals are difficult to obtain. Parents may not see or may underplay abusive behavior. Until recently, many assessments of violent children neglected to ask about animal abuse or included only one vaguely worded item in a checklist: "is cruel to animals." There is no scholarly or popular consensus on just what behaviors constitute "cruelty." For example, is taunting, screaming at, or teasing an animal, without causing physical injury, also cruelty? Different studies may or may not take into account the following aspects of animal abuse: frequency, severity, duration, intentionality, and pleasure derived. Until recently, scholars believed that animal cruelty occurred along with firesetting and bedwetting as a "triad" of symptoms predicting later antisocial violence. However, more careful analyses of patterns of symptoms have challenged this view. See Randall Lockwood and Frank R. Ascione, eds., *Cruelty to Animals and Interpersonal Violence: Readings in Research and Application*, (West Lafayette, Ind.: Purdue University Press, 1998), pp. 245–288.

12. This is probably an underestimate, since some youths had been incarcerated for less than twelve months; personal communication from Frank R. Ascione.

13. D. O. Lewis, S. S. Shanok, M. Grant, and E. Ritvo, "Homicidally Aggressive Young Children: Neuropsychiatric and Experiential Correlates," *American Journal of Psychiatry* 140 (1983): 148–153.

14. Ascione, "Children Who Are Cruel to Animals." We do not know what percentage of children with conduct disorder have abused animals.

15. Phil Arkow, *Breaking the Cycles of Violence: A Practical Guide* (Alameda, Calif.: Latham Foundation, 1998), p. 5.

16. Stephen R. Kellert and Alan R. Felthous, "Childhood Cruelty toward Animals among Criminals and Noncriminals," *Human Relations* 38 (1985): 1113–29. Kellert and Felthous also interviewed fifty young men with no criminal histories from New Haven,

Connecticut, and Topeka, Kansas, as a comparison group to the prison sample. None of these noncriminals reported five or more childhood acts of cruelty toward animals. However, 56 percent acknowledged one or two acts of cruelty. Generally, these were less severe—pulling wings off bugs was common—than those described by the aggressive criminals.

17. With one exception, there are no studies of girls' cruelty to animals or of women's childhood histories of animal abuse. Boys are much more likely than girls to have problems with aggression and impulse control; rates of conduct disorder are five times higher for boys than for girls. In addition, forms of female aggression have been underplayed and ignored. Only recently have psychologists begun studying teasing, taunting, isolation, ostracism, and scapegoating as verbal, relationship-harming aggressive acts that girls are more likely to perpetrate against other children than boys.

18. For example, Felthous compared nonaggressive psychiatric inpatients with patients admitted to the same hospital for urological problems; Alan Felthous, "Childhood Antecedents of Aggressive Behaviors in Male Psychiatric Patients," *Bulletin of the American Academy of Psychiatry and the Law* 8 (1979): 104–110.

19. The comparison groups of nonviolent adult men drawn from the general population have been too small to allow inferences to the general population.

20. There is one Canadian census-based study, which found a 2 percent prevalence rate for mothers' reports but a 10 percent rate based on children's self-reports. Only a single item, "is cruel to animals," was used, and the meaning of this phrase is open to many interpretations. See D. R. Offord, M. H. Boyle, and Y. A. Racine, "The Epidemiology of Antisocial Behavior in Childhood and Adolescence," in Deborah J. Pepler and Kenneth H. Rubin, eds., *The Development and Treatment of Childhood Aggression* (Hillsdale, N.J.: Erlbaum, 1991). Another way to gauge the prevalence of children's cruelty to animals is to review all complaints of abuse and neglect reported to a society for the prevention of cruelty to animals (SPCA). In an example of this approach, Arnold Arluke and Carter Luke reviewed the records of the Massachusetts SPCA from 1975 to 1996 and found that 27 percent of all prosecuted cases of physical abuse of animals involved boys under eighteen years of age. Only a small fraction of complaints resulted in prosecutions. See "Physical Cruelty toward Animals in Massachusetts, 1975–1996," *Society and Animals* 5 (1997): 195–204.

21. Frank Ascione, Teresa Thompson, and Tracy Black have developed a comprehensive interview protocol, the Cruelty to Animals Assessment Instrument (CAAI), to gain detailed information on both maltreatment of and kindness toward animals by children over four years of age. CAAI cruelty scores can range from zero (no instances of cruelty) to 30 (severe, chronic, and recent cruelty, without any empathy, toward a variety of animals). In a small sample of fifteen boys and five girls drawn from programs for emotionally disturbed youth, incarcerated teens, and children accompanying their mothers to shelters for battered women, most of the children received cruelty scores in the 10–20 range. See "Childhood Cruelty to Animals: Assessing Cruelty Dimensions and Motivations," *Anthrozoös* 10 (1997): 170–173.

22. Unpublished report from the Wisconsin Humane Society, 1997; interview with Jill DeGrave of the Wisconsin Humane Society, July 1, 1998; telephone interview with Randall Lockwood, July 15, 1998.

23. Interview with Randall Lockwood, July 15, 1998.

24. Arkow, *Breaking the Cycles of Violence*, p. 5.

25. Randall Lockwood and Ann Church, "Deadly Serious," *Humane Society News,* Fall 1996, pp. 1–4; reprinted in Lockwood and Ascione, *Cruelty to Animals,* pp. 241–244; quotation pp. 242–243.

26. Aquinas quoted in K. Thomas, *Man and the Natural World* (New York: Pantheon, 1983). Michel de Montaigne, *Complete Essays of Montaigne,* trans. Donald M. Frame (Stanford, Calif.: Stanford University Press, 1998). Montaigne counted himself among the "theriophiles," literally "animal lovers."

27. John Locke, "Cruelty," in *Some Thoughts concerning Education,* in *The Works of John Locke in Nine Volumes,* 12th ed. (London: C. & J. Rivington), 8: 112–114; reprinted in Lockwood and Ascione, eds., *Cruelty to Animals,* p. 5.

28. Gillian Avery, *Nineteenth-Century Children: Heroes and Heroines in English Children's Stories, 1780–1900* (London: Hodder and Stoughton, 1965).

29. Quoted in Margaret Blount, *Animal Land: The Creatures of Children's Fiction* (New York: William Morrow, 1975), p. 47.

30. Bernard Unti, "The History of Humane Education: Lessons for Today from the Past," paper delivered at the Humane Education Symposium, Animal Expo '99, Orlando, Florida, February 24, 1999.

31. Margaret Marshall Saunders, *Beautiful Joe* (New York: A. L. Burt, 1922), p. 176.

32. The misuse of horses in England and America is ably documented in Gerald Carson, "Horses Are Cheaper than Oats," in *Men, Beasts, and Gods* (New York: Charles Scribner, 1972), pp. 87–94.

33. Blount, *Animal Land,* p. 252.

34. Andreas-Holger Maehle, "Cruelty and Kindness to the 'Brute Creation': Stability and Change in the Ethics of the Man-Animal Relationships, 1600–1850," in Aubrey Manning and James Serpell, eds., *Animals and Human Society: Changing Perspectives* (New York: Routledge, 1994), p. 94. Jerrold Tannenbaum points out that court cases in the nineteenth century related to animal mistreatment often exempted the owners of the animals in question; "Animals and the Law: Property, Cruelty, and Rights," in Arien Mack, ed., *Humans and Other Animals* (Columbus: Ohio State University Press, 1995), pp. 125–193.

35. A charming example is *Some Swell Pup, or Are You Sure You Want a Dog?* by Maurice Sendak and Matthew Margolis (New York: Farrar, Straus and Giroux, 1976). A querulous brother and sister shift from effusive hugs and kisses for their new puppy to curses and kicks as soon as the puppy poops on the floor and chews up the furniture. A mysterious stranger—beneath the long robes, we glimpse an adult dog—tutors the children in the ways of normal puppydom, with lessons on being gentle, speaking softly, having patience, and waiting until the puppy is twelve weeks old to begin training.

36. Sigmund Freud, "Three Contributions to the Theory of Sex" (1905), in A. A. Brill, ed. and trans., *The Basic Writings of Sigmund Freud* (New York: Random House, 1938), p. 594.

37. Randall Lockwood and Guy R. Hodge, "The Tangled Web of Animal Abuse: The Links between Cruelty to Animals and Human Violence," *Humane Society News,* Summer 1986, pp. 1–6.

38. Telephone interview with Laurie Rovin, July 1, 1998.

39. Frank R. Ascione and Claudia V. Weber, "Animal Welfare and Domestic Violence," in *Final Report to the Geraldine R. Dodge Foundation*, April 25, 1997. See also Frank R. Ascione, "Battered Women's Reports of Their Partners' and Their Children's Cruelty to Animals," *Journal of Emotional Abuse* 1 (1998): 119–133.

40. 1994–95 survey, Community Coalition Against Violence, LaCrosse, Wisconsin; figures provided by Phil Arkow.

41. Elizabeth DeViney, Jeffery Dickert, and Randall Lockwood, "The Care of Pets within Child Abusing Families," *International Journal for the Study of Animal Problems* 4 (1983): 321–329.

42. Arnold Arluke, Jack Levin, Carter Luke, and Frank Ascione, "The Relationship of Animal Abuse to Violence and Other Forms of Antisocial Behavior," *Journal of Interpersonal Violence* 14 (1999): 963—975.

43. L. B. Costin, "Unraveling the Mary Ellen Legend: Origins of the 'Cruelty Movement,'" *Social Service Review* 65 (1991): 203–223; S. Zawistowski, "The Legacy of Mary Ellen," ASPCA *Animal Watch* 10 (1992); Carson, *Men, Beasts, and Gods*.

44. Locke, "Cruelty," p. 5.

45. Alan R. Felthous, "Aggression against Cats, Dogs, and People," *Child Psychiatry and Human Development* 10 (1980): 169–177; Stephen R. Kellert and Alan R. Felthous, "Childhood Cruelty toward Animals among Criminals and Noncriminals," *Human Relations* 38 (1985): 1113–29.

46. Personal communication from Jill DeGrave, Wisconsin Humane Society, July 2, 1998.

47. Interview with Mary Pat Boatfield, Executive Director, Toledo Humane Society, July 15, 1998; interview with Doug Allen, Toledo Police Department, July 16, 1998.

48. Interview with Peggy Smith, school psychologist, Washington High School, Milwaukee, July 6, 1998.

49. Interview with Jill DeGrave, July 2, 1998.

50. Telephone interview with Robert Bierer, July 1, 1998.

51. In an analysis of MSPCA abuse prosecutions, adolescents who abused animals were male (over 96 percent), acted in groups as often as alone, and, more than half the time, abused cats. By contrast, adult males tended to act alone, and most abused dogs. See Arluke and Luke, "Physical Cruelty toward Animals in Massachusetts."

52. Telephone interview with Donna Straub, July 9, 1998.

53. Only Colorado mandates veterinarians by law to report suspected child abuse or neglect to law enforcement or social services. See Phil Arkow, "The Correlations between Cruelty to Animals and Child Abuse and the Implications for Veterinary Medicine," *Canadian Veterinary Journal* 33 (1992): 518–521.

54. Charlotte A. Lacroix, "Another Weapon for Combating Family Violence," in Frank R. Ascione and Phil Arkow, eds., *Child Abuse, Domestic Violence, and Animal Abuse* (West Lafayette, Ind.: Purdue University Press, 1999).

55. Randall Lockwood, "HSUS Launches 'First Strike,'" *HSUS News*, Summer 1997, pp. 7–8.

56. G. Stanley Hall, *Adolescence*, vol. 2 (New York: D. Appleton, 1904), p. 228; quoted in Frank R. Ascione, "Humane Education Research: Evaluating Efforts to Encourage

Children's Kindness and Caring toward Animals," *Genetic, Social, and General Psychology Monographs* 123 (1997): 73.

57. An overview of humane education programs and an evaluation of their effectiveness may be found in Ascione, "Humane Education Research." See also Frank R. Ascione, "Enhancing Children's Attitudes about the Humane Treatment of Animals: Generalization to Human-Directed Empathy," *Anthrozoös* 5 (1992): 176–191.

58. Not surprisingly, longer, more intensive school programs produce more attitude change, at least immediately after the program, which is often the only assessment time. See Thomas A. Fitzgerald, "Evaluating Humane Education: The Jefferson County Study," *Humane Education,* September 1981, pp. 21–22; Vanessa Malcarne, "The Boston Study," *Humane Education,* March 1983, pp. 12–13.

59. Interview with Jean McGroarty, Lafayette Humane Society, Lafayette, Ind., March 12, 1998.

60. Brenda K. Bryant, "Regard for Our Environment Is in Part a Family Affair: A New Perspective on a Humane Education Curriculum," paper delivered at the annual conference of the Delta Society, Houston, October 11–13, 1990.

61. Michael Robin, Robert ten Bensel, Joseph S. Quigley, and Robert K. Anderson, "Childhood Pets and the Psychosocial Development of Adolescents," in Aaron H. Katcher and Alan M. Beck, eds., *New Perspectives on Our Lives with Companion Animals* (Philadelphia: University of Pennsylvania Press, 1983), p. 441.

62. 1994–95 survey, Community Coalition Against Violence, LaCrosse, Wisconsin.

63. Susan Isaacs, *Intellectual Growth in Young Children* (London: Routledge and Kegan Paul, 1930), pp. 204–205.

64. Estimates of animals euthanized at shelters vary widely, since no national or standardized figures are collected. I am relying on Andrew Rowan's estimates for 1992 in "Companion Animal Demographics and Unwanted Animals in the United States," *Anthrozoös* 5 (1992): 222–225; and editorial, "Shelters and Pet Overpopulation: A Statistical Black Hole," *Anthrozoös* 5 (1992): 140–143.

65. Gary J. Patronek, Lawrence T. Glickman, Alan M. Beck, George P. McCabe, and Carol Ecker, "Risk Factors for Relinquishment of Dogs to an Animal Shelter," *Journal of the American Veterinary Medical Association* 209 (1996): 572–581. Of those who relinquished pet cats to shelters, 37 percent strongly agreed that the cats were family members, and 43 percent carried or displayed a picture of the cat. In this survey, relinquishment of kittens, including entire litters, was excluded from study because "relinquishment of kittens is typical." See Gary J. Patronek, Lawrence T. Glickman, Alan M. Beck, George P. McCabe, and Carol Ecker, "Risk Factors for Relinquishment of Cats to an Animal Shelter," *Journal of the American Veterinary Medical Association* 209 (1996): 582.

66. G. Francione, "Animals as Property," *Animal Law* 2 (1996): 1–6.

67. Isaacs, *Intellectual Growth in Young Children,* p. 161.

68. Margaret Mead, "Cultural Factors in the Cause and Prevention of Pathological Homicide," *Bulletin of the Menninger Clinic* 28 (1964): 11–22; reprinted in Lockwood and Ascione, *Cruelty to Animals,* quotation pp. 30–31.

69. See Carson, *Men, Beasts, and Gods,* for excellent historical treatment of cruelty to animals.

70. James Serpell rightly notes that our evolutionary history as hunter-gatherers incorporated an ethic of respect for animals. This respect began its fateful erosion with animal domestication 11,000 years ago. See "Working Out the Beast: An Alternative View of Western Humaneness," in Ascione and Arkow, *Child Abuse, Domestic Violence, and Animal Abuse,* pp. 38–49.

71. Douglas Martin, "Caution: Exploding Donkey," *New York Times,* May 9, 1999, p. WK3.

72. Carson, *Men, Beasts, and Gods,* p. 156.

73. Andrew Rowan argues that there is no societal consensus on what constitutes cruelty or neglect toward animals. He advocates that only when people gain satisfaction by harming an animal should the terms *cruelty* or *abuse* be used. Careless or ignorant mistreatment or excessively hard obedience training should be termed *neglect.* He labels socially accepted practices, such as hunting, livestock production, and medical research, as animal "use." See "Cruelty to Animals," *Anthrozoös* 6 (1993): 218–220.

8. Deepening the Animal Connection

1. Jeanne Brooks and Michael Lewis, "Infants' Responses to Strangers: Midget, Adult, and Child," *Child Development* 47 (1976): 323–332.

2. I borrow the term *biophobia* from David W. Orr, *Earth in Mind: On Education, Environment, and the Human Prospect* (Washington, D.C.: Island Press, 1994), p. 131.

3. As Margot Lasher points out, relational theorists such as Daniel Stern, Donald Winnicott, and Heinz Kohut emphasize optimal psychological growth through connectedness or attunement of self and other. Because animals, especially interactive pets like dogs and cats, express their attunement openly and wholeheartedly, Lasher notes that human-animal connections can provide the experience of "two living creatures responding to the core self of each other . . . a safe, responsive setting for inner growth"; "A Relational Approach to the Human-Animal Bond," *Anthrozoös* 11 (1998): 133.

4. This typical textbook definition is from Laura E. Berk, *Child Development,* 4th ed. (Boston: Allyn and Bacon, 1997), p. 281.

5. Ibid., p. G-1.

6. Theodore E. Wachs and Gerald E. Gruen, *Early Experience and Human Development* (New York: Plenum, 1982).

7. Gary Paul Nabhan and Stephen Trimble, *The Geography of Childhood: Why Children Need Wild Places* (Boston: Beacon Press, 1994), p. 97.

8. David Hutchison, *Growing Up Green: Education for Ecological Renewal* (New York: Teachers College, Columbia University, 1998), p. 84.

9. Orr, *Earth in Mind,* p. 27.

10. Dilafruz R. Williams and Sarah Taylor, "From Margin to Center: Initiation and Development of an Environmental School from the Ground Up," in Gregory A. Smith and Dilafruz R. Williams, eds., *Ecological Education in Action* (Albany: SUNY Press, 1999), pp. 79–102.

11. An evaluation of the Caretaker Classroom program showed that after a school year, participants increased positive environmental attitudes but not knowledge of environmental

issues. Program effects were greater in grades one through three than in grades four through seven. Frank C. Leeming, Bryan E. Porter, William O. Dwyer, Melissa K. Cobern, and Diana P. Oliver, "Effects of Participation in Class Activities on Children's Environmental Attitudes and Knowledge," *Journal of Environmental Education* 28 (1997): 33–42.

12. Joseph Kiefer and Martin Kemple, "Stories from Our Common Roots: Strategies for Building an Ecologically Sustainable Way of Learning," in Smith and Williams, *Ecological Education in Action,* pp. 21–45; C. A. Bowers, *Educating for an Ecologically Sustainable Culture* (Albany: SUNY Press, 1995), p. 196.

13. Gregory Cajete, "Reclaiming Biophilia: Lessons from Indigenous Peoples," in Smith and Williams, *Ecological Education in Action,* pp. 189–206.

14. Telephone interview with Jill DeGrave, July 2, 1998. Descriptions of J. and T. from Jill DeGrave.

15. Videotaped interview provided by Nancy Katz, Shiloh Project, Fairfax, Va.

16. Interview with Rice Lilly, Director, Fairfax County Boys' Probation Home, Fairfax, Va., July 16, 1998. Lilly reiterated the refrain of most professionals on the front lines of interventions using animals: "We need to quantify the impact of programs like Shiloh."

17. For a discussion of multiple "targets" of nurturance, see Alan Fogel, Gail F. Melson, and Jayanthi Mistry, "Conceptualizing the Determinants of Nurturance: A Reassessment of Sex Differences," in Alan Fogel and Gail F. Melson, eds., *Origins of Nurturance: Developmental, Biological, and Cultural Perspectives on Caregiving* (Hillsdale, N.J.: Erlbaum, 1986), pp. 53–67.

18. Roger Ulrich, "Biophilia, Biophobia, and Natural Landscapes," in Stephen R. Kellert and Edward O. Wilson, eds., *The Biophilia Hypothesis* (Washington, D.C.: Island Press, 1993), pp. 73–137. These findings have not been replicated with children.

19. Carol Rathmann and Lynn Loar, "A Humane Garden of Children, Plants, and Animals Grows in Sonoma County, California," *Latham Letter,* Spring 1994, pp. 6–9.

20. The term *extinction of experience* comes from Robert Michael Pyle's *The Thunder Tree* (Boston: Houghton Mifflin, 1993). Gary Paul Nabhan coined the expression "vicarious view of nature" in Nabhan and Trimble, *The Geography of Childhood,* p. 86.

21. Nabhan and Trimble, *Geography of Childhood,* p. 75.

22. Roger Hart, *Children's Experience of Place* (New York: Irvington, 1979), p. 3.

INDEX